Meaningful Teaching Interaction at the Internationalised University

This edited collection draws together the latest thinking, research and practical case studies related to classroom interaction at internationalised universities.

Through evidence-based approaches which involve the analysis of and reflection on classroom interaction practices, this book examines issues related to classroom interaction in disciplinary higher education contexts, whilst addressing the question of how teachers and students can develop their ability in orchestrating and taking part in classroom interaction.

Covering topics such as classroom interactional competence, 'silent' students, interaction and integration in multicultural classes, social factors in classroom talk, group interaction, oracy development and anti-bullying interventions, this title is ideal reading for postgraduate students, teacher trainers in higher education, scholars and researchers and anyone interested in higher education pedagogy and its development.

Doris Dippold is Senior Lecturer in Intercultural Communication at the University of Surrey, UK.

Marion Heron is Senior Lecturer in Higher Education at the University of Surrey, UK.

Meaningful Teaching Interaction at the Internationalised University

Moving From Research to Impact

Edited by
Doris Dippold and Marion Heron

Routledge
Taylor & Francis Group

LONDON AND NEW YORK

First published 2021
by Routledge
2 Park Square, Milton Park, Abingdon, Oxon OX14 4RN

and by Routledge
52 Vanderbilt Avenue, New York, NY 10017

Routledge is an imprint of the Taylor & Francis Group, an informa business

British Library Cataloguing-in-Publication Data
A catalogue record for this book is available from the British Library

Library of Congress Cataloging-in-Publication Data
Names: Dippold, Doris, editor. | Heron, Marion, editor.
Title: Meaningful teaching interaction at the internationalised university: moving from research to impact / Edited by Doris Dippold and Marion Heron.
Description: Abingdon, Oxon ; New York, NY : Routledge, 2021. | Includes bibliographical references and index.
Identifiers: LCCN 2020048023 (print) | LCCN 2020048024 (ebook) | ISBN 9780367350864 (hardback) | ISBN 9780367350888 (paperback) | ISBN 9780429329692 (ebook)
Subjects: LCSH: Teacher-student relationships–Great Britain. | Teacher-student relationships–Great Britain–Case studies. | Classroom environment–Social aspects–Great Britain. | Education, Higher–Research–Great Britain. | Muliticultural education–Great Britain.
Classification: LCC LB1033 .M353 2021 (print) | LCC LB1033 (ebook) | DDC 371.102/3–dc23
LC record available at https://lccn.loc.gov/2020048023
LC ebook record available at https://lccn.loc.gov/2020048024

ISBN: 978-0-367-35086-4 (hbk)
ISBN: 978-0-367-35088-8 (pbk)
ISBN: 978-0-429-32969-2 (ebk)

Typeset in Times New Roman
by Taylor & Francis Books

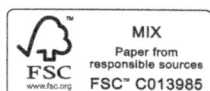

Contents

Illustrations

Boxes

Contributors

Jane G. Bell, Heriot-Watt University, is an Assistant Professor and has taught English for Academic Purposes (EAP) at Heriot-Watt University for over 20 years. Besides co-ordinating Pre-sessional and Foundation English courses, other commitments include contributing sessions to the HWU LEADS Programme for PhD students on the (inter)cultural aspects of teaching and learning; developing and teaching on undergraduate and postgraduate Cultural Studies and Scottish Studies courses, dissertation supervision and embedded in-sessional academic skills provision for undergraduate and postgraduate courses. Her research interests include student diversity and classroom interaction, intercultural communication, bullying prevention and affective pedagogy. She is working towards an HEA Fellowship.

Dr Florence Bonacina-Pugh, University of Edinburgh, is a Lecturer in Language Education in the Institute for Education, Teaching and Leadership at the Moray House School of Education and Sport, University of Edinburgh. She is a member of the Language Education Research Hub at Edinburgh. Florence started her academic career by being awarded a Post-Doctoral Research Fellowship (PTA-026-27-2638) from the Economic and Social Research Council (ESRC) hosted by the department of Linguistics and English Language at the University of Edinburgh. She then worked as a Teaching Fellow in TESOL in the School of Education at the University of Edinburgh. Before working in academia, Florence taught French as a foreign language at all levels for nine years in various institutions across the UK and was regularly hired for curriculum and teaching material development.

Qi Chen, Hangzhou Normal University/University of Edinburgh, is currently an Associate Tutor in TESOL at the Moray House School of Education and Sports, University of Edinburgh and has recently joined the School of International Studies at Hangzhou Normal University, China, as a Lecturer in Applied Linguistics. She obtained an MA in Applied Linguistics and TESOL in 2012, and a PhD in Educational and Applied Linguistics in 2017, both at Newcastle University. Her current research interests include: 1) multilingual language use and language ideologies in internationalised universities, 2) teachers' beliefs, teacher autonomy and classroom teaching practices in EFL contexts, and 3) talk-and-bodies-in-interaction in multilingual and multicultural social contexts.

Dr Philippa Cranwell, University of Reading, is an organic chemist with a strong interest in chemistry education. She completed her undergraduate studies at the University of Southampton, her PhD studies at the University of Cambridge and postdoctoral work at ETH in Zürich, Switzerland. Her current research focuses on looking at the differences in complexity of oral discourse that students face when transitioning to university from their previous education, and the integration of transnational education students into the final year of highly specialised STEM degree programmes.

Dr Daniel Dauber, University of Warwick, is an Associate Professor in the Department of Applied Linguistics at the University of Warwick. His main areas of expertise revolve around organisational behaviour, international management and intercultural aspects related to these two fields. His most recent publications focus on the higher education sector and provide insights and guidance on how universities can manage, enhance and maintain a healthy internationalisation strategy. Daniel Dauber is also the co-developer of the Global Education Profiler, a diagnostic tool which is widely used in Europe to assess various aspects of internationalisation at diversified higher education institutions.

Dr Doris Dippold, Senior Lecturer in Intercultural Communication, University of Surrey, is Senior Lecturer in Intercultural Communication in the School of Literature and Languages at the University of Surrey. Doris' published research includes monographs and articles on English as a lingua franca, internationalisation in higher education, and interlanguage and intercultural pragmatics. Her research pursues a language-led perspective on interaction in international settings. Doris is also Programme Director of the MA in Intercultural Business Communication and Marketing and lead educator of the Futurelearn MOOC "Communicating with Diverse Audiences".

Dr Jill Doubleday's research interests include intercultural communication, internationalisation of higher education, English as a medium of instruction and English as a lingua franca. She runs professional development workshops for academics related to these areas and to teaching diverse student groups. Jill also teaches subject-specific academic English and contributes to MA programmes in Applied Linguistics and English Language Teaching.

Dr Fufy Demissie, Sheffield Hallam University, is Senior Lecturer in Primary and Early Years at Sheffield Hallam University and is a registered trainer for SAPERE (Society for the Advancement of Philosophical Enquiry and Reflection in Education). Her primary research focus is on philosophical enquiry and teacher development and she is currently conducting a project on teachers' classroom interactions.

Dr Jan Hardman, University of York, is Associate Professor in Language Education in the Department of Education, University of York. Her research focuses on classroom interaction, discourse analysis, dialogic pedagogy and teacher education across all phases of education. She has worked on a range of international research projects and published widely on dialogic pedagogy and teacher professional development. More recently, she was involved in a large-scale study of a teacher professional development intervention designed to improve the quality of classroom talk, learning and student attainment in primary schools serving socially deprived areas of England. Informed by her research, Jan contributes to staff professional development courses on teaching and learning in schools and higher education.

Dr Marion Heron, Senior Lecturer in Higher Education, University of Surrey, has worked in higher education for over 30 years in Turkey, Dubai and the UK. Her background is in applied linguistics and she has carried out research in the areas of classroom discourse, classroom interaction, oracy skills, academic literacies and academic writing. She has published in a number of journals focusing on educational linguistics and presented her work at conferences. She teaches on the Graduate Certificate in Learning and Teaching, the MA in Higher Education, the MA TESOL and supervises PhD students in language teacher education and applied linguistics.

Dr Daguo Li, University of Reading, is Programme Co-Director of the University of Reading's MA in English Language Education at Guangdong University of Foreign Studies, China. His areas of research interest include international education/transnational education, intercultural communication, and professional development for second language teachers. He has published research articles in these areas in international journals, including *System, Language Teaching Research*, and the *Journal of Research in International Education*. He has also co-authored a chapter on professional development of Chinese teachers of English in the *Encyclopedia of Education: Second and Foreign Language Education* by Springer (2017).

Elizabeth Long, the American International University in London, has designed and delivered a suite of first-year university modules covering a range of skills to empower students to achieve their goals both at university and beyond, working alongside student services colleagues to provide a strong focus on employability. These skills include oracy in a range of situations, digital fluency, service learning and self-reflection. As university teaching adapts and evolves, the importance of oracy skills at university and in the world of work is on a par with literacy and numeracy, so her aim is to push it to the forefront of pedagogical innovation.

Dr Elizabeth M. Page, University of Reading, was formerly professor of Chemical Education at the University of Reading and author of several textbooks on general and inorganic chemistry. In her role as Director of

Undergraduate Studies, Elizabeth was responsible for establishing a successful articulated degree programme in chemistry with Nanjing University of Information Science and Technology (NUIST). She has several years of experience in transnational education and supporting international students both in the UK and abroad.

Dr Benjamin Poore, University of York, theatre research includes publications on British playwriting about the Victorians and on empire, and on adaptations of Victorian novels and the Sherlock Holmes stories. Ben's professional background is in teaching English and drama in secondary schools as well as higher education. He is currently Director of Learning and Teaching for his academic department and sits on the university's Learning and Teaching Committee where he is editor of the university magazine on learning and teaching, *Forum*.

Jane Richardson, Heriot-Watt University, is an EAP teacher, co-ordinating and teaching pre-sessional and foundation programmes and providing in-sessional support in key critical and literacy skills for postgraduate programmes in the social sciences. She also developed and teaches an undergraduate module on Global Englishes. Her research interests include EAP in the internationalised university, intercultural communication in the classroom and groupwork assessment in higher education.

Lee-Ann Sequeira, London School of Economics, is an academic developer at the Eden Centre for Education Enhancement at the LSE, where she advises departments on curriculum design and pedagogy. She leads the Eden Centre's academic development programme, Atlas, and is also the editor of the LSE Higher Education Blog. She is interested in exploring and researching contemporary higher education using a critical lens. Having lived, studied and taught in different education systems and countries, she is passionate about fostering all forms of diversity (including intellectual and cultural diversity) in higher education.

Dr Olcay Sert, Mälardalen University, is an Associate Professor of TESOL and Applied Linguistics at Mälardalen University, Sweden. His research focuses on classroom discourse, L2 interaction and language teacher education. His book *Social Interaction and L2 Classroom Discourse* (Edinburgh University Press, 2015) was shortlisted for the BAAL Book Prize in 2016 and was a finalist for the AAAL First Book Award in 2017. He is leading the **M**älardalen **IN**teraction & **D**idactics (MIND) Research Group and is the editor of the *Classroom Discourse* journal (Routledge). He has also worked as a language teacher in Turkey and the UK and has been actively involved in teacher education in Turkey and Sweden.

Dr Bong-gi Sohn, Simon Fraser University, is a Postdoctoral Fellow at Simon Fraser University, Canada. Her research focuses on international student mobilisation in higher education and multilingual/minority family language policy and practices. In her doctoral study, she elaborated how current scholarship on global chains of care and so-called feminised multilingual development explains the ways in which immigrant wives selectively move on to become bilingual workers in service of the host country's preparation for its global future. In her current work, focusing on experiences of international/multilingual education, she is playing a role in co-designing a discipline-specific content-language integrated learning (CLIL) curriculum with teachers and students.

Dr Helen Spencer-Oatey, University of Warwick, is a Professor in the Department of Applied Linguistics, University of Warwick. Having lived and worked abroad for many years, one of her main research interests is in the internationalisation of higher education and the lived experiences of international students. She researches in many aspects of this field, and has published her findings extensively in both books and journal articles. Helen is particularly interested in the applied relevance of her research and, with colleagues, has developed extensive intercultural resources for practitioners, including frameworks, assessment tools and e-training modules, available via the GlobalPeople website.

Dr Valia Spiliotopoulos, University of British Columbia, is Assistant Professor of Teaching in the Department of Language and Literacy Education. Her research focuses on content and language-integrated learning, academic literacy and assessment, and teacher and faculty development in multilingual and multicultural contexts.

Dr Steve Walsh, University of Newcastle, has been involved in English language teaching and English language teacher education for more than 30 years in a range of overseas contexts. Steve's research interests include classroom discourse, teacher development, second language teacher education, and professional communication. He has published ten books and more than 100 research papers. His most recent publications, with Steve Mann, are the monograph *Reflective Practice for English Language Teaching: Research-based Principles and Practices* (Routledge, 2017) and *The Routledge Handbook of English Language Teacher Education* (Routledge, 2019).

Dr Karin Whiteside, University of Reading, is an EAP practitioner, specialising in specific-purposes (ESAP) provisions, having completed a PhD related to this area and developed courses for a range of disciplines including Politics, Business, Psychology, Law and Construction Management. Currently, she is Programme Director of the University of Reading's in-sessional programme, and teaches doctoral research writing.

Aaron Woodcock, University of Reading, is a Lecturer in Transnational Education with a particular interest in the linguistic and sociolinguistic aspects of transnational education within STEM subjects.

Foreword

Classroom discourse and interaction: a field in transformation

Olcay Sert

MÄLARDALEN UNIVERSITY

Interactional repertoires and competencies are central to the existence and development of humans and other agents. These repertoires, enacted in the material world, facilitate and are the site of knowledge co-construction – especially in settings where learning is mediated, including classrooms. The scientific study of "discourse and interaction in settings where activity is deliberately organised to promote learning" (Classroom Discourse, online) gives (us) access to the dynamics of learning-oriented and pedagogical practices. There is, however, a problem of language to talk about discourse and interaction in teaching and learning, as six different terms have been used in these investigations to address similar and related issues: (1) classroom discourse, (2) classroom interaction, (3) classroom talk, (4) classroom dialogue, (5) educational dialogue, and (6) pedagogical interaction. Do all these six terms point to the same research field though? Are they being used interchangeably, or do they represent different research agendas as well as theoretical and methodological standpoints? Do we need a common language, a research 'lingua franca' so to speak, to facilitate interdisciplinary and cross-subject co-operation? (see Buckholtz et al., 2016). In this foreword, I will argue that establishing co-operation and possibly a common language to study classroom discourse and interaction will help us tackle future challenges for research and education together. In order to achieve this, we need to (1) address the 'language bias', (2) reconceptualise classroom discourse in the digital world, and (3) be open but very critical towards big data and artificial intelligence. My aim is not, at least in this foreword, to offer solutions, but rather to raise questions for debate.

A citation analysis[1] based on author keywords shows that 'Classroom Interaction' and 'Classroom Discourse' have by far been the most commonly used keywords to describe the field (see Figure 0.1). This is also why most of the researchers in the field use these two terms together. For instance, Markee's (2015) edited volume is entitled *The Handbook of Classroom Discourse and Interaction*, and Chapter 1 of the present volume includes a section with the following heading: Frameworks for analysing classroom interaction and classroom discourse. Yet, the other four terms in Figure 0.1 are not uncommon, and the keyword 'classroom dialogue' received the highest average number of citations per article between 2015 and 2019. Furthermore, one of the influential

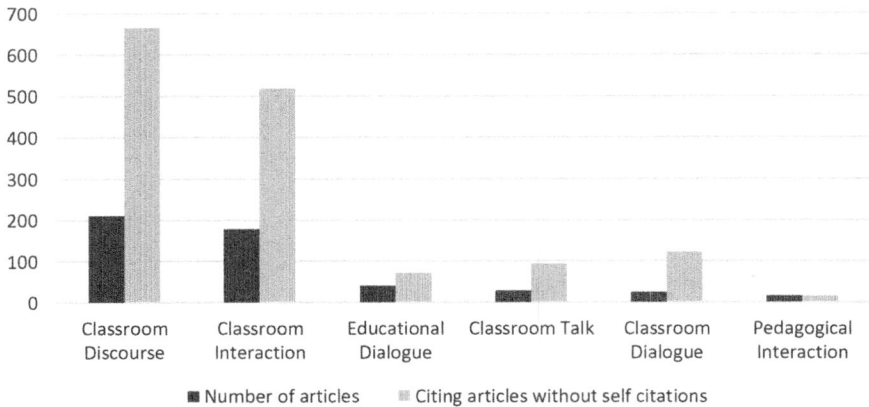

Figure 0.1 Author keywords and citations in Web of Science, 2015–2019

publishing houses published two volumes this year: *Research Methods for* **Classroom Discourse** (Ingram and Elliott, 2020) and *Research Methods for* **Educational Dialogue** (Kershner et al., 2020). A closer investigation into the contents of the articles using these six keywords shows that there are methodological, theoretical and contextual differences. However, the phenomena being investigated overlap greatly, that is, the interactional aspects of pedagogical practices. The articles that come from a 'classroom interaction' trend, which predominantly use conversation analysis methodology, do not interact with those that have the keywords 'educational dialogue' or 'classroom dialogue' (and the other way around). The gap can be theoretical and methodological, but is also clearly disciplinary.

Classroom Discourse and Interaction (CDI) research seems to have a 'language bias' as many more published articles have a language pedagogy focus (Dippold and Heron, this volume, Chapter 6). The present volume is therefore a welcome contribution to the field, with its focus on conceptual development in higher education that goes beyond second/foreign/additional languages (L2s). Furthermore, the contributions go beyond 'English' language teaching, as they also cover higher education disciplinary contexts. However, the problem of language bias goes beyond disciplinary boundaries: there is a traditional understanding of language as a linguistic system that leads researchers to focus only on the verbal aspects of CDI. However, conversation analytic research on discourse and interaction in instructed learning settings have shown that any study of CDI should consider translingual and embodied resources deployed by teachers and students. CDI cannot just involve a process of coding language structures because within educational settings we perform actions that are co-constructed within verbal, visual and material modalities, in a locally situated manner.

Another aspect of the language bias is that research on CDI mostly focuses on 'English' as L2 or comes from English-speaking countries. It is, however, clear that we will see more English as a medium of instruction (EMI) in higher education research coming from different parts of the globe. While conceptual development and learning outcomes in relation to interaction are obvious topics of future research from EMI settings, more micro-analytic research looking into the interactional dynamics of these settings (e.g. Duran et al., 2019) is required. The concept of an educational lingua franca, or an EMI, is (also) a policy issue, so language policies at macro and micro levels need to remain as part of the research agenda. How these policies are enacted in such classrooms through daily interactions and how we train teachers in higher education will need to be investigated thoroughly. These investigations at local educational and classroom levels, when coupled with macro-level policy research, will also help us develop a more in-depth understanding of the process of internationalisation. The present volume, therefore, is a key contribution to the field with its focus on internationalisation. Internationalisation in higher education is key to solving many social issues in the world, and CDI research that focuses on internationalisation is more than welcome.

In the last decade, CDI research has not been limited to physical classrooms with walls– we have a great number of studies on interactions that take place online, as well as research on many other forms of digital and distance education. However, the recent pandemic once again reminded us of the importance of research into how learning is facilitated and students are engaged through online classroom interaction. Online classroom interaction is not necessarily a replacement for or a virtual model of pre-technology classroom interaction. We need to, however, reconceptualise some of the aspects of CDI that are inherited from traditional classroom research. For instance, earlier research findings on interactional phenomena like silences (see Chapter 4 in this volume) and wait-time need to be reconsidered, or the boundaries of synchronous and asynchronous interaction need to be reinvestigated. The use of modalities afforded by online classrooms is rich, and what interactional data is needs to be considered from a multimodal perspective. Technology is not only pushing methods of teaching forward, it is not just a matter of material science or medium of communication, but it is also pushing research methodologies forward, and more data-driven research on educational outcomes is timely. While conversation analysis methodology is teaching us more about microscopic aspects of (online) classroom interaction, corpus linguistics and artificial intelligence are bridging big data and pedagogical interaction. For instance, Kelly et al. (2018) combined speech recognition, natural 'language' processing and machine learning to automatically measure question authenticity in classroom interaction, which has been a very welcome and innovative contribution to the field. However, what kind of limitations does this research have due to its focus on audio and verbal data only? What are the limitations of the coding schemes used by researchers who want to tackle big data? One potential future-looking solution might be to replace natural language processing with Natural Action Processing (Housley et al., 2019).

It is now established that multimodal aspects of classroom discourse and interaction are key to understanding teaching and learning practices (e.g. Sert, 2015; Gardner, 2019). Therefore, any tool that is designed to help teachers based on their classroom discourse or any coding scheme that aims to link classroom interaction and learning outcomes will need to acknowledge the multimodal nature of CDI. The risk, otherwise, is obvious: conclusions on learning outcomes or teacher performances would be built on an incomplete understanding of underlying human actions. A volume like this one on higher education CDI is an important step forward, as the chapters are illuminating and point towards two important contributions of CDI research: 1) CDI and learning outcomes, and 2) CDI and teacher education. In order to build the bridges between these two future projects, we need a common language, a lingua franca between researchers who use different methodologies. What kind of interactional designs enhance student engagement and thus what needs to be integrated into teacher education are two complementary research and development agendas that meet at the level of classroom interaction. If we want to bridge the micro-interactional detail and big data in responding to educational challenges, researchers who use the keyword 'classroom interaction' and researchers who use the keywords 'educational dialogue'/'classroom dialogue' need to interact. For example, researchers that integrate coding schemes like SEDA (Hennessy et al., 2016) into teacher education (Vrikki et al., 2019) and researchers who use CA informed teacher education schemes (Walsh, this volume; Sert, 2019; Waring, 2020) can learn from each other. Given that teachers are educated in higher education settings, higher education classrooms as a research context might be even more important than many think.

Note

1 For this analysis, I searched for 'Author keywords' in Web of Science (SCI, SSCI, AHCI and ESCI), with research articles published from 2015 to 2019.

References

Buckholtz, J., Reyna, V. F., & Slobogin, C. (2016). A neuro-legal lingua franca: bridging law and neuroscience on the issue of self-control. *Mental Health Law & Policy Journal*, Working Paper Number 16–32.

Classroom Discourse online (nd). Aim and scope. Accessed 12 May 2020. Duran, D., Kurhila, S., & Sert, O. (2019). Word search sequences in teacher-student interaction in an English as medium of instruction context. *International Journal of Bilingual Education and Bilingualism*, 1–20. https://doi.org/10.1080/13670050.2019.1703896.

Gardner, R. (2019). Classroom interaction research: the state of the art. *Research on Language and Social Interaction*, 52(3), 212–226.

Hennessy, S., Rojas-Drummond, S., Higham, R., Márquez, A. M., Maine, F., Ríos, R. M., ... & Barrera, M. J. (2016). Developing a coding scheme for analysing classroom dialogue across educational contexts. *Learning, Culture and Social Interaction*, 9, 16–44.

Housley, W., Albert, S., & Stokoe, E. (2019). Natural action processing: conversation analysis and big interactional data. In *Proceedings of Halfway to the Future (HTTF 2019), November 19-20, 2019, Nottingham, United Kingdom*. ACM. https://doi.org/10.1145/3363384.3363478.

Ingram, J., & Elliott, V. (2020). *Research methods for classroom discourse*. Bloomsbury Publishing.

Kelly, S., Olney, A. M., Donnelly, P., Nystrand, M., & D'Mello, S. K. (2018). Automatically measuring question authenticity in real-world classrooms. *Educational Researcher*, 47(7), 451–464.

Kershner, R., Hennessy, S., Wegerif, R., & Ahmed, A. (2020). *Research methods for educational dialogue*. Bloomsbury Publishing.

Markee, N. (2015). *The handbook of classroom discourse and interaction*. John Wiley & Sons.

Sert, O. (2015). *Social interaction and L2 classroom discourse*. Edinburgh University Press.

Sert, O. (2019). Classroom interaction and language teacher education. In S. Mann & S. Walsh (Eds.), *The Routledge handbook of English language teacher education* (pp. 216–238). Routledge.

Vrikki, M., Kershner, R., Calcagni, E., Hennessy, S., Lee, L., Hernández, F., ... & Ahmed, F. (2019). The teacher scheme for educational dialogue analysis (T-SEDA): developing a research-based observation tool for supporting teacher inquiry into pupils' participation in classroom dialogue. *International Journal of Research & Method in Education*, 42(2), 185–203.

Waring, H. Z. (2020). Harnessing the power of heteroglossia: how to multi-task with teacher talk. In S.Kunitz, N.Markee, & O. Sert (Eds.), *Classroom-based conversation analytic research: Theoretical and applied perspectives on pedagogy* (pp. 275–295). Springer.

Introduction

This edited volume on classroom interaction was conceived as a result of the two editors' shared interests in analysing language, interaction and discourse in classroom settings. Doris' interests in the subject were primarily guided by her wider interests in internationalisation and its implications for the interaction between teachers and students in a linguistically and culturally diverse space. In contrast, Marion's perspective on classroom interaction was led by an interest in dialogic teaching and in how students and teachers co-construct understanding through classroom talk. In December 2018, we held a symposium at the University of Surrey entitled "Classroom Interaction at the Internationalised University", bringing together both these perspectives. This volume features chapters by many of the contributors to this symposium.

Interaction and classroom talk have long been studied in school contexts (Alexander, 2001; Mercer & Howe, 2012) and second language (L2) learning contexts (Tsui, 2001; van Lier, 2014; Walsh, 2013). However, there is little focus on classroom interaction in higher education research. The field of higher education has yet to take notice of a research approach which draws on authentic data, with leading HE journals (e.g. *Studies in Higher Education, Teaching in Higher Education*) having no history of publishing such papers. This edited collection is an attempt to examine issues related to classroom interaction in disciplinary higher education contexts, whilst at the same time addressing the question of how teachers and students can develop their ability in orchestrating and taking part in classroom interaction.

The internationalisation of higher education is a daily reality which requires a range of competencies from students and staff. In today's international university, differences between the varieties of English spoken by members of the classroom community have the potential to lead to misunderstanding and emotive reactions (Björkman, 2013; Chiang, 2009). The chapters in this book attest to the importance of recognising issues of language, culture and (native speaker) power in the management of the classroom discourse (Dippold, 2015).

A further significant development is that universities today, and the staff who teach in them, are under increasing scrutiny regarding the quality of teaching they provide (French & O'Leary, 2017). A recent UK government initiative, the Teaching Excellence and Student Outcomes Framework (TEF) (2017), has placed greater emphasis on teaching quality and 'excellence'. The TEF was established to "open up the sector" (French & O'Leary, 2017, p. 13) by giving students greater flexibility in their decision making through access to data on teaching excellence. However, the term 'teaching excellence' is highly contested, largely because the concept is "context specific, meaning different things in different disciplines and institutions" (Gunn, 2018, p. 134). This book provides an unpacking of teaching and learning in a micro-context through an examination of classroom interaction, arguably central to considerations of excellence as it scaffolds learning and mediates relationships between teachers and staff. As a result of TEF and other quality assessments such as the National Student Survey and module evaluation questionnaires (MEQs), student learning and therefore pedagogy and teacher development are gaining prominence. However, few studies to date have focused on teacher development in higher education through analysis of and reflection on classroom interaction practices. A number of chapters in this book provide empirically based suggestions for teacher development, culminating in a knowledge base of approaches to teacher training in HE.

Part I of the book, *Theoretical considerations*, describes a number of core concepts fundamental to a study of a classroom interaction in an internationalised context. Chapter 1: *Overview of classroom interaction: definitions, models, practices and challenges* considers the role of talk in conceptual learning and its relationship to classroom interaction. The chapter also provides an overview of theoretical frameworks used to describe classroom interaction, arguing that we have much to learn from the research and scholarship in compulsory education. Chapter 2: *Classroom Interactional Competence and evidence-based reflection* focuses on teacher development and argues that teachers can develop an understanding of their own Classroom Interactional Competence when they have something to reflect on and with. The chapter also presents the case for embracing a Scholarship of Teaching and Learning (SoTL) approach to our work. Chapter 3: *Pedagogic renewal: promoting a dialogic pedagogy in the internationalised 21st century higher education* argues that teaching in higher education to date remains heavily reliant on knowledge transmission methods. Introducing the principles of dialogic pedagogy based on social interaction and language, the chapter argues that implementing these principles can lead to transformative learning experiences in the internationalised higher education space. Chapter 4: *The problem with silent students: it's us not them* critiques the view of the silent learner as one who is shy and lacks confidence and communication skills. Using a multi-dimensional view of silence and contesting the current higher education trends such as performativity and student engagement, the chapter frames silence as a critical pedagogy. Chapter 5: *Global competencies and classroom interaction: implications for student and staff training* asks whether, and to what extent, higher education classrooms are offering opportunities which allow students to develop global competencies. Discussing the results of a survey administered to home and international students at six English-speaking universities, the chapter argues that students and staff need additional support for using classroom interaction to foster global competencies.

Part II of the book, *Classroom interaction and disciplinary contexts*, presents specific research projects on classroom interaction in a disciplinary context. Chapter 6: *Classroom interaction: Disciplinary contexts* presents an overview of existing research on classroom interaction in a disciplinary context. The chapter demonstrates the bias of existing research in the area of second language learning and notes the paucity of research in the area of classroom interaction and disciplinary knowledge construction. Chapter 7: *Scaffolding peer interaction within a language-and-content integrated business curriculum: a case study in a Western Canadian University* presents an ethnographic case study of interaction in student groups comprising multilingual students. The chapter shows that interactional practices have the risk of marginalising multilingual students, with linguistic difference seen as deficit rather than a resource. Chapter 8: *Challenges faced by transnational education students (TNE) in advanced STEM practical classes* focuses on the discipline of chemistry, and describes, through empirical research, how transnational education students navigate the interactional challenges when studying in lab classes in a UK context. Chapter 9: *Spotlights on 'practiced' language policy in the internationalised university* continues the theme of transnational education in a postgraduate context and argues how the language choices made by teachers and students in a language education classroom interaction reflect and legitimise a 'practiced' language policy in higher education. Chapter 10, *We (don't) need to talk: communication among international students in group projects* uses ideas and principles derived from English as a lingua franca research to investigate business student perceptions of group interaction in international groups in higher education. The chapter shows that national culture alone is not sufficient to account for how students engage in international group work, and argues for student and staff training which acknowledges group diversity beyond the 'home' and 'international' student divide.

The final part of the book, Part III, *Classroom interaction: interventions and reflections*, highlights research which aims to develop interactional strategies for both students and teachers with the purpose of contributing to more quality classroom dialogue. Chapter 11: *Developing practice through intervention* summarises pedagogic intervention studies in school as well as higher education contexts. The chapter shows that there is still a dearth of such studies in the higher education sphere, despite them providing opportunities for teacher education in particular, which could be fruitfully integrated into teacher training initiatives. Chapter 12: *Dialogic interaction in the higher education classroom: a philosophy for children (P4C) approach* describes and argues for a teaching approach designed to scaffold students' thinking and allow opportunities for argumentation and reasoning. The chapter presents a number of empirical studies which point to the success of such an approach and draws on both teacher and student perspectives. Chapter 13: *Implementing a dialogic pedagogy in university seminar-based teaching* presents a case study of the implementation of dialogic pedagogy in higher education drama seminars. Drawing on teacher journals, qualitative and quantitative surveys as well as module marks, the chapter shows that implementation of dialogic pedagogy led to improved student assessment results. However, the chapter also shows that students can be uncomfortable with teaching formats which are discussion rather than transmission focused. Chapter 14: *Reflecting on the cultural assumptions we bring to teaching: one strategy for improving classroom interaction* puts a spotlight on the need for teaches to be aware of diversity (linguistic and neurodiversity) in their classes and how this impacts on classroom interaction. The chapter reports on a successful intervention in the form of a diversity awareness induction workshop for teachers which resulted in more emphasis on affective pedagogy. Chapter 15: *An experiment in how to teach strategies for effective classroom interaction: are we getting it right?* presents an summary of a pedagogic intervention by which students were systematically taught oracy skills for higher education classroom contexts. The chapter shows, using student feedback, that students benefited from explicit instruction in all dimensions of oracy combined with opportunities for reflection, provided for example by watching video-recorded performances. Chapter 16: *Conclusion: taking classroom interaction forward* provides a summary of the chapters in the book and argues that each of the contributions reflects a field of transformation. The transformation is reflected in the wide range of methodologies used by the authors, in the scope of learning opportunities and in the innovative pedagogies placing classroom interaction at the centre of the teaching and learning. In looking forward, the chapter reflects on how teaching and learning in online spaces is being reconfigured and argues for the key role of classroom interaction research in informing this emerging and innovative environment.

This book was conceived prior to Covid-19 and as such does not consider the growing field of literature and research on online interaction. As has been pointed out in both the Foreword and Chapter 16, this is an area which will benefit from further scholarship as both teachers and students accept online interaction as an increasingly familiar pattern of communication. We hope that this book will be used to inspire further research and develop teaching and interaction practices in the classroom, both face to face and online.

References

Alexander, R. J. (2001). *Culture and pedagogy: International comparisons in primary education*. Blackwell.

Björkman, B. (2013). *English as an academic lingua franca: An investigation of form and communicative effectiveness*. Walter de Gruyter.

Chiang, S. (2009). Dealing with communication problems in the instructional interactions between international teaching assistants and American college students. *Language and Education*, 23(5), 461–478.

Dippold, D. (2015) *Classroom interaction: the internationalised Anglophone university*. Palgrave.

French, A., & O'Leary, M. (Eds.). (2017). *Teaching excellence in higher education: Challenges, changes and the teaching excellence framework*. Emerald Group Publishing.

Gunn, A. (2018). Metrics and methodologies for measuring teaching quality in higher education: developing the Teaching Excellence Framework (TEF) . *Educational Review*, 70 (2), 129–148.

Mercer, N., & Howe, C. (2012). Explaining the dialogic processes of teaching and learning: the value and potential of sociocultural theory. *Learning, Culture and Social Interaction*, 1(1), 12–21.

Teaching Excellence and Student Outcomes Framework (TEF) (2017). Available from https://assets.publishing.service.gov.uk/government/uploads/system/uploads/attachm ent_data/file/658490/Teaching_Excellence_and_Student_Outcomes_Framework_Spe cification.pdf.

Tsui, A. B. (2001). Classroom interaction. In Carter, R. & Nunan, D. (Eds.), *The Cambridge guide to teaching English to speakers of other languages* (pp 120–125). Cambridge University Press.

Van Lier, L. (2014). *Interaction in the language curriculum: Awareness, autonomy and authenticity*. Routledge.

Walsh, S. (2013). *Classroom discourse and teacher development*. Edinburgh University Press.

Part I
Theoretical considerations

1 Overview of classroom interaction

Definitions, models, practices and challenges

Marion Heron and Doris Dippold

Introduction

Considering that the main aim of higher education (HE) learning and teaching is the development of disciplinary understanding, both conceptual development and skills, it is remarkable that classroom interaction and classroom talk have largely been underexplored in this context (Hardman, 2019; Heron, 2018; O'Keeffe & Walsh, 2010; Stokoe, 2000). This omission is concerning for a number of reasons. Firstly, classroom interaction where students are engaged in academic speaking has been found to be key to developing disciplinary understanding (Mah, 2016). Secondly, a considerable proportion of students' time is spent in seminars, tutorials and other learning environments in which students are expected to interact with each other. Thirdly, group work and other interactive activities are becoming increasingly common due to developments in HE pedagogy. Finally, research has shown that classroom talk "has the power to shape knowledge through participant engagement with a range of processes: hypothesising, exploration, debate and synthesis" (Barnes, 2010, p. 7), arguably key skills necessary for successful HE classroom participation. All these arguments underscore the importance of understanding classroom interaction in the HE context

Similarly, despite a large body of research on classroom interaction and classroom talk in compulsory school settings (Howe et al, 2019; Vrikki et al, 2019) and a strong tradition of exploring classroom interaction in second language learning contexts (Seedhouse, 1996; Tsui, 2001; Walsh, 2013), the general literature on HE, for example in high-impact journals such as *Studies in Higher Education* and *Teaching in Higher Education*, makes little mention of classroom interaction. There is much to be learned from studies examining how students learn a second language, or how school children construct understanding of concepts.

For this reason, it is timely we explore how classroom interaction works in an HE context. This chapter seeks to address the following questions:

- What are key terms in the study of classroom interaction?

- What is the relationship between classroom talk, classroom interaction and learning/conceptual development?
- What theoretical frameworks can be drawn on to explore classroom interaction?

Background

This chapter, and the book in general, takes a sociocultural perspective which places social interaction at the centre of learning. In an educational context, students construct understanding and knowledge through interacting with each other, both listening and speaking. As Vygotsky (1986) famously noted, there are two stages to learning. Firstly, we learn on an inter-psychological level (interacting with others) and then we learn on an intra-psychological level (interacting with ourselves). Language is a significant tool which is used to mediate our understanding of new concepts (Daniels, 2016): "…without language, we would not have, so to speak, general ideas; for it is the word which, in fixing them, gives to concepts a consistency sufficient for them to be able to be handled conveniently by the mind" (Durkheim, 1956 in Lauder et al, 2006, p. 82). This quote highlights the key role of language in interaction and learning.

The term interaction is generally understood to mean the *communication* between teacher, students and between students themselves (Tsui, 2001). Alexander (2020) notes that there are five ways of organising classroom interaction: whole-class teaching, teacher-led group work, student-led group work, teacher–student one-to one, and student–student one-to-one. In an English language learning context, Allwright (1984, p. 156) points out that "it is through this joint management of interaction in the classroom that language learning is itself jointly managed. The importance of interaction in classroom language learning is precisely that it entails this joint management of learning". The arguments posed here in a second language learning context also hold true for disciplinary contexts.

The term discourse is concerned with the 'text', in other words, the classroom *talk*. According to Tsui (2001), classroom discourse refers to the linguistic and non-linguistic elements of discourse which takes place in the classroom. Cazden (2001) puts forward several reasons for the significance of classroom discourse to teaching and learning and a rationale for empirical study. One is that the classroom discourse is the medium through which teaching and learning takes place. As Alexander (2001, p. 430) states: "The talk that takes place between a teacher and pupil and – less commonly among pupils themselves – is not merely a vehicle for the exchange of information. It is a vital tool of learning". Classroom interaction in which students participate orally with each other has been found to develop critical thinking skills and intellectual processing (Fassinger, 2000). Furthermore, students spend a considerable amount of time engaging in classroom discourse in their learning contexts. In HE, most students will spend several hours a day engaged in large-group and small-group learning contexts, as well as tutorials and labs.

Yet despite the centrality of quality classroom discourse to learning, the ubiquitous Initiation–Response–Feedback (IRF) exchange developed by Sinclair and Coulthard (1975) has traditionally prevailed in schools and HE. Recently, there have been some developments in adapting the IRF model to incorporate more dialogic moves through expanding the F-move. Consequently, as the chapters in this book demonstrate, IRF in its original teacher-fronted, lock-step mode no longer dominates. In fact, the IRF framework has provided a theoretical basis on which to elaborate the basic exchange pattern, taking into account the different ways in which teachers and students can exploit the F-move (Hardman, 2016, 2019).

In the next section, we outline a number of ways in which we might conceptualise classroom interaction and classroom discourse. The examples in the first section are drawn from the literature on research in compulsory education. We then present the scant work that has been carried out in HE contexts with a view to highlighting how we might draw on the former to enrich and develop research into HE classroom interaction.

Compulsory school settings

Exploratory talk

Exploratory talk is a way of viewing the dual activities of 'talk for learning' and 'learning to talk'. Mercer (1995) describes exploratory talk as classroom talk in which students make their thinking visible. This involves classroom discourse which specifically challenges, asks questions, defends, supports and gives justifications. It is argued that exploratory talk can be supported by establishing Talk Rules in which students agree, for example, to challenge each other's ideas. The ideas generated by exploratory talk have had considerable impact on the teaching of oracy skills in schools (Mercer, Warwick & Ahmed, 2017). A large body of research stemming from a project called Thinking Together has established that students' use of exploratory talk results in improvement in the quality of group work, group talk and individual attainment (see https://thin kingtogether.educ.cam.ac.uk/projects/).

Dialogic teaching

Dialogic teaching is an approach developed by Alexander (2004) and comprises dialogic teaching repertoires. According to Alexander, dialogic teaching is:

- Collective – i.e. teachers and learners address learning tasks together.
- Reciprocal – teachers and learners listen to each other, share ideas and consider alternative viewpoints.
- Supportive – children articulate their ideas freely without fear or embarrassment, and they help each other reach common understandings.
- Cumulative – children build on each other's ideas.

- Purposeful – teachers plan and guide learning activities with specific educational goals in mind.

In a recent study (see Alexander, 2018; Alexander, Hardman & Hardman, 2017; reported in Jay et al, 2017; Hardman, 2019), it was clear that interventions with teachers to develop their dialogic teaching skills resulted in more classroom interaction in which students were encouraged and able to engage in justification, elaboration and reasoning. A further result of the dialogic interaction was seen in higher achievements in maths and English.

Accountable talk

Michaels, O'Connor and Resnick (2008) argue for a notion of classroom talk which is accountable to:

- the community: all participants listen and build on each other's contributions.
- reasoning: participants explain and justify their ideas.
- knowledge: participants base their talk and contributions on fact and evidence.

Their ideas have been applied to subjects such as English and literacy (Richardson, 2010; Wolf, Crosson & Resnick, 2006) and science (Michaels & O'Connor, 2012). Michaels et al (2008) argue that developing students' accountable talk leads to greater academic achievement for diverse groups of students. Accountable talk is particularly relevant to an HE context due to its focus on knowledge, evidence and reasoning. Indeed, all three frameworks for viewing classroom interaction are entirely transferrable to the HE context. In HE we want students to challenge, debate and work together to solve problems, not just for academic achievement and beyond their higher education experience, but also to enable equitable participation and democratic engagement.

Higher education contexts

Whilst we have found that there has been little research into classroom interaction in HE settings, there are a few notable exceptions which have explored HE classroom interaction from a sociocultural perspective, with particular emphasis on classroom discourse.

Using a Conversation Analysis approach, Stokoe's (2000) research explored how students decide on the relevance, appropriacy and legitimacy of topics in their academic conversations. She summarises that explicating students' understanding of the task in which they are engaged is crucial to successful interaction. Whilst this research does not explicitly focus on the role of classroom interaction in developing conceptual understanding, it does provide an examination of how students interact in an HE context. The justification for exploring topic management is made by highlighting the lack of research in an HE context: "few studies have focused on discourse at this level and, as a result, little is known about the dynamics of adult educational talk" (Stokoe, 2000, p. 188).

O'Keeffe and Walsh (2010) also used a Conversation Analysis and Corpus Linguistics lens to examine HE seminar discourse. Their study revealed that in small-group teaching there are a number of classroom discourses, described as organisational talk, argumentative talk and discursive talk. The latter is highlighted as classroom discourse in which students discuss, challenge and carry out rhetorical moves associated with critical thinking. Here we see a direct link to dimensions of accountable talk and exploratory talk, as described above, and classroom discourse through which students develop their conceptual understanding.

Utilising the IRF framework, Hardman (2016) explored the classroom interaction of an undergraduate and postgraduate engineering management class. She found that there was little opportunity for students to explain their answers or engage in critical thinking. Her study revealed the limited IRF interaction prevalent in the HE classroom and she calls for more research on how to support HE tutors in using classroom interaction which engages students in "intellectually stimulating classroom talk" (p. 63).

Frameworks for analysing classroom interaction and classroom discourse

A number of studies have developed frameworks, systems and coding to analyse classroom discourse as well as several research approaches and methodologies for the study of classroom talk (Mercer, 2010). These frameworks have derived from studies in both the HE second language learning context and school settings. However, due to limitations of space, we present a few frameworks below which we believe to have had considerable impact on the field of classroom interaction.

Flanders Interaction Analysis Categories (FIAC)

FIAC (Freiberg, 1981) is an attempt to analyse the observable and verbal behaviour in the classroom. There are ten codes, mostly for teacher talk, with one for pupil talk and one for silence.

IRF

The IRF framework was developed by Sinclair and Coulthard in 1975, with the aim of coding classroom discourse into exchanges, moves and acts. The IRF pattern is considered to be the basic unit of interaction, and studies generally find that this pattern is common in all classrooms, regardless of context (primary, secondary, HE) and discipline. Although the IRF pattern has been heavily criticised (Clifton, 2006), it has provided a basis on which to develop frameworks which reframe the F-move as a more probing and exploratory move (Hardman, 2016, 2019) and to highlight the learning opportunities afforded by the F-move (Waring, 2008). The IRF exchange has also stimulated thinking around a focus on functions of classroom discourse rather than form (see for example the work of Boyd & Markarian, 2011, 2015) to inform notions of dialogic stance.

Self-evaluation of teacher talk (SETT)

The SETT framework was developed by Walsh (2006) for second language learning contexts and, in particular, for second language teacher development. The framework is organised into modes, pedagogic goals and interactional features. The interactional features are further broken down into descriptions. For example, in a managerial mode, the pedagogic goal may be to explain something, which is realised by an absence of learner contributions and an overdominance of teacher talk. The framework was developed to allow teachers to analyse their classroom interaction and classroom discourse for professional developmental purposes.

T-SEDA

T-SEDA was developed by Vrikki et al (2019) to support teacher development in primary and secondary schools, although the project has recently been utilised in HE contexts (see www.educ.cam.ac.uk/research/projects/tseda/). The framework comprises codes of talk moves, which may be attributed to teacher or student talk. The coding system is part of a wider scheme which aims to raise teacher and student awareness of classroom talk. Based on their research, the project team identified the codes of elaborate and query, across sustained participation, as crucial for developing conceptual knowledge (Vrikki et al, 2019). Using the tools developed in the scheme, teachers are encouraged to identify what types of classroom talk they use and how to incorporate more of the codes associated with supporting conceptual development and higher attainment.

A coding system for higher education

Hardman (2016) developed a coding system for analysing the classroom discourse in an HE context. Based on the three-part interactional exchange IRF, it includes further options for teacher and student questions, and in particular recognises the myriad of ways the teacher or student may provide the feedback move, such as probing or building on an answer. The coding system is applicable to a whole-class teaching context in which it is generally the teacher who provides the F-move. Hardman has since developed a more detailed coding system which acknowledges student feedback moves, which are more likely in a seminar or tutorial context. Hardman's (2019) work elaborates on the earlier model (see Chapter 3 in this volume) by including student moves, allowing for a more fine-grained analysis of classroom interaction, dialogic teaching and student learning outcomes. The latter framework was developed from empirical work in the school context.

The sociocultural context of classroom interaction

So far, we have mainly considered the linguistic elements of classroom interaction and classroom discourse. But as the chapters in this book bear testimony to, classroom interaction exists in a particular sociocultural context and this must be recognised in research studies (Engin, 2017). In the models presented above, there is acknowledgement of the importance of the classroom dynamics and atmosphere. Alexander's (2004) model of dialogic teaching identifies this through his features of reciprocity and support. Lefstein (2010) writes of the need to acknowledge the dialogic tensions which may be at play in exploring classroom dialogue and interaction. In other words, teachers may wish to create an environment in which there are opportunities for dialogic teaching and learning, but due to constraints such as the curriculum, institutional expectations and other practical considerations, the teacher may not be able to manage this. In this case, a realistic and pragmatic approach needs to be taken (see Heron, 2018 for an example of this in HE). The chapters in this book will surface these dialogic tensions and explore how classroom interaction can be managed and nurtured in a variety of sociocultural and educational contexts.

Classroom interaction at the internationalised university

A further dimension of the sociocultural context of classroom interaction in HE is internationalisation. Internationalisation has two different indications: *internationalisation abroad* relates to student (and staff) flows (Unesco, 2020), and *internationalisation at home* describes efforts for creating a cohesive and inclusive culture on the home campus (Turner & Robson, 2008). The growing number of mobile students has led to the creation of undergraduate and postgraduate programmes taught in English in countries where the majority language is not English, described with the term *English as a medium of instruction (EMI)* (Macaro, 2018). In these programmes, students as well as teachers often engage in learning in a second language. Similarly, in Anglophone HE environments, students and staff from different lingua-cultural backgrounds also come together to create diverse classroom communities. This creates issues and tensions in terms of language skills, expectations for classroom discourse, and student and staff willingness to adapt and accommodate to different ways of interacting in the classroom, which will be discussed in different chapters of this book.

Conclusion

Within a sociocultural perspective on learning, it is through articulating ideas that students co-construct understanding of disciplinary concepts. Classroom discourse is therefore at the heart of learning, yet it is woefully clear that there is little research on classroom interaction and discourse in HE disciplinary classrooms. The chapters in this book represent innovative and impactful work in this area. In view of the internationalised contexts in which students study, the development of disciplinary terminology is key to disciplinary understanding and accessing threshold concepts (Meyer & Land, 2006). Research has pointed out that speaking is a crucial skill in an EMI context to develop this disciplinary terminology (Arkoudis & Doughney, 2014); therefore, a closer look at how HE classrooms work together, the interaction patterns which prevail, and the discourse which unfolds, is timely and crucial.

References

Alexander, R. J. (2001). *Culture and pedagogy: International comparisons in primary education*. Oxford: Blackwell Publishing.

Alexander, R. (2004). *Dialogic teaching*. York: Dialogos.

Alexander, R. (2018). Developing dialogic teaching: Genesis, process, trial. *Research Papers in Education*, 33(5), 561–598.

Alexander, R. (2020). *A dialogic teaching companion*. London: Routledge.

Alexander, R. A., Hardman, F. C., & Hardman, J. (2017). *Changing Talk, Changing Thinking: Interim report from the in-house evaluation of the CPRT/UoY Dialogic Teaching Project*. Available from http://eprints.whiterose.ac.uk/151061/1/Alexander_Hardman_hardman_2017_.pdf.

Allwright, R. L. (1984). The importance of interaction in classroom language learning. *Applied Linguistics*, 5(2), 156–171.

Arkoudis, S., & Doughney, L. (2014). *Good Practice Report–English Language Proficiency*. Office for Learning and Teaching, Sydney. Available from https://melbourne-cshe.unimelb.edu.au/__data/assets/pdf_file/0004/1489162/GPR_English_language_2014.pdf.

Barnes, D. (2010). Why talk is important. *English Teaching*, 9(2), 7–10.

Boyd, M. P., & Markarian, W. C. (2011). Dialogic teaching: Talk in service of a dialogic stance. *Language and Education*, 25(6), 515–534.

Boyd, M. P., & Markarian, W. C. (2015). Dialogic teaching and dialogic stance: Moving beyond interactional form. *Research in the Teaching of English*, 49(3), 272–296.

Cazden, C. B. (2001). *The language of teaching and learning*. Portsmouth, NH: Heinemann.

Clifton, J. (2006). Facilitator talk. *ELT Journal*, 60(2), 142–150.

Daniels, H. (2016). *Vygotsky and pedagogy*. London: Routledge.

Durkheim, E. (2006). Education: Its nature and its role. In H. Lauder, P. Brown, J. Dillabough, & A. A. Halsey (Eds.), *Education, globalisation, and social change* (pp. 76–87). Oxford: Oxford University Press..

Engin, M. (2017). Contributions and silence in academic talk: Exploring learner experiences of dialogic interaction. *Learning, Culture and Social Interaction*, 12, 78–86.

Fassinger, P. A. (2000). How classes influence students' participation in college classrooms. *The Journal of Classroom Interaction*, 35(2), 38–47.

Freiberg, H. J. (1981). Three decades of the Flanders interaction analysis system. *The Journal of Classroom Interaction*, 16(2), 1–7.

Hardman, J. (2016). Tutor–student interaction in seminar teaching: Implications for professional development. *Active Learning in Higher Education*, 17(1), 63–76.

Hardman, J. (2019). Developing and supporting implementation of a dialogic pedagogy in primary schools in England. *Teaching and Teacher Education*, 86, 102908.

Heron, M. (2018). Dialogic stance in higher education seminars. *Language and Education*, 32(2), 112–126.

Howe, C., Hennessy, S., Mercer, N., Vrikki, M., & Wheatley, L. (2019). Teacher–student dialogue during classroom teaching: Does it really impact on student outcomes? *Journal of the Learning Sciences*, 28(4–5), 462–512.

Jay, T., Willis, B., Thomas, P., Taylor, R., Moore, N., Burnett, C., & Stevens, A. (2017). *Dialogic teaching: Evaluation report and executive Summary.* Available from https://educationendowmentfoundation.org.uk/public/files/Projects/Evaluation_Reports/Dialogic_Teaching_Evaluation_Report.pdf.

Lefstein, A. (2010). More helpful as problem than solution: Some implications of situating dialogue in classrooms. In K. Littleton and C. Howe (Eds.) *Educational dialogues: Understanding and promoting productive interaction* (pp. 170–191). Abingdon, UK: Routledge.

Macaro, E. (2018). *English medium instruction.* Oxford: Oxford University Press.

Mah, A. S. H. (2016). Oracy is as important as literacy: Interview with Christine CM Goh. *RELC Journal*, 47(3), 399–404.

Mercer, N. (1995). *The guided construction of knowledge: Talk amongst teachers and learners.* Clevedon: Multilingual Matters.

Mercer, N. (2010). The analysis of classroom talk: Methods and methodologies. *British Journal of Educational Psychology*, 80(1), 1–14.

Mercer, N, Warwick, P., & Ahmed, A. (2017). An oracy assessment toolkit: Linking research and development in the assessment of students' spoken language skills at age 11–12. *Learning and Instruction*, 48, 51–60.

Meyer, J., & Land, R. (Eds.) (2006). *Overcoming barriers to student understanding: Threshold concepts and troublesome knowledge.* Abingdon, Oxon: Routledge.

Michaels, S., & O'Connor, C. (2012). *Talk science primer.* Cambridge, MA: TERC.

Michaels, S, O'Connor, C., & Resnick, L. B. (2008). Deliberative discourse idealized and realized: Accountable talk in the classroom and in civic life. *Studies in Philosophy and Education*, 27(4), 283–297.

O'Keeffe, A., & Walsh, S. (2010). Investigating higher education seminar talk. *Novitas-ROYAL (Research on Youth and Language)*, 4(2), 141–158.

Richardson, A. E. (2010). Exploring text through student discussions: accountable talk in the middle school classroom. *English Journal*, 100(1), 83–88.

Seedhouse, P. (1996). Classroom interaction: Possibilities and impossibilities. *ELT Journal*, 50(1), 16–24.

Sinclair, J. M., & Coulthard, M. (1975). *Towards an analysis of discourse: The English used by teachers and pupils.* Oxford: Oxford University Press.

Stokoe, E. H. (2000). Constructing topicality in university students' small-group discussion: A conversation analytic approach. *Language and Education*, 14(3), 184–203.

Tsui, A. B. (2001). Classroom discourse: Approaches and perspectives. In J. Cenoz & N. H. Homberger (Eds.), *The encyclopedia of language and education* (Vol. 6: *Knowledge about language*) (pp. 261–272). New York: Springer.

Turner, Y., & Robson, S. (2008). *Internationalizing the university*. London: Continuum.

UNESCO (2020). *Global flow of tertiary-level students*. Available from http://uis.unesco.org/en/uis-student-flow.

Vrikki, M., Kershner, R., Calcagni, E., Hennessy, S., Lee, L., Hernández, F., ... & Ahmed, F. (2019). The teacher scheme for educational dialogue analysis (T-SEDA): Developing a research-based observation tool for supporting teacher inquiry into pupils' participation in classroom dialogue. *International Journal of Research & Method in Education*, 42(2), 185–203.

Vygotsky, L. S. (1986). *Thought and language*. Cambridge, MA: MIT Press.

Walsh, S. (2006). *Investigating classroom discourse*. Abingdon, Oxon: Routledge.

Walsh, S. (2013). *Classroom discourse and teacher development*. Edinburgh: Edinburgh University Press.

Waring, H. Z. (2008). Using explicit positive assessment in the language classroom: IRF, feedback, and learning opportunities. *The Modern Language Journal*, 92(4), 577–594.

Wolf, M. K., Crosson, A. C., & Resnick, L. B. (2006). *Accountable talk in reading comprehension instruction*. CSE Technical Report 670. University of Pittsburgh, National Center for Research on Evaluation, Standards, and Student Testing (CRESST).

2 Classroom Interactional Competence and evidence-based reflection

Steve Walsh

Introduction

This chapter makes the case for university teachers to become researchers of their teaching practice by reflecting on the interactions which take place in seminars and tutorials. For many university lecturers, much of their work is occupied by research, which is typically prioritised over teaching. At the same time, this same group of professionals has, typically, developed a set of research skills and expertise which enable them to produce quality research outputs. The argument in this chapter is that academics should be able to transfer these research skills to their teaching; becoming a researcher of one's own practice is not, I suggest, such a big step given that most of these teachers already have research skills.

The notion of scholarship of teaching and learning (SoTL) is gaining credence in many higher education (HE) contexts (see, for example, McKinney 2006). Essentially, SoTL entails studying one's own teaching and highlighting those elements which constitute good or even exemplary practice. What is needed, then, is a methodology for advancing scholarship; a means of researching professional practice that will enhance the quality of teaching and learning and improve the experience of our students. As in many disciplines, researching SoTL entails the identification of an issue or problem, the selection of a methodology for studying that issue or problem, and data to provide findings and evidence for any change to practice.

The central argument of this chapter is that SoTL can be advanced through reflective practice, providing university teachers are given something to reflect *on* and something to reflect *with*. Here, the focus of reflection is classroom interaction, which underpins much of what is learnt in any classroom. As previous studies have shown convincingly, understandings of teaching and learning can be enhanced through a detailed understanding of interaction. In this chapter, I make the case for university teachers to study and improve their Classroom Interactional Competence (Walsh 2013) through evidence-based reflection.

The chapter falls into three main sections:

- Classroom Interactional Competence
- Evidence-based reflection
- The SETTVEO research project

In the final part of the chapter, implications for university teaching and learning are discussed.

Classroom Interactional Competence

Classroom Interactional Competence (CIC) is defined as, 'teachers' and learners' ability to use interaction as a tool for mediating and assisting learning' (Walsh 2013, p 65). It puts interaction at the centre of teaching and learning and argues that by improving their CIC, both teachers and learners will immediately improve learning and opportunities for learning. The central argument of a focus on CIC is that by helping teachers better understand classroom interaction, there will be a corresponding impact on learning, especially where learning is regarded as a social activity which is strongly influenced by involvement, engagement and participation. The starting point of an understanding of CIC is to acknowledge the centrality of interaction to teaching and learning.

CIC focuses on the ways in which teachers' and learners' interactional decisions and subsequent actions enhance learning and learning opportunity. It addresses questions such as:

- How are new concepts, ideas and knowledge co-constructed through interaction?
- What do participants do to ensure that understandings are reached?
- How do interactants address 'trouble' and repair breakdowns?
- What is the relationship between CIC and learning in a university context?
- How is 'space for learning' (Walsh & Li 2012) created and maintained?

The relevance of CIC is clear. If our aim as university educators is to promote dialogic, engaged and 'safe' classroom environments where students are actively involved and feel free to contribute and take risks, we need to study the interactions which take place and learn from them. The proposal here is that we need to acquire a fine-grained understanding of what constitutes Classroom Interactional Competence and how it might be achieved. This can be accomplished by using data from our own context; the starting point has to be evidence from the seminar or tutorial in the form of a video- or audio recording, self- or peer observation. Only by starting to describe interactional processes can we begin to understand in some detail our local context. Not only will such an understanding result in more engaged and dynamic interactions in classrooms, it will also enhance learning (see, for example, Mercer 2009; Walsh 2019).

While it is true to say that CIC is highly context specific, there are a number of features which are common to all contexts. Firstly, pedagogic goals and the language used to achieve them are convergent: they work together. This is clearly particularly important in more technical subjects where students must acquire the metalanguage of the discipline in order to access that discipline. Put simply, students need to learn to 'talk the talk' of their subject if they are to gain a closer understanding of it. From a university teacher's perspective, this entails developing an understanding of the interactional strategies which are appropriate to the unfolding agenda of a seminar or lecture. This position assumes that pedagogic goals and the language used to achieve them are inextricably intertwined and constantly being re-adjusted (see Seedhouse 2004; Walsh 2006;). Any evidence of CIC must therefore demonstrate that interlocutors are using discourse which is both appropriate to specific pedagogic goals and to the agenda of the moment.

Secondly, CIC facilitates interactional space: students need space to participate in the discourse, to contribute to seminar debates and to receive feedback on their contributions. In short, CIC creates 'space for learning' (Walsh & Li, 2012). There are a number of ways in which space for learning can be maximised. These include increasing wait time: by resisting the temptation to 'fill silence' (by reducing teacher echo), by promoting extended learner turns and by allowing planning time. By affording learners space, they are better able to contribute to the process of co-constructing meanings – something which lies at the very heart of learning through interaction.

Thirdly, CIC entails *shaping* learner contributions. Shaping involves taking a learner response and doing something with it rather than simply accepting it. For example, a response may be paraphrased, using more technical language or a particular code or metalanguage; it may be summarised or extended in some way, or linked to a specific reference; a response may require scaffolding so that learners are assisted in saying what they really mean; it may be recast (c.f. Lyster 1998): 'handed back' to the learner but with some small changes included. By shaping learner contributions and by helping learners to articulate what they mean, teachers are performing a more central role in the interaction, while, at the same time, maintaining a student-centred, decentralised approach to teaching. This position chimes with much of the recent research on feedback, which has been shown to be central to good practice in HE teaching and learning.

In this section, I have discussed the 'what' of professional development by proposing a focus for reflection in the form of CIC. The next section looks at the 'how' of reflective practice and proposes a methodology for researching SoTL using dialogic reflection.

Evidence-based reflection

Few practitioners and teacher educators would question the value of reflection and reflective practice (RP). Professionals have been reflecting on their practice for many years, since the inception of RP by Dewey (1933) and its subsequent elevation to its present position, which, arguably, is one of orthodoxy or widespread acceptance (Mann & Walsh 2013; Walsh & Mann 2015). In a body of work which now spans around 10 years, Walsh and Mann have endeavoured to re-position RP as a process which requires evidence – in the form of data; dialogue with another professional; appropriate tools and a collaborative approach to research.

There are three elements to current approaches to reflection, often referred to as peer observation of teaching, or POT, in many universities:

a   There is both a lack of data-led research on RP and a need for data-led practice in RP (Mann & Walsh 2017). Essentially, there is a need for more evidence from the perspectives of both research and professional development.
b   Current thinking in teacher education emphasises approaches which foster teacher autonomy and self-development. For this to be effective, there is a pressing need for teachers to acquire the skills and practices which will allow them to develop as teacher-researchers, using evidence from their own contexts.
c   Following on from (a) and (b), the argument here is that teacher efficacy will be heightened when teachers develop closer and better-grounded understandings of their contexts. Evidence-based reflection is, I suggest, the most appropriate means of ensuring that such understandings occur.

Much of the work on RP over a long period has focused on written forms of reflection (c.f. Farrell 2006). My focus here is on *dialogic reflection* (Walsh 2006; Walsh & Mann 2015; Mann & Walsh 2017), whereby professional development is enhanced through collaboration and dialogue with a colleague or critical friend. The claim is not so much that one form of reflection is in any way better than another, rather that there needs to be a rebalancing of written reflection – which tends to be solitary – towards something spoken. Dialogic reflection is a collaborative process of professional learning which entails interaction, discussion and debate with another professional. It emphasises learning (and professional development more broadly) as a social process whereby meanings and new understandings of complex phenomena are mediated by language. Dialogue allows meanings to be co-constructed, new understandings to emerge and professional learning to develop. Dialogic processes can either be intrapersonal or interpersonal (private or public, c.f. Vygotsky 1978), entailing interactions between individuals or between an individual and an artefact or tool. It draws heavily on sociocultural theories of learning, which highlight the importance of language as a mediating tool, stressing the value of social interaction in professional learning.

Current thinking on best practice in SoTL emphasises discovery-based learning through problem-solving; the value of 'talk' in promoting new understandings; and the importance of publicly derived knowledge becoming privately internalised or appropriated. Much of the current thinking recognises the value of interaction and dialogue in the process (Johnson 2009). Arguably, the quality of that interaction is very much dependent on the teacher's ability to manage complex interactional processes and 'correctly' interpret the learning environment. Dialogue facilitates understanding by allowing interactants space and support to express their ideas and arrive at new or different takes on a particular practice, issue or concern. Opportunities for reflection and learning are maximised when new concepts, or the metalanguage used to realise them, can be both understood and verbalised. However, the centrality of speech to learning has another, more significant dimension: consciousness, considered by Vygotsky as being central to learning, is developed through social interaction. Teachers become more aware, through participation in social activity, of themselves, their practices and actions. Dialogic reflection may lead to deeper, longer-lasting professional development and can facilitate the appropriation of good practice (Mann & Walsh 2017; Walsh 2019).

A second key element of dialogic reflection is collaboration, seen here as being highly relevant to the reflective cycle (c.f. Schön 1983). While for some, the process of reflection may be seen as a solitary practice (see, for example, Osterman & Kottcamp 1993), it is not always easy to be critical when reflecting on one's own behaviour or practice. As Osterman and Kottcamp put it, 'analysis occurring in a collaborative and cooperative environment is likely to lead to greater learning' (1993, p 6).

In addition to dialogue and collaboration, another central feature of dialogic reflection are the tools and artefacts which can be used as a catalyst (e.g. metaphors, critical incidents, video) and help promote more systematic and focused professional dialogue. Examples include the use of transcripts and recordings of classroom talk, though more recently there has been an effort to move away from transcription on the basis that it is too time-consuming and not always representative of what 'really happens'. One alternative is the use of 'snapshot' lesson excerpts: short 7–10-minute recordings which are then ana-lysed without transcription (Walsh 2011). In the next and final section of this chapter, I demonstrate how this might work in a report on a British Council project which has just concluded.

The SETTVEO project

The aim of this British Council funded ELTRA (English Language Teaching Research Award) project was to enable HE teachers to reflect on their practice through the use of SETT (Self Evaluation of Teacher Talk) and VEO (Video Enhanced Observation) – henceforth 'SETTVEO'. Participating teachers used the SETTVEO app to collect data, reflect on their practice by studying their developing CIC and share their reflections through an online community of practice.

The VEO app was developed by teacher educators at Newcastle University; it allows users to record and tag videos which can be uploaded and saved into a portal (see www.veo-group.com). By enabling the live tagging of video, the VEO app goes further, generating data and evidence which is both quantitative and qualitative in nature. Predefined tags are used by practitioners to time-stamp video and classify moments in a manner that allows their aggregation and quick recall. On review, automatic categorisation of these micro-events builds up a profile of practice for the entire episode, while facilitating easy access to each individual moment. The tags allow the user to jump to the exact instance within the video, presenting a rich view of action, interaction and context that can be shared for further analysis and evaluation.

This tagging functionality allows for systematic data collection over time, supported by illuminating video evidence that can be interpreted and analysed by multiple practitioners and researchers. An intuitive, easy-to-use system enhances teachers' understanding by presenting data in a readily under-standable format, providing a base on which reflective processes can occur. The data tags pick a path through the relative chaos of a teaching episode while maintaining access to video for situated recall of interactions. Resul-tant conversations can heighten awareness to drive changes in, and build understanding of, interaction for professional practice.

VEO has been trialled in numerous geographical locations and educational contexts across the globe for various purposes, including: improving initial teacher education in the UK and Finland; enabling ongoing teacher CPD in the USA, China and Ghana; researching university-level medical education; and evaluating pupil understanding of taught concepts. The advantages that VEO brings to analysing complex situations make it highly appropriate for studying interaction, where multiple perspectives are possible and where relevant frameworks can clarify and enhance its understanding.

The SETT framework was originally developed in 2006 as a means of helping HE English language teachers to reflect on their use of language and interaction while teaching. It has been used in a range of educational settings since its publication and further development in 2011 and 2013. The SETT framework comprises four classroom micro-contexts (called *modes*) and 14 interactional fea-tures (called *interactures*). Classroom discourse is portrayed as a series of complex and inter-related micro-contexts or modes, where meanings are co-constructed by teachers and learners and where learning occurs through the ensuing talk of teachers and learners (Walsh 2013). The key to developing good practice is for teachers to acquire detailed profiles of the interactions which take place in their classes as a means of understanding how learning opportunities are created, how 'space for learning' (Walsh & Li 2012) can be opened up, and in order to create the kind of dialogic, engaged learning environments which have been advocated for more than 10 years (see, for example, Alexander, 2008; Mercer, 2009).

In this study, SETT and VEO were combined in order to help university teachers profile their interactions, improve their Classroom Interactional Competence (CIC) and enhance learning and learning opportunity. By sharing their reflections in an international online community of practice, it was possible to develop a global network of reflections, with teachers identifying and talking about common problems and issues in a range of contexts. In this way, it was possible to share understandings of CIC – which is highly context specific – and acquire insights into professional practices from a range of contexts. By making comments and comparisons and by engaging in reflective accounts, the goal was to increase awareness and understanding of the types of interaction that help learning. Communicating via the VEO social/professional network, these processes and the communities involved were able to operate at distance, thus exposing practitioners to a wider range of different interaction styles and offering a clearer view of their own practice.

The British Council ELTRA project was guided by the following research questions:

1   How do VEO and SETT networks promote evidence-based reflection?
2   To what extent are teachers able to improve their classroom interactional competence through the use of SETTVEO?
3   What evidence is there that the process of using SETTVEO, combined with reflection and online discussion, results in more dialogic, engaged learning environments?

Using outcomes from a previous research project, a total of four partner countries were included in the study (Spain, Turkey, Chile, Thailand). From each country, five university teachers volunteered to participate, giving a total of 20 teachers in all.

The following approaches to data collection were adopted:

Phase 1. In this phase of the project, baseline data were collected to include a short, video-recorded lesson segment plus a short reflective commentary by each teacher, and an online interview with the research team. In this phase, the aim was to provide an overview of teachers' professional practices in each of the four contexts.

Phase 2. In the second phase of the study, participating teachers each made four 'snapshot' recordings of their teaching (7–10 minutes per recording). Online training in the use of SETTVEO was provided. Each recording was then reviewed and evaluated using SETTVEO. The recordings and reflective commentaries were uploaded to the VEO platform and made available to the entire community comprising four country partners.

Phase 3. In the final phase of the study, participating teachers took part in online focus groups and individual interviews to evaluate the extent to which their reflective practices had changed and to consider any changes in CIC.

Data were analysed using the following combination of approaches:

1   Profiles of each teacher's classroom practices were created using the VEO software and SETT tags. These provided detailed qualitative and quantitative information about teachers' interactional practices, use of language, levels of learner involvement, use of language in relation to pedagogic goals and so on.

2   Conversation analysis was used to transcribe and analyse a sample of the video-recorded classroom data.
3   Thematic analysis was used to analyse focus group and interview data.
4   Reflective commentaries from teachers' interactions in the online community, together with their posts, were analysed using thematic content analysis.

Owing to limitations of space, a brief summary of the findings is presented here. (For a full report of this project, the reader is referred to Walsh 2019.)

A number of teachers commented on their developing CIC; Teacher A, below, for example, talks about her elicitation strategies and gives reasons for her particular use of display or referential questions. Of interest in this extract is the extent to which this teacher uses an appropriate metalanguage to describe her practices – she talks about question types and (indirectly) teacher echo ('I repeated the same phrases several times'). She goes on to include two additional interactures: content feedback and form-focused feedback. It is also of interest to note that she is able to rationalise her use of particular features which helped and supported her students.

Indications of CIC include an ability to use an appropriate metalanguage and to be able to justify 'online decision making' (Walsh 2013) – both of which are evidenced by this teacher in her reflective commentary. She refers to five of the 14 interactional features included in the app and is able to both justify her interactional decisions and explain how level is an important determiner of these practices.

Extract 1

> I asked mostly display questions to help them do brainstorming about the topics and to make most of the students be able to speak about the topics. At the beginning I needed to ask some referential questions (00.20) to refer to the exercises we did in our former lessons. After watching myself in the video I saw that I repeated the same phrases several times, but I think this helped them speak better and self-confidently because they were elementary level students and needed to hear too many repetitions and examples. Firstly, I used content feedback to emphasise how they would find relevant supporting ideas for the topics we discussed, how they would agree/disagree with each other, how they would organise their ideas and list them. Secondly, I mostly preferred form-focused feedback because they were in need of hearing correct forms and learning how to make correct sentences.
>
> (Teacher A)

An important feature of the SETTVEO app is the tagging function, which allows users to 'tag' (i.e. mark) specific features of their interactions and then review these features later. The software then prepares a statistical breakdown showing how features are used, which ones occur most frequently and how the use of certain interactional features affected the interaction. In Extract 2 below, Teacher C is talking about her use of teacher echo, commenting on her excessive use of discourse markers (sometimes referred to as transition markers). Note too the statistical breakdown of specific features, making a valid comparison between display and referential questions – the former dominate most classroom talk, while teachers often miss opportunities to ask genuine, or referential, questions. Again, she demonstrates a high level of CIC through her ability to use an appropriate metalanguage and justify her actions, even being quite critical of her decisions at times.

Extract 2

> Looking at the tagging session report, I observed that the teacher echo was excessive to my standards. It made me realise that I should put an effort to reduce it, because I found it annoying to watch myself saying so many "oks", "alrights". The amount of display questions on the report was high at 40%, compared to the referential questions at 15%. The amount of content feedback and seeking clarification were quite similar at approximately 15%. The lowest rate was form focused feedback with only about 3%. Although I was a bit disappointed at myself for making the tagging session a bit long because of the wait times for the reading and watching the videos, the extended wait time was quite low in the report, with only 5%.
>
> (Teacher C)

In a project which focuses on reflective practice, there is clearly an interest to note any changes to practice, or rather, if any changes to practice were reported. In Extract 3, the emphasis is very much on the students rather than on teacher performance (*the best way of creating self-sufficiency; the better they feel and learn*). One of the main advantages of tagging software like the SETTVEO app is that, while the user may be focusing on their own use of language and interactional features (i.e. the teacher's), they cannot ignore what students are doing; one aspect of CIC is to understand how teacher and learner interaction are inextricably linked.

Extract 3

> Speaking and helping them speak is the best way of creating self-sufficiency. The more they speak, the better they feel and learn.
>
> (Teacher M)

The extent to which SETTVEO promoted a focus on learners – a point made in relation to Extract 3 – is illustrated in the next extract. Teacher G in Extract 4 focuses on the need to vary tasks more. She is able to highlight the main problem or issue in her class (*not all the students talked about the topic*) and suggest a possible way forward: the use of pair/group work and a more interesting worksheet. Of interest too is the reference to 'learning more instinctively', which suggests that – for this teacher at least – certain task types promote more 'instinctive' opportunities for learning. While this idea would need to be explored further with Teacher G, this extract highlights the extent to which a focus on speaking helps students to gain confidence and become more independent as learners.

Extract 4

> When it comes to the question "What would I change If I taught the same lesson again?" It would definitely be task variety. I criticise myself about sticking to the same type of task, which can be really boring for unmotivated learners. As far as I observed in my class, due to some personal factors, lack of task variety and restricted time, not all the students talked about the topic which was not my expectation before the class. Had there been small pair or group works, students could have participated and been more productive. I could have distributed worksheets; therefore, they could have felt more inspired and orientated to learning more instinctively.
>
> (Teacher G)

It is clear when reading the final extract that for some of the participants at least, the use of video in SoTL is of great benefit. Teacher B, with 16 years' experience, emphasises the value of self-observation as a means of understanding classroom dynamics and understanding student feelings and attitudes. Of importance in this observation is the fact that she seems to suggest that her own strengths and weaknesses can be gleaned by focusing on her learners; an acute and mature observation. Rather than 'blaming the learner', this teacher takes responsibility for her professional practice, acknowledging that while her understanding of teaching and learning can be developed through self-observation, a focus on her students will clearly highlight her strengths and weaknesses as a teacher.

Extract 5

> I had an opportunity to reflect on my teaching as a teacher having sixteen years' experience considering my classroom video as a part of SETTVEO Project. During this period, I found a chance to make a self-observation which enabled me to be deeply aware of my classroom dynamics, students' attitudes and feelings during the class and as a matter of course my strengths and weaknesses.
>
> (Teacher B)

Conclusion

The aim of this chapter was to suggest a methodology which might contribute towards an understanding of the SoTL in HE, with a particular focus on classroom interaction. The reader is reminded that SoTL entails studying one's own practice and highlighting those elements which constitute good or even exemplary practice. In the first two sections, the chapter advocated two key elements of this methodology: evidence-based reflection and Classroom Interactional Competence. In the final section, an example of the methodology was reported via a recently completed research project.

I believe that there are three main conclusions to be drawn from the evidence presented here; each has relevance for teaching and learning in the internationalised university.

Firstly, there is considerable evidence to highlight the importance of video in any future work on SoTL. Recent studies (see, for example, Mann et al 2018) confirm the value of video in mediating understandings of teaching and in unpacking the complexities of that process. By giving teachers a tool and focus, reflection becomes extremely 'doable' and useful. Note too that relatively short 'snapshot' recordings have value in heightening awareness and deepening understandings; given an appropriate tool and a clear focus, there is no need for wholesale transcription of lessons. Put simply, video creates opportunities for professional development in a relatively short space of time and without an enormous investment of energy.

Secondly, teaching in HE would benefit from a closer understanding of CIC; while many introductory university teacher education programmes highlight the importance of subject knowledge and pedagogical skills, hardly any – to my knowledge – promote an understanding of interaction. Given its centrality to learning, it seems vital to foster up-close and 'ecological' (van Lier 1996) understandings of classroom interaction. If we accept that interaction is where the action is, the place to look for evidence of learning, then surely it warrants closer scrutiny. Advances in technology and the widespread use of video make this so much easier to achieve. And yet course providers, materials designers and curriculum and policy planners have not, to my knowledge, seized this opportunity by integrating interactional competence into their courses and degrees. By making CIC a core requirement, course providers would be taking an important step in highlighting the need for a detailed understanding of interaction.

Finally, any attempts to advance SoTL in HE would be well-advised to make data and evidence key components; university teachers are extremely aware of the need for data in their research and writing. It would not be too much of a leap to make data, evidence and dialogue key components of their teaching practice. By using appropriate tools like SETTVEO, university teachers can easily collect evidence and engage in meaningful dialogic reflection with a colleague or critical friend.

The potential from what was essentially a small-scale study reported here is enormous; it would not be difficult, for example, to build an international corpus of professional practice in HE, comprising video recordings and reflections from every corner of the globe. The ability to offer such a product is with us now; there are clearly enormous advantages in developing an online resource through which teachers comment on and compare teaching practices from around the world. Not only would such a resource promote greater understandings of teaching and learning, it would result in closer and deeper understandings of context, surely one of the most important elements in any internationalised university.

24   *Steve Walsh*

References

Alexander, R. J. (2008). *Towards dialogic teaching: rethinking classroom talk* (4th ed.). York: Dialogos.

Dewey, J. (1933). *How we think: a restatement of the relation of reflective thinking to the educative process* (Revised ed.). Boston, A: D. C. Heath.

Farrell, T. S. C. (Ed.) (2006). *Language teacher research in Asia.* Alexandria, VA: TESOL.

Johnson, K. E. (2009). *Second language teacher education: a sociocultural perspective.* London and New York: Routledge.

Lyster, R. (1998). Recasts, repetitions and ambiguity in L2 classroom discourse. *Studies in Second Language Acquisition*, 20, 51–81.

Mann, S. et al (2018). Video in language teacher education. *ELT Research Papers*, 19/01. London: The British Council.

Mann, S. and Walsh, S. (2013). RP or 'RIP': a critical perspective on reflective practice. *Applied Linguistics Review*, 4(2), 291–315.

Mann, S. and Walsh, S. (2017). *Reflective practice in English language teaching: research-based principles and practices.* London and New York: Routledge.

McKinney, K. (2006). Attitudinal and structural factors contributing to challenges in the work of the scholarship of teaching and learning. *New Directions for Institutional Research*, 129(Summer), 37–50.

Mercer, N. (2009). *Words and minds: how we use language to think together.* London: Routledge.

Osterman, K. F. and Kottkamp, R. B. (1993). *Reflective practice for educators: improving schooling through professional development.* Thousand Oaks, CA: Corwin Press Inc.

Schön, D.A. (1983). *The reflective practitioner.* London: Temple Smith.

Seedhouse, P. (2004). *The interactional architecture of the second language classroom: a conversational analysis perspective.* Oxford: Blackwell.

van Lier, L. (1996). *Interaction in the language curriculum: awareness, autonomy and authenticity.* New York: Longman.

Vygotsky, L. S. (1978). *Mind in society: the development of higher psychological processes.* Cambridge, MA: Harvard University Press.

Walsh, S. (2006). *Investigating classroom discourse.* London: Routledge.

Walsh, S. (2011). *Exploring classroom discourse: language in action.* London and New York: Routledge.

Walsh, S. (2013). *Classroom discourse and teacher development.* Edinburgh: Edinburgh University Press.

Walsh, S. (2019). SETTVEO: evidence-based reflection and teacher development. *ELT research papers.* London: The British Council.

Walsh, S. and Li, L. (2012). Conversations as space for learning. *International Journal of Applied Linguistics*, 23(2), 247–266.

Walsh, S. and Mann, S. (2015). Doing reflective practice: a data-led way forward. *ELT journal*, 69(4), 351–362.

3 Pedagogical renewal

Promoting a dialogic pedagogy in the internationalised 21st-century higher education

Jan Hardman

Introduction

Higher education in the 21st century has become a fully global entity linked internationally through teaching, research, and impact activity. UK universities place a high premium on internationalisation as it drives recruitment of international staff and students, study-abroad programmes, and cross-border research and impact collaborations. The main goals of higher education are to provide students from diverse backgrounds with a holistic experience at the personal, academic, and social level and to prepare them for studying, living, and working in the globalised world. There is, therefore, a need to rethink the pedagogy of higher education to align it with these goals. This chapter calls for a paradigm shift in the way in which teaching and learning is delivered in higher education and argues that a dialogic pedagogy needs to be central in transforming teaching and learning in higher education.

The chapter begins with a discussion of the globalised landscape of higher education in the 21st century. It goes on to explain what a dialogic pedagogy is and to discuss the benefits and challenges of implementing such a pedagogy in the higher education sector. It also offers a critically reflective professional development scheme to help lecturers adopt a dialogic pedagogy in their lectures and seminars. It concludes with a call for more research into the implementation of a dialogic pedagogy in higher education.

Internationalised higher education

The remit of higher education has broadened extensively to not only develop students' personal, academic, and intellectual growth but also to prepare them well for living and working in the globalised world. Its mission is to provide students with an excellent learning environment in which they are taught to develop a range of transferable and employability skills needed by employers, such as communication, problem-solving, collaborative teamwork and enterprise (Shapiro, 2006; Nixon, 2011; Teo, 2019). However, it can be argued that the economic purpose of higher education cannot be fulfilled without addressing the growth of students at the personal, intellectual, and academic levels. Students need to develop a sense of self, curiosity, criticality, agency, and active citizenship, and to be well-informed in their academic subjects if they are to become well-rounded individuals and members of an internationalised workforce in the 21st century.

The internationalisation agenda of UK universities has attracted large numbers of students from different countries who bring with them diverse identities, experiences, dispositions, expectations, and perspectives. The diversity of ideas and perspectives offers a rich source of learning for all students and needs to be maximised in the classroom through dialogue and discussion that are central to a dialogic pedagogy (Alexander, 2016, 2020).

However, it has to be acknowledged that learning through dialogue and discussion can present a challenge to students enrolling in higher education if they have not had much exposure to a co-constructive approach to learning in school. For international students, the challenges could be even greater if they have experienced teacher-centred approaches where students are often passive recipients of knowledge (Chen, 2014; Engin, 2017). International students need to adapt to a new way of learning and negotiate the unspoken rules of engagement and discourse norms of the UK culture of learning (Jin & Cortazzi, 2006). A dialogic pedagogy offers a way of addressing these types of challenges as it makes explicit the agreed ground rules for collaboration in whole-class and group-based learning through discussion and dialogue.

Another challenge for non-western international students revolves around the English language. Second language acquisition research suggests that it may take between five and seven years for learners to develop a good level of academic language competence in a foreign language (Cummins & Swain, 1986). International students are not only required to learn English as a foreign/second language, but also to learn the subject content through the medium of English. Furthermore, having acquired the academic content, they then need to be able to display the learning and knowledge visibly in appropriate academic discourse forms. However, it is important to stress that the challenges described here are not a reflection of deficiency in intellectual ability on the part of international students (Trenkic & Warmington, 2019).

A dialogic pedagogy can address the language-based challenges in two main ways: firstly, it can provide a safe and supportive classroom environment where students are not made to feel embarrassed when making a mistake, and secondly, it makes explicit the discourse moves that facilitate respectful, productive discussion and dialogue (Alexander, 2016, 2020). Therefore, a dialogic pedagogy is well placed for dealing with such barriers to learning and for enhancing the student experience through exposure to a diverse range of ideas and perspectives.

Classroom research in higher education

Classroom research in higher education (Boyle, 2010; De Klerk, 1995; Engin, 2017; Hardman, 2016a, 2016b; Simpson, 2016; Teo, 2016) points to three main findings: a limited range of teaching methods being used; the dominance of lecturer-centred knowledge transmission and recitation; and a lack of dialogue-rich collaborative group work. For example, Hardman (2016a) carried out a case study of seminar teaching with British third-year undergraduate and international postgraduate students on an engineering management course. The findings showed that, despite the small-group teaching, the discourse was predominantly lecturer-led, with little room being provided for extended student contributions, as the lecturer rarely probed, built on or challenged student responses. The recitation is illustrated in Extract 1 below (taken from Hardman, 2016a:67).

Extract 1

(T = university tutor; S = student)

1	T:	got a balance sheet? so first thing to do is try and find the balance sheet
2	S1:	[gives positive response]
3	T:	OK, great, good
4	T:	So can you see tangible fixed assets, yep?
5	S1:	Yeah
6	T:	OK, is it called anything different?
7	S2:	Group balance sheet
8	T:	OK

As can be seen in Extract 1, the discourse exchange is short, led by the lecturer asking closed questions (lines 1, 4, and 6). In response, the students provide brief (expected) answers. The interaction is mainly to check students' knowledge of the already presented teaching content. Such orchestration of the classroom talk by the lecturer closes down students' authentic contributions and thinking, resulting in stilted and fragmented discourse exchanges.

Hardman's study also showed that little opportunity was provided for students to work in small groups or pairs, and when they did occur, the length of discussions was brief (5 minutes on average). The student group discussions were largely focused on the exchanging of ideas without any real attempts to build on or critically evaluate the ideas being presented.

De Klerk's (1995) analysis of postgraduate seminars in a Faculty of Arts revealed that the teaching was dominated by long lecturer monologues interspersed with short question–answer sequences. There was a distinct lack of substantive feedback on student responses and also feedforward to propel conceptual understanding and cognitive development. Boyle's (2010) study of 15 seminars covering ten subjects – architecture, chemistry, computer science, education, engineering, English, management, music, pharmacy, and politics – showed that lecturers asked far more questions than students and that student turns were significantly shorter than those of the lecturers. Similarly, Teo's study (2016) in the context of pre-university language classrooms showed that tutors closed down student talk through excessive use of display questions. These findings suggest that lecturers, regardless of subject disciplines, do most of the talking in class and that students are provided with few opportunities to share their thinking, offer alternative ideas and perspectives, and talk with other students. This situation exacerbates the issue of (deadly) silence in the classroom, particularly on the part of international students who, as discussed above, may have problems with language and/or acculturation into the UK culture of learning (Jin & Cortazzi, 2006; Engin, 2017).

Overall, classroom research in higher education suggests that there are missed opportunities for enhancing the student learning experience. The heavy reliance on traditional knowledge transmission and recitation methods denies students the opportunity for deepening their understanding of the academic content as they encounter it in class. It also hinders lecturers from being able to diagnose students' misconceptions of the curriculum content. Furthermore, the lack of group work restricts students from building relationships with the lecturer and peers, which are necessary for creating students' sense of belonging and community. This leads to a widespread reporting of problems with poor participation and engagement in learning in higher education (Rocca, 2010). A lack of collaborative discussions as part of the classroom experience also denies students the opportunity for developing a sense of confidence, agency, critical thinking, curiosity, communication, and teamwork skills. In light of these shortcomings, there is a need to place a dialogic pedagogy at the centre of teaching and learning in higher education.

What is a dialogic pedagogy?

Dialogic pedagogy is influenced by a sociocultural theory of learning and development (Vygotsky, 1962) that highlights the role of social interaction and language as crucial mediators of the learning process. Five principles underpin the dialogic teaching framework (Alexander, 2016). A dialogic pedagogy is:

- collective – the lecturer and students work together as a team through whole-class, small-group and one-to-one discussions
- reciprocal – participants listen actively and respect different viewpoints
- supportive – a safe, positive classroom climate is created
- cumulative – knowledge is co-constructed to develop shared understanding
- purposeful – classroom tasks are planned with specific educational goals in mind

The first three principles – collective, reciprocal, and supportive – help to create a safe, open, and inclusive space for students to learn comfortably, which is vital for their sense of confidence, agency, and wellbeing, and for promoting social and academic integration in multicultural classrooms (Spencer-Oatey & Dauber, 2019). A positive classroom climate can also be reinforced by ground rules that are negotiated and agreed upon by both the lecturer and students, such as 'giving people time to talk', 'listening carefully to each other', 'asking questions', 'giving evidence or reasoning for ideas', 'building on own and other's contribution', and 'respectfully challenging ideas'. The explicit ground rules are beneficial to students who are new to the higher education classroom as it helps them to negotiate the implicit rules of engagement, discourse norms, and expectations. They are particularly helpful to non-western international students whose former cultures of learning may be very different from the ethnocentric concept of classroom participation (Murray & McConachy, 2018)

The fourth principle – cumulative – focuses on discourse moves (questioning, feedback, and follow-up talk moves) that make up a productive classroom dialogue. These discourse moves are, in effect, the pedagogical and cognitive tools of dialogic teaching. They are responsible for improving the quality of interactions through the use of open (and authentic) questions and substantive feedback and feedforward that deepens students' conceptual understandings and thinking. They transform a discussion, where ideas are simply exchanged and accumulated, into dialogue, where the merits of ideas and evidence are deliberated on and a case is argued (Alexander, 2020).

Finally, the fifth principle of dialogic teaching is that it is purposeful, whereby the lecturer carefully designs talk-rich activities (for example, whole-class discussions, collaborative group work, and think-pair-share activities) to meet specific learning objectives. These different activities generate different talk patterns and also ideas and perspectives that suit different learning styles and preferences. Research into multilingual classrooms suggests that UK and European students prefer to interact with the lecturer in whole-class teaching rather than in small groups. In contrast, Asian students feel more comfortable in small-group situations than speaking publicly in front of the class (Spencer-Oatey and Dauber, Chapter 5, this volume).

As discussed above, a dialogic pedagogy places discussion and dialogue at the centre of the learning process. However, it is also acknowledged that traditional rote, lecture, and recitation also have a key role to play in the classroom, for example, when introducing new facts and concepts, reviewing previously taught content, and checking memorisation and comprehension. In other words, a dialogic pedagogy widens the repertoire of teaching methods and enriches the student learning experience.

Dialogic talk moves

Using classroom dialogue as a cognitive and pedagogical tool requires a good understanding and knowledge of a range of talk moves (corresponding with the dialogic principle of cumulation). For example, lecturers can create a mutual space for dialogue by making use of a balance of closed/test questions and open/authentic questions and a mixture of talk-extending moves that feed back, build on, probe, and challenge student contributions. Examples of dialogic talk moves are provided in Table 3.1 below (adapted from Hardman, 2019:13).

The identification of the talk moves in Table 3.1 draws heavily on the framework of accountable talk by Michaels and O'Connor (2012). Open initiation questions invite students to think and provide non-specified information, as opposed to recalling known information. Follow-up talk moves, also referred to by Alexander (2020) as 'ingredient x' (p. 150), play a particularly critical role in that they sustain, deepen, and enrich the unfolding discourse. They represent high-order questions to frame students' elaborated contributions, requiring them to deeply engage in learning by providing explanation, expansion, evaluation, justification, argumentation, speculation, and so on. Using this repertoire of dialogic talk moves, lecturers create space in the classroom discourse for students to take responsibility for and stretch their curiosity and learning and, at the same time, show appreciation for their contributions. This process, in turn, facilitates student voice and their sense of identity and agency, contributing to their personal growth and active citizenship.

An example of how dialogic talk moves can be used in a university classroom is presented in Extract 2 below (taken from Hardman, 2016b:11). It is taken from a seminar on a Teaching English to Speakers of Other Languages course, which mainly consists of Chinese students and is taught by a lecturer who has undergone training in dialogic teaching.

Table 3.1 Lecturer question and follow-up talk moves

Lecturer talk moves	*Descriptions*
Initiation questions	
Closed L question	Lecturer asks a closed/test question – allows one possible response
Open L question	Lecturer asks an open or authentic question – allows various (expected or original) responses
Follow-up talk moves	
L expand question	Lecturer stays with the same student and asks to say more
L add-on question	Lecturer asks a student to add on to other's contribution
L rephrase question	Lecturer asks a student to repeat or reformulate own or other's contribution
L revoice question	Lecturer verifies his/her understanding of a student contribution, which requires a student response
L agree/disagree question	Lecturer asks if a student or students agree or disagree with other's contribution
L why question	Lecturer asks for evidence or reasoning
L challenge question	Lecturer provides a challenge or a counter-example

Extract 2

1	T:	OK, I think we've had plenty of time to talk about it, so let's just see if we can get some kind of ideas about what is the value of the coursebook for students from your own experience as students?
2	S1:	I think they made the knowledge part more visible. You can look at the words... (inaudible 00:20:46)... pictures.
3	T:	What do you think? This is what you think: it makes the knowledge point more visible.
4		T: Any comments on that? Can you see what Wendy is trying to say there?
5	SS:	[silence]
6	T:	Tell us more about this making it visible now, Wendy. In what way is it more visible?
7	S1:	Maybe when they listen to the part they don't quite know, maybe the material can make it more visible.
8	T:	Yes, Lin, go on...
9	S2:	Just like, you give us a handout; it helps us follow what you are saying.
10	T:	So that's the support; that's kind of what you are saying. It's good support to the teaching point.
11	T:	Any others? Good. Any more?

Extract 2 illustrates the use of dialogic talk moves in a whole-class interaction. The lecturer encourages students to draw on their own experiences in the discussion, and he starts the interaction with an open question *'what is the value of the coursebook?'* (line 1), thus allowing for various responses from the students. A reasonably extended response, containing an explanation, is provided by Wendy (S1 in line 2). Rather than moving on immediately to another student, the lecturer stays with Wendy and probes her answer further (line 3). At the same time, he revoices Wendy's response to verify his understanding and to ensure that other students can hear and that they contribute to the discussion. The lecturer is mindful of engaging the whole group in the discussion, and this is evident in his question to the rest of the class (line 4). However, there is no student response (silence) to that question. Instead of closing the discussion prematurely, the lecturer returns to Wendy by asking her to expand her previous contribution (line 6). Wendy says more about her earlier contribution (line 7), and this, in turn, is picked up by Lin (S2 in line 9) who builds on Wendy's contribution. The lecturer keeps the discussion going by inviting other students to contribute *'Any others? Good. Any more?'* (line 11).

The lecturer–student interaction illustrated above extends and, to a degree, deepens the discussion. The lecturer creates space for students to participate by scaffolding their contributions with open questions, revoicing, probing, and asking questions that build on student answers. This leads to greater reciprocity in the exchanges, whereby students provide elaborated responses, make their reasoning explicit, and build on their own and other's contribution.

By incorporating the use and modelling of dialogic talk moves (in Table 3.1) into their teaching, lecturers can provide more space for students to participate in and practise the academic discourse. Hardman has identified student talk moves that mostly correspond with lecturer talk moves (2019:16–17). Student talk moves are provided in Table 3.2.

These talk moves enable students to share ideas, discuss alternative viewpoints, deliberate on reasoning, and argue their case. Using an extensive repertoire of student talk moves is not only essential for maximising learning, but also for practising and refining communication, negotiation, teamwork, and problem-solving skills. Students will also become well-rounded individuals and be able to function effectively and creatively in the global context of the 21st century.

Impact of a dialogic pedagogy on learning

Most of the research into a dialogic pedagogy has mainly been carried out in school contexts. However, the five principles of dialogic pedagogy – collective, reciprocal, supportive, cumulative, and purposeful – have a universal appeal and resonate strongly with the goals of 21st-century higher education (Teo, 2019).

In the school context, a growing body of international research shows positive relationships between classroom dialogue, participation, and educational outcomes (Hattie 2009; Howe & Abedin, 2013; Resnick, Asterhan & Clarke, 2015). For example, in secondary education in Finland, the quality of classroom dialogue has been associated with student academic attainment in physics, chemistry, and language arts (Muhonen et al., 2017). In the

Table 3.2 Student talk moves

Student talk moves	Descriptions
S connect	Student makes an intertextual reference to something else, e.g. a previous discussion, another text, event, experience, or resource
S explain/analyse	Student explains something in some detail or examines own or other's contribution (not to convince or persuade)
S rephrase	Student repeats, reformulates, or summarises own or other's contribution
S recount	Student gives an account of an event or experience
S evaluate	Student makes a judgement
S argue	Student states a position/opinion/argument (to convince or persuade)
S justify	Student provides reasoning/evidence
S speculate	Student predicts/hypothesises an idea or situation
S imagine	Student creates an analogy, mental image, or scenario
S challenge	Student provides a challenge or counter-example
S shift position	Student indicates a change of mind or perspective

Czech Republic, research shows that middle school students who participate more in classroom talk perform better in reading literacy in language arts (Sedova et al., 2019).

In the UK, a large-scale observational study of 72 Year 6 (aged 10–11) primary English, mathematics, and science classes showed that classroom dialogue is positively correlated with higher learning outcomes and with positive attitudes to schooling (Howe et al., 2019). Another large-scale study – a randomised controlled trial of a 20-week dialogic teaching intervention with Year 5 primary English, mathematics, and science classes in 78 primary schools serving socio-economically deprived areas of England – also showed significant gains in learning engagement and test scores (Alexander, Hardman & Hardman, 2017; Hardman, 2019). An independent evaluation of the RCT study showed that the student attainment in the intervention schools was on average two months ahead of their control peers in all three subjects (Jay et al., 2017).

Research into a dialogic pedagogy in the higher education sector is somewhat limited as it is relatively new to this context. Simpson (2016) carried out a study in dialogic pedagogy in the context of a BA in Education (Primary) programme and showed a positive impact in terms of the student teachers' conceptual change about learning and changes to their pedagogical practices. From a different perspective, the study by Engin and Donanci (2015) looked at the relationship between iPad use and opportunities for dialogic teaching in the context of English for Academic Purposes and found that iPads served as a catalyst for lively group discussions. Poore (Chapter 13, this volume) carried out a year-long case study in a BA in Theatre: Writing, Directing and Performance programme to address the theme of effective seminar teaching. The results showed improved assessment outcomes as a result of implementing dialogic principles. Student feedback indicated that they found reflection on the quality of the talk to be valuable. While these studies show positive results in the higher education context, more research is needed in different subject disciplines at all levels of degree programmes.

Implementing a dialogic pedagogy

Dialogic pedagogy is a broad and versatile approach and so is predisposed to the different interpretations and enactments of the dialogic teaching principles, influenced by such factors as class size, teaching experience, mastery of subject knowledge, and disciplinary content. For example, a case study of two UK secondary school teachers' understanding of dialogic teaching and classroom practice (Van de Pol, Brindley & Higham, 2017) showed that the history teacher paid special attention to becoming a co-learner and engaging in a symmetrical relationship with students, as historical discussions have no clear right or wrong answers. On the other hand, the mathematics teacher emphasised democratising the learning process to accommodate the students' different ways of arriving at the correct answer. Similarly, a study in the Czech Republic lower secondary school context (Sedova, Salamounova & Svariceck, 2014) showed that attempts to promote real dialogue in the literacy classrooms can be challenging due to a lack of rational argumentation and frequent misunderstandings of the (English) words used by students. Lefstein (2010) also argues that it is difficult to realise Alexander's five principles of dialogic teaching all at the same time in everyday classroom practice as it is constrained by teachers' own interactional practices and lesson objectives. However, Hardman (2019) argues that, over time, with practice and professional development support, teachers can become more skilful and confident in embedding the dialogic talk moves into their practice.

Professional development in a dialogic pedagogy

To embed a dialogic pedagogy into higher education, there is a need to provide professional development opportunities for lecturers with a focus on peer support. Peer support involves connecting a lecturer (or two) with a peer who functions as a critical friend (or mentor). The participants need first to develop a good grasp of the dialogic teaching principles and the relevant talk moves (as presented in Tables 3.1 and 3.2) to support its implementation in the classroom. The lecturer being mentored is then required to video-record their seminar teaching. Video clips of critical moments from seminars (and, if possible, seminar transcripts too) can be used for critical reflections by the lecturer, supported by the mentor, on what went on in the seminar or lecture to set targets for improvement. This collaborative viewing of video footage provides the lecturer with the opportunity to monitor how the dialogic teaching principles are being realised in class through self-evaluation and peer feedback. The peer support follows a four-step process, as illustrated in Figure 3.1.

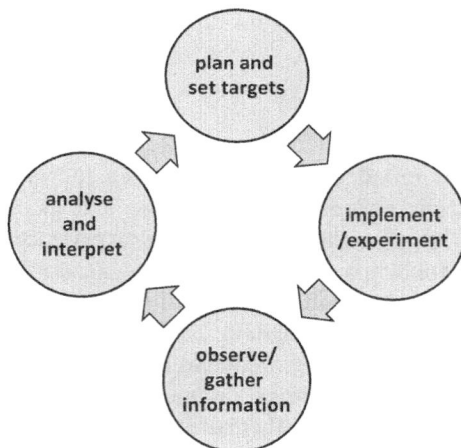

Figure 3.1 Peer support for dialogic teaching scheme

The four-step process makes up a learning cycle:

1   Formulate a plan and set targets – planning what will happen during the cycle and what changes and outcomes are to be achieved
2   Implement – teaching the planned seminar with the targets in mind
3   Observe and gather information – collaborative viewing of video footage of selected seminar episodes by the lecturer and mentor
4   Analysis and interpretation – a collaborative discussion of what happened during the selected seminar episodes

The cycle needs to be repeated several times with at least two-week intervals (depending on circumstances) to provide the lecturer with a sustained period of time to try out the dialogic teaching approaches, practise using the associated talk moves, and receive feedback on their efforts. The scheme should also include strategies for raising students' meta-talk awareness and supporting their development of, and confidence in, using the repertoire of student talk moves.

Conclusion

The chapter presents the case for a dialogic pedagogy to be at the heart of teaching and learning in the higher education sector. It argues that a dialogic pedagogy can bring together the social, epistemological, cognitive, and communicative elements that embody the transformative learning experience demanded by a globalised world in the 21st century.

A dialogic pedagogy can create a safe space and promote social inclusion, which have been shown to facilitate the making of friendships and instil a sense of belonging to the university. This is crucial in helping students to settle in, remain engaged in learning, and to sustaining a sense of wellbeing (Hardy & Bryson, 2016; Masika & Jones, 2016; Maunder, 2018). A dialogic pedagogy can enhance students' epistemological and cognitive development by transforming traditional knowledge transmission and recitation into productive discussion and dialogue, leading to positive educational outcomes. The mechanisms for this transformation lies in lecturers broadening their teaching repertoire. By extension, the quality and repertoire of student talk moves also improve. It also provides a way of ensuring the oracy skills called for by many scholars are embedded into the internationalised higher education curricula (Dippold et al., 2018; Heron, 2019).

The chapter has argued for the need for a dialogic pedagogy, delivered through professional development for lecturers involving peer support, to be central to a pedagogical renewal in higher education. Finally, it calls for more research into a dialogic pedagogy to build a strong evidence base for its impact on student learning experiences and outcomes, which can be used to inform university policy and practice with regard to teaching and learning.

References

Alexander, R. (2016). *Towards dialogic teaching: Rethinking classroom talk*. York: Dialogos.

Alexander, R. (2020). *A dialogic teaching companion*. New York: Routledge.

Alexander, R. J., Hardman, F., & Hardman, J., with Rajab, T., & Longmore, M. (2017). *Changing talk, changing thinking: Interim report from the in-house evaluation of the CPRT/UoY Dialogic Teaching Project*. York: University of York. http://eprints.whiterose.ac.uk/151061/.

Boyle, A. (2010). *The dialogic construction of knowledge in university classroom talk: A corpus study of spoken academic discourse*. Unpublished PhD Thesis. Queen's University, Belfast.

Chen, T. H. R. (2014). East Asian teaching practices through the eyes of Western learners. *Teaching in Higher Education*, 19 (1), 26–37. https://doi.org/10.1080/13562517.2013.827652.

Cummins, J. & Swain, M. (1986). Linguistic interdependence: a central principle of bilingual education. In J. Cummins & M. Swain (Eds.), *Bilingualism in Education* (pp. 80–95). New York: Longman.

De Klerk, V. (1995). Interaction patterns in postgraduate seminars: tutor versus student. *Language and Education*, 9 (4), 249–264. https://doi.org/10.1080/09500789509541418.

Dippold, D., Bridges, S., Eccles, S., & Mullen, E. (2018). Developing the global graduate: how first year university students narrate their experiences of culture. *Language and Intercultural Communication*, 4, 313–327. https://doi.org/10.1080/14708477.2018.1526939.

Engin, M. (2017). Contributions and silence in academic talk: exploring learner experiences in dialogic interaction. *Learning, Culture and Social Interaction*, 12, 78–86. https://doi.org/10.1016/j.lcsi.2016.11.001.

Engin, M. & Donanci, S. (2015). Dialogic teaching and iPads in the EAP classroom. *Computers and Education*, 88, 268–279. https://doi.org/10.1016/j.compedu.2015.06.005.

Hardman, J. (2016a). Tutor-student interaction in seminar teaching: implications for professional development. *Active Learning in Higher Education*, 17 (1), 63–76. https://doi.org/10.1177/1469787415616728.

Hardman, J. (2016b). Opening-up classroom discourse to promote and enhance active, collaborative, cognitively-engaging student learning experiences. In C. Goria, O. Speicher, & S. Stollhans (Eds.), *Innovative language teaching and learning at university: Enhancing participation and collaboration* (pp. 5–16). Dublin: Research-publishing.net.

Hardman, J. (2019). Developing and supporting the implementation of a dialogic pedagogy in primary schools in England. *Teaching and Teacher Education*, 86, 1–14. https://doi.org/10.1016/j.tate.2019.102908.

Hardy, C. & Bryson, C. (2016). The salience of social relationships and networks in enabling student engagement and success. *Student Engagement in Higher Education Journal*, 1 (1), 1–20. Retrieved from http://195.201.33.159/raise/article/view/376.

Hattie, J. (2009). *Visible learning: A synthesis of 800+ meta-analyses on achievement*. Abingdon: Routledge.

Heron, M. (2019). Making the case for oracy skills in higher education: practices and opportunities. *Journal of University Teaching & Learning Practice*, 16 (2). https://ro.uow.edu.au/jutlp/vol16/iss2/9.

Howe, C. & Abedin, M. (2013). Classroom dialogue: a systematic review across four decades of research. *Cambridge Journal of Education*, 43(3), 325–356. https://doi. org/10.1080/0305764X.2013.786024.

Howe, C., Hennessey, S., Mercer, N., Vrikki, M. & Wheatley, L. (2019). Teacher-student dialogue during classroom teaching: Does it really impact upon student outcomes? *The Journal of the Learning Sciences*. doi:10.10.1080/100508406.2019.1573730.

Jay, T., Willis, B., Thomas, P., Taylor, R., Moore, N., Burnett, C., … Stevens, A. (2017). *Dialogic teaching: Evaluation report and executive summary*. London: Education Endowment Foundation. https://educationendowmentfoundation.org.uk/public/files/ Projects/Evaluation_Reports/Dialogic_Teaching_Evaluation_Report.pdf.

Jin, L. & Cortazzi, M. (2006). Changing practices in Chinese cultures of learning. *Language, Culture and Curriculum*, 19 (1), 5–20. https://doi.org/10.1080/07908310608668751.

Lefstein, A. (2010.) More helpful as problem than solution: Some implications of situating dialogue in classrooms. In K. Littleton, C. Howe (Eds.), *Educational Dialogues: Understanding and promoting productive interaction* (pp. 171–190). London: Routledge.

Masika, R. & Jones, J. (2016). Building student belonging and engagement: insights into higher education students' experiences of participating and learning together. *Teaching in Higher Education*, 21 (2), 138–150. https://doi.org/10.1080/13562517. 2015.1122585.

Maunder, R. (2018). Students' peer relationships and their contribution to university adjustment: the need to belong in the university community. *Journal of Further and Higher Education*, 42 (6), 756–768. https://doi.org/10.1080/0309877X.2017.1311996.

Michaels, S. & O' Connor, C. (2012). *Talk science primer*. Cambridge, MA: TERC.

Muhonen, H., Pakarinen, E., Poikkeus, A-M., Lerkkanen, M-K., & Rasku-Puttonen, H. (2017). Quality of educational dialogue and association with students' academic performance. *Learning and Instruction*, 55, 67–79. https://doi.org/10.1016/j.learninstruc.2017.09.007.

Murray, N., & McConachy, T. (2018). "Participation" in the internationalised higher education classroom: an academic staff perspective. *Journal of International and Intercultural Communication*, 11 (3), 254–270. https://doi.org/10.1080/17513057. 2018.1459789.

Nixon, J. (2011). *Higher education and the public good: Imagining the university*. London: Continuum.

Poore, B. (2021). Implementing a dialogic pedagogy in university seminar-based teaching. In D. Dippold & M. Heron (Eds.), *Meaningful teaching interaction at the internationalised university: Moving from research to impact*. Abingdon, Oxon: Routledge.

Resnick, L., Asterhan, C. & Clarke, S. (Eds.). (2015). *Socialising intelligence through academically productive talk and dialogue*. Washington, DC: American Education Research Association.

Rocca, K.A. (2010). Student participation in the college classroom: an extended multidisciplinary literature review. *Communication Education*, 59 (2), 185–312. https:// doi.org/10.1080/03634520903505936.

Sedova, K., Salamounova, Z. & Svariceck, R. (2014). Troubles with dialogic teaching. *Learning, Culture and Social Interaction*, 3 (4), 271–285. https://doi.org/10.1016/j. lcsi.2014.04.001.

Sedova, K., Sedlacek, M., Svaricek, R., Majcik, M., Navratilova, J., Drexlerova, A., Kychler, J. & Salamounova, Z. (2019). Do those who talk more learn more? The relationship between student classroom talk and student achievement. *Learning and Instruction*, 63, 1–11. https://doi.org/10.1016/j.learninstruc.2019.101217.

Shapiro, H. T. (2006). *A larger sense of purpose: Higher education and society.* Princeton, NJ: Princeton University Press.

Simpson, A. (2016) Dialogic teaching in the initial teacher education classroom: "Everyone's Voice will be Heard". *Research Papers in Education*, 31 (1), 89–106. https://doi.org/10.1080/02671522.2016.1106697.

Spencer-Oatey, H. & Dauber, D. (2019). What is integration and why is it important for internationalisation? A multidisciplinary review. *Journal of Studies in International Education*, 23 (5), 515–534. https://doi.org/10.1177/1028315319842346.

Spencer-Oatey, H. & Dauber, D. (2021). Global competencies and classroom interaction: implications for students and staff training. In D. Dippold & M. Heron (Eds.), *Meaningful teaching interaction at the internationalised university: Moving from research to impact.* Abingdon, Oxon: Routledge.

Teo, P. (2016). Exploring the dialogic space in teaching: A study of teacher talk in the pre-university classroom in Singapore. *Teaching and Teacher Education*, 56, 47–60. https://doi.org/10.1016/j.tate.2016.01.019.

Teo, P. (2019). Teaching for the 21st century: a case for dialogic pedagogy. *Learning, Culture and Social Interaction*, 21, 170–178. https://doi.org/10.1016/j.lcsi.2019.03.009.

Trenkic, D. & Warmington, M. (2019). Language and literacy skills of home and international university students: how different are they, and does it really matter? *Bilingualism: Language and Cognition*, 22 (2), 349–365. https://doi.org/10.1017/S136672891700075X.

Van de Pol, J., Brindley, S. & Higham, R. J. E. (2017). Two secondary teachers' understanding and classroom practice of dialogic teaching: a case study, *Educational Studies*, 43 (5), 497–515. https://doi.org/10.1080/03055698.2017.1293508.

Vygotsky, L. S. (1962). *Thought and language.* Cambridge MA: MIT.

4 The problem with silent students

It's us not them

Lee-Ann Sequeira

"Fourth-year history courses are often billed as seminars, where participation can be worth a whopping 40 per cent. In our educational system, silent students pay a heavy academic price indeed."[1]

"The more quiet students you have, the less dynamic your session will be."[2]

"Tactics to draw quiet students in:

- Invite them to summarize conflicting points of view or positions taken by others. This offers a relatively low-risk opportunity to talk.
- Ask if they understand what someone else just said.
- At the end of a class, ask the quiet students which other students helped them with the biggest impact on their learning that day."[3]

"At the time I thought (class participation marks) were **BS**, but now as a teacher, I see the value of it. It forces students to read the material and come prepared to articulate their thoughts... this is when real learning can take place..."[4]

The four quotes above reveal a range of attitudes towards silence and its role in learning and how we view silent students. These are attitudes and perceptions held by teachers, students, and staff that operate at social, cultural, psychological, academic, disciplinary, and institutional levels. In this chapter, I aim to trace the foundation of these perceptions, to interrogate the underlying assumptions, and to examine their implications for higher education. Instead of adopting an educational development approach which would focus primarily on pedagogy and practice, I have chosen to take a broader, multi-dimensional view of silence – the origins and context of silence in society, the influence of psycho-medical trends, and the role of silence in teaching and learning – in order to locate it in the contemporary higher education context. The critical stance is consolidated in the final section, where I attempt to frame silence as a critical pedagogy that disrupts the status quo; interposing notions of values and identity with power and agency; arguing for "a better balance between speech and silence, contemplation and contribution in our classes" (Sequeira, 2020a). The chapter is divided into four sections: silence in our culture, silence in psychology, silence as pedagogy, and silence as a critical pedagogy.

Silence in our culture

Early civilisation up to modernity is full of examples of wise men and women who were sages, thinkers, and mystics such as the Buddha and Teresa of Avila who sought extended periods of solitude and reflection. With the Enlightenment, colonisation, and the Industrial Revolution, things started to change; scientists, explorers, and adventurers were in the ascendant. Fast-forward to contemporary society and the 'man of letters' has given way to the 'man of action'. To get up to speed with our post-modern times, we need to think in terms of influencers and creators.

In Western society particularly, there is a primacy accorded to speech and oracy, which has become the dominant culture in schools and universities. From a young age, public speaking, presentation, and communication skills are emphasised and valued. And while there is no doubt about their usefulness, their value often is at the cost of silent, contemplative, and private or solitary activities. Thoughtful commentary has given way to the gift of the gab. The 2019 British election is a case in point. The Tory campaign was reduced to a slogan, Get Brexit Done, rendering the issue devoid of its inherent complexity: "a deliberate oversimplification", "an illusion", as an article in *The Times* put it (Perrigo, 2019). Pundits and laypeople often surmised that one of the reasons Labour did not win is because they didn't have a similar catchy election mantra. What started off decades ago as quotes in the national newspaper are now soundbites on television, or more aptly, tweets or a meme on social media. Given that social media interactions occur asynchronously, one would think this medium would afford the opportunity for concentration and deep reflection, but "the majority of digital interactions – tweets, posts, and pictures – are instant communication, much like vocal engagement in a classroom setting" (Sequeira, 2020a). While some social media champions feel it has democratised accessibility and levelled the playing field for more users to participate, it mostly privileges a certain form of content – content that elicits rapid interaction rather than thoughtfulness or criticality (Ollin, 2008).

Academics and students, the overwhelming majority of whom are active on social media in some form, bring these same traits and expectations to the classroom. The second quote at the beginning of this chapter sums it up: "The more quiet students you have, the less dynamic your session will be." The false equivalence between silence and a lack of dynamism creeps into our classroom and is a view shared by students and academics, and often the quieter students themselves (Skinner et al, 2016). If we think of great teachers – from Socrates to Robin Williams' John Keating in *Dead Poets Society* – they are remembered as charismatic teachers who used debate, emotion, and passion to reach their students. In recent studies that attempt to gauge the effect of lecturer fluency and expressiveness on student learning, findings indicate that students feel that the fluent and expressive lecturer is more effective, even though they may not have actually learned significantly more (Carpenter et al, 2013).

Another key stakeholder in the higher education sector – employers – also view communication skills, particularly oral communication skills, as very important and relevant. For the second year running, LinkedIn, the online job board, has listed 'persuasion' (aka oral communication skills) as the second most transferable skill in demand from companies (Pate, 2020). Silence, which is often a guise for good listening skills, on the other hand, is not a transferable skill that employers value. It is not unheard of for university students to seek out private coaching to work on their presentation and communication skills when looking for a job (Rajan and Hix, 2019). The job search process for most students and graduates – from the networking stage to the final interview stage – values strong speaking skills with not much demand for contemplative silence or listening skills. Consequently, universities who aim to inculcate 21st-century employment skills such as communication skills, teamwork, and collaboration in their students through regular coursework and assessment are settling on more authentic assessment methods such as group projects and presentations, which again privilege oracy and communication skills.

Susan Cain, in her moving TED talk, *The Power of Introverts* (2012), explains how introverts are constantly given the message that a "quiet and introverted style of being is not necessarily the way to go." A number of positive traits such as creativity and productivity are (falsely) associated with gregariousness. She discusses how the 'culture of character' has given way to the cult of personality, and how this has influenced classroom layout and interaction in schools with desks being arranged café-style or in pods, and collaboration, groupwork, and interaction seen as the cornerstone of learning. The message that extroverts are the way to be or are happier has taken hold in the public imagination. In a recent article in a national newspaper, a young, self-professed introvert fakes it as an extrovert for a week because of a recent study she read where extroverted behaviour claims to make people happier (Kale, 2019). She is not the only one to have tried this 'conversion therapy' with others having tried it for longer periods (Pan, 2019).

Not surprisingly, given the primacy of oracy and speech in wider society and education, silence in the university classroom is not looked upon favourably. Teachers and lecturers "often equate silence with shyness, lack of confidence, fear of speaking up, lack of preparation, avoidance of work, and lack of fluency in the medium of instruction" (Sequeira, 2020a). In this way, silence is pathologised and silent students are viewed as problem students who are struggling and need rescuing. Tellingly, in a *Times Higher Education* article, Bruce Macfarlane decries the current trend of reification of speech and public performance in higher education, only for two other contributors to the same article (also academics) to reinforce common stereotypes associated with shy students and silence in learning – a journey of struggling and being denied success until you speak up (Macfarlane, 2014). Silence is seldom viewed as a valid learning preference for some students who may be more inclined towards introversion or reflection, just as other students may be inclined towards extraversion or hands-on learning activities.

We see how silence can be characterised at a basic level as the absence of speech (Ollin, 2008) or a conversational silence (Bilmes, 1994, p. 74); more benignly, as a form of non-vocal listenership (McCarthy, 2002, p. 52) or non-verbal communication; and its significance in Western culture, where it is mostly associated with problematic, pejorative connotations.

Silence in psychology

Like several aspects of the contemporary higher education student experience, silence, and by extension, silent students are subject to therapeutic treatment – an increasingly prevalent trend in the sector (Ecclestone, 2004). Hazard, anxiety, failure, and silence are a few facets of the student learning experience that have been pathologised, cloaking their subjects in fragility and dysfunction (Sequeira, 2020). This therapeutic culture has grown and become pervasive on university campuses in the UK with an increase in counselling services, mentors, and support groups which students are referred to and encouraged to attend. Higher education institutions increased their spending on mental health provision to £50 million in response to increasing demand (Watts et al, 2018; Universities UK, n.d., p. 8), and have broadened their provision with third-party providers (Lightfoot, 2018) and drafting and training cleaners and security staff among others (Angel, n.d.) to respond to mental health issues. As the saying goes, when you have a hammer, everything begins to look like a nail; similarly, with such a significant increase in mental health resources, 'problems in living' acquire a malignancy that must be treated (Szasz, 2003).

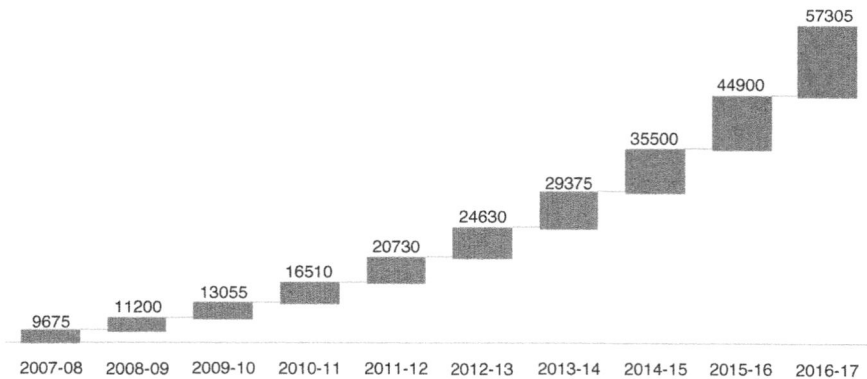

Figure 4.1 A six-fold increase in students reporting a mental health condition over 10 years

Source: Universities UK. Minding our future: starting a conversation about the support of student mental health. p. 8. (Screenshot) www.universitiesuk.ac.uk/policy-and-analysis/reports/Documents/2018/minding-our-future-starting-conversation-student-mental-health.pdf

Out of 2.3 million students in the UK, which includes undergraduates and postgraduates, 2.5% disclosed a mental health condition to their higher education institution. This represents an increase of 83% over 10 years.

If we use shyness as a proxy for silence, Susie Scott's (2006) work on the medicalisation of shyness illuminates the issue from a sociological perspective. She defines shyness as "a socially intelligible response to the dramaturgical stresses of everyday interaction" (p. 134) and distinguishes normal shyness from DSM-sanctioned social anxiety and avoidant personality disorder. Incidence of chronic shyness is accelerating and is often mentioned in the media and popular imagination in sexist ('female malady') and neuro-discriminatory ('social autism') terms. Scott explains how psychiatry works to reinforce culturally valued norms and traits such as loquaciousness, assertiveness, and extraversion. She shows how, using medication, cognitive behavioural therapy, and self-help resources, shyness is managed at a superficial and individual level rather than at a social, systemic level. The emergence and existence of shyness clinics tap into what is referred to as the 'MacDonaldization of emotion' – quick-fix tips and tricks that promise (short-term) cures. One can see how seductive this kind of conversion therapy is for shy students, and how convenient it is for university administrators who are under pressure to appear caring and concerned. However, there is a long-term implication as the new converts subscribe to and reinforce problematic notions of what it means to be shy and socially outgoing, setting in motion a vicious cycle that clamours for the eradication of normal human adversity. Silence is subject to similar treatment – a benign and normal human response labelled as a personal deficiency or behavioural disorder that requires corrective action or medical intervention.

However, not all psychiatrists and university administrators agree. Simon Wessely, a psychiatrist and academic, cautioned universities against pathologising the normal everyday emotions of students such as stress and loneliness (Turner, 2018). Wessley also underlined the need for robust evaluation of ongoing wellbeing programmes in institutions. Steve West, Vice-Chancellor at the University of West England, warned that if universities "jump to a medical model without necessarily understanding a social component... [they] are in danger of creating the wrong response." As a sector, we need to be rigorous about the science, the detail, and whether it works. Efforts to this end are underway with a Higher Education Policy Institute (HEPI) report that unpacks the difference between mental wellbeing and mental health, and how this needs to be factored into our metrics and programme evaluation (Hewitt, 2019). I would suggest taking it a step further and elevating the level of our discourse on these topics. When referring to these issues, we should exercise greater care: acknowledge their complexity and nuance rather than use terms loosely or rely on pop psychology explanations.

From the class and seminar observations I have conducted and from exchanges with fellow academics, academic developers, and students, one thing that always struck me is the use of binaries and proxies in framing our perception and thereby our teaching approaches. (I am sure I am no exception to the rule; it's just that I have not had the misfortune of being a dispassionate observer of my own teaching.) In the case of silence, it is often not silence per se that many teachers take issue with. In most lectures, periods of silence from the audience are valued and actively encouraged; in classes and small-group settings, not so much. From my understanding, it has to do with how silence is framed and how we are conditioned to think about its role in the classroom.

Terms and theories from psychology find their way into popular imagination and shape our (teachers and students) perceptions and attitudes. Take for instance the term 'extrovert'. It is a popularisation of the term 'extravert', which is a Jungian term that can be translated as outward-facing. Since Carl Jung introduced the term, not only has its spelling but also its meaning has changed. While in popular parlance, the term 'extrovert' is used primarily in reference to a personality type – "an outgoing, socially confident person" (Lexico.com), the term 'extravert' is used almost exclusively in scientific journals and writing, and has evolved to reflect just one dimension of personality (there are four others), which in reality is on a continuum, and 'extraversion' itself is broken down into multiple aspects subject to different interactions, constraints, and triggers (Kaufman, 2015). Unfortunately, it is the popular understanding of 'extrovert–introvert' that prevails in teaching practice which is based on a simplistic, reductive binary that is not in keeping with the latest research or good practice in the field of psychology. As a result, students are labelled either as introverts or extroverts – something that is unfair, unscientific, and unproductive for learning. This pseudo-psych creep in contemporary higher education, which is most often well-intentioned, is not unique to the approach to silence, but can be seen in the sector's perception of self-esteem (Emler, 2001) and the use of trigger warnings (Sequeira, 2020b; Flaherty, 2019) to provide a couple of examples. This kind of psychologised curricular and extra-curricular structure (Malcolm and Zukas, 2001) provides the ideal substrate for such dichotomous thinking to thrive.

Silence as pedagogy

In most societies and civilisations across the world, the transmission of knowledge was oral. Even after the invention of papyrus and the printing press, the oral tradition held sway with the teacher lecturing and students taking notes. A version of this continues today with the lecture as the mainstay in most courses in formal higher education. (The massification of higher education has ensured its continuation despite the lecture as a mode of teaching not being fit for purpose in certain conditions.) There is an authority and credibility that is synonymous with lecturing and speaking, and in turn, lecturing confers authority and credibility on the lecturer. In job titles too, the lecturer role has higher status in the hierarchy compared to a graduate teaching assistant. In this way, through the history, format, and hierarchy of teaching, the dominance of lecture or speech is established.

However, the student role has changed quite dramatically, at least in Anglo-American settings, and the student is no longer cast as a passive recipient of knowledge – the biblical empty vessel. Lev Vygotsky's social development theory began to gain prominence in the 1980s along with other active learning and social constructivist approaches. This trend found its way into higher education, and traditionally didactic seminars and classes began featuring small-group activities and peer-to-peer interaction. In the active learning classroom of the 21st century, a good student must participate enthusiastically in small-group discussions, share opinions and feelings, collaborate on group projects, and make presentations. Macfarlane (2014) discusses the "performative drama of the oral presentation" and how "reflective assignments require a confessional performance". Outward-facing portfolios allow students to curate a "unique personal learning story" for various stakeholders that might include prospective employers, advocacy groups, and the general public (Fung, 2017, p. 103). As Ros Ollin puts it, "social learning theory has been confused with 'sociable' learning theory" where talk and interaction, as opposed to silent learning, is culturally desirable and rewarded (2008, p. 278).

Underlying this form of social learning is the performative element, the mark of a neoliberal higher education agenda and policy. The emphasis in learning and teaching is on overt, visible behaviours and attitudes, which can be observed, measured, and possibly showcased as evidence of the student's learning journey. In cases where the numbers, marks, and grades do not convey the appropriate progress, the narrative takes on greater importance. This would explain why reflective assignments can sometimes take on a confessional quality – it behoves the student and teacher to show that the learning progress can be demonstrated. And therein lies the irony. Reflective assignments in higher education, which by their nature should be deep, personal, metacognitive, and evaluative, often turn into personal learning journeys of positive transformation. This is anathema not just for introverts, but also for those who are critically minded and value their privacy (Macfarlane, 2017).

It is not surprising that silence is stigmatised in such a performative learning culture where 'doing learning' is seen as more important than learning. Nowhere is this more apparent than in the widely adopted practice of awarding a grade for class participation. When designed and implemented thoughtfully and fairly, I can see the merit, but very often it is designed as a throw-away grade to incentivise students to attend and participate however superficially (see the fourth quote at the beginning of this chapter). Students, especially those who have been socialised in a competitive learning environment, are likely to view participation as a competitive rather than collaborative activity (Remedios et al, 2008). Sometimes despite having a grading rubric, the emphasis during implementation tends to be on quantity of contribution rather than quality. As the first quote in this chapter indicates, students who are more reticent, not overconfident about making knowledge claims, and process more deeply or for longer will be disadvantaged in such an environment.

Awarding a grade for what should be a formative learning experience so that students feel free to make mistakes, try out new articulations, and take risks seems counterproductive in some respects.

Teachers also subscribe to a culture of performativity, where doing (learning activities) or getting students to produce an output – something tangible and observable (a poster, a worksheet) – is seen as desirable. Even teachers who adopt a more student-centred approach do not tend to explicitly design time for internal reflection, deep cognitive processing, or behavioural silence. From some of my classroom observations, I have noticed that teachers are sometimes so keen to get students to participate that they prize anecdote and opinion over substance and rigour, resulting in a disappointing learning experience for students who were expecting more than social engagement. The second quote at the beginning of the chapter shows how some lecturers hold quiet students responsible for ruining the vibe in their classroom.

Teachers' own personalities and inclinations also play a role. For an extravert teacher, a silent classroom could take them out of their comfort zone. Expressions such as an 'awkward pause' and 'uncomfortable silence' come to mind. Furthermore, teachers tend to impute negative reasons for students' silence – passivity, disinterest, shyness, lack of preparation, and lack of fluency in English.

Ollin (2008, p. 277), in her research on how teachers value talk and silence, observed that some teachers felt "silences were often misunderstood and undervalued by those observing the teaching process". Given the outcomes-oriented nature of contemporary teaching and academic development, this does not come as a surprise to me. As an academic developer, I see a marked slant towards small-group teaching and active learning techniques, which more often than not neglect to include the beneficial effects of silence. Occasionally, there will be a mention of think-time and wait-time, but in the context of getting students to contribute vocally. Learning activities such as think-pair-share are a departure from the norm as they explicitly allocate time for thinking and reflection, enabling all students to practise generative silence, speaking, and active listening (Skinner et al, 2016). More broadly, educational developers need to recalibrate their approach to speech and silence in pedagogy and practice, so that future generations of teachers appreciate the role of both in the classroom. Silence needs to be viewed as a rich and generative space where students are encouraged to engage in deep learning. Given the demands on students' time and as the collective attention span becomes more fragmented and accelerates (Lorenz-Spreen et al, 2019), it becomes increasingly important to provide students with the headspace to develop deep cognitive processing skills during classes and seminars.

Given how speaking is valorised in the current environment, it is not surprising that higher education institutions, teachers, and academic developers often apply the deficit model. Silence in students is viewed as a deficiency stemming from timidity, fear, lack of preparation, avoidance of work, and lack of language skills. Silent students are viewed as problematic – social loafers and lurkers that drain energy from the class without contributing (Macfarlane, 2014). As a result of applying the deficit model, well-intentioned teachers and administrators aim to draw silent students out of their shells. The third quote at the beginning of this chapter ("Tactics to draw quiet students in...") underlines the almost missionary zeal to rescue silent students and bring them back into the fold. Silences imposed by teachers acquire a constructive, positive quality; while when the silence is student generated, it is viewed as problematic (Reda, 2009).

Seeing silence as a deficiency that needs to be remedied is patronising and harmful. It deprives silent students of agency and imposes society's and the teacher's values on the student. It is possible that the student deliberately chose to be silent – out of disinterest, not being challenged enough, being in a reflective or introspective mood, not in agreement with the teacher's views – none of which have pejorative connotations. Vicki Skinner and her colleagues (2016) in their study of dominance and quietness in problem-based learning groups advise against teachers singling out reticent students "as this risks situating the *problem* with the individual and devaluing silence" (emphasis added).

The detrimental effects of the primacy of speech in contemporary society and the modern university are experienced not just by silent students. Loquacious students who dominate discussions, and are rewarded for it, are led to believe that bluster and confidence count for more than thoughtful reflection. The important skill of active listening that is a key element of learning and constructing knowledge on our own or with peers is often missing from grading rubrics that assess class participation, despite it being a cornerstone of social constructivism (Rogers and Farson, 1987). Listening skills are considered to be important in a number of professions – psychotherapy, medicine, business, management, leadership – but its use and development tends to be devalued in teaching and learning. Rather than trying to understand peers' contributions or building on them, some students dominate class discussions and ignore other students' contribution unchecked. The teacher's role as facilitator is called into question here. But often instead of getting students to talk to one another, the teacher steps in to weave together contributions from different students. This kind of practice reinforces the existing status quo where speech is elevated over silence. As a result, students – both voluble and reticent – are not inculcated in the art of active listening. Teachers' biases towards students who tend to dominate seminar discussions are evident in other ways: greater eye contact with them, looking to them to answer when a question is put to the class, consistently inviting them to contribute before others, not adopting think-time or wait-time after posing a question, to name a few. This sets a tone and expectation of what is considered acceptable and desirable behaviour in class. Here again, mainstream academic development practices must be called into question. Just as educational developers helped introduce active learning to classrooms, they must similarly advocate for and promote active listening techniques.

Silence as a critical pedagogy

Silence, as we have seen, is characterised as passive, unprepared, unengaged in mainstream education. For the reasons outlined above, we need to challenge these unfounded stereotypes and subvert silence into a radical critical pedagogy that disrupts the status quo in the classroom, rebalancing the role of speech and silence, and the importance of contemplation and contribution. But the bias against silence is pervasive and operates at multiple and intersecting levels in higher education: across the curriculum – in seminars and assessment; across disciplines – the use of disciplinary pedagogies such as the Socratic method, debate, and the case study; across different tiers of the institution – teaching assistants, tutors, lecturers, mentors; and across the student experience – training in assertiveness, public speaking, communication. There appears to be a systemic bias on the part of teaching staff and institutions that could, in many cases, ultimately have a deleterious effect on learning outcomes for silent students – scoring lower on oral presentations, class participation, and group work; receiving less-than-stellar references and mediocre job offers. Beyond the university, the UK government and its higher education quangos, employers and wider society in general contribute in reinforcing this stigmatisation of silence, as we've seen in previous sections. In this way, neoliberal, performative forces work to maintain the status quo and subjugate silence to oracy. This is why we have to move beyond mere instrumental outcomes, whether imposed by the government, employers, or institutions, and focus on the big issues – the crisis of hope (Amsler, 2011, p. 49) in higher education.

The big issues facing higher education today are the marketisation of higher education, the student as customer resulting in a paradoxical loss of agency and autonomy as they are now subject to market forces, precarity, disparity of income and outcomes in the sector, and the backlash against expertise and knowledge, to mention a few. In what Gourlay (2015) refers to as the "tyranny of participation", do students really have the agency and autonomy to choose their mode of engagement? Similarly, teachers have been domesticated into adhering to sectoral standards of good practice (Macfarlane, 2011). In both cases, for students and teachers, their choice in terms of how and what knowledge to acquire or teach is undermined. In peer discussions which are often dominated by the mainstream or prescribed point of view, silence can be used to create space for alternative viewpoints and other modes of participation. Requiring students to engage with silence and reflection is an effective antidote to groupthink and conformism. The message should be that students who dominate discussions have as much to learn from reticent students as vice versa.

In a higher education culture that reproduces the status quo in terms of learning gain and employment or further study outcomes, silence can be seen as an inclusive pedagogy which does not depend upon social capital nor adherence to dominant cultural values. The sector enacts paradoxical policies, in that the agenda of inclusion does not problematise the practice of pathologising and dismissing the value of silence in the classroom. Critiques that are levelled at the conceptualisation of inclusion and inclusive pedagogies – that it is fragmented and procedurally enacted – apply here (Stentiford and Koutsouris, 2020). In a neoliberal economy, where instrumental outcomes take precedence, there isn't much appetite to challenge the status quo; it is easier to adapt to the existing status quo. Therefore, we need to interrogate the notion of silence not just at a pedagogic or practitioner level, but to understand and engage with it at a deeper and higher level – epistemologically and philosophically – to ward off the crisis of hope in neoliberal institutions.

Western education has long prided itself on validating theory through enquiry and critique rooted in the agonistic tradition, and more recently based on the empirical tradition. As a society, as the importance of evidence grows (a trend fuelled in academia), what passes for critical enquiry in higher education is often merely analytical or reflective without ever challenging the dominant paradigm (Anon, 2020; Macfarlane, 2017). And sometimes, even when the dominant paradigm is questioned or problematised, it is within the safe bubble of the 'alternative' discipline or sub-discipline. For students who have no wish to partake in this lip service to critical enquiry, silence, reticence, and disengagement are valid choices and need to be viewed as resisting the dominant pedagogy.

Silence can, at times, appear to be at odds with the precepts of free speech and social justice. Civil rights, critical pedagogy, and culturally responsive teaching, with their emphasis on the emancipatory effects of dialogue eschew silence with its history of subjugation and construe using voice as liberating and powerful (Reda, 2009). Not surprisingly in classrooms where the pedagogy subscribes to the principles of feminist or critical race theory, giving voice and speaking up are seen as disrupting the status quo – literally speaking truth to power. Viewed through such a lens, silence has no currency, no value, and in this way is counter-cultural, and sometimes counter-critical pedagogy too.

The evidence and anecdotal data I draw on are primarily from Western higher education contexts where English is the long-standing medium of instruction. I do not see silence as an issue unique to international students even though the language barrier is frequently raised as an issue (Skinner et al, 2016). Without doubt, there is a dimension where speaking in a second language and understanding local colloquialisms, slang, and humour are compounding factors; but personality and attitudes and values (personal and cultural) seem to play a more pervasive role and transcend the processual and technical issues of language.

The cultural context and values of students and teachers are also factors in classroom interactions. In Confucian-heritage countries, reticence and thoughtful reflection are personal traits that are valued and cultivated. The Japanese proverb, *ichi wo ieba juu ga wakaru* ("make one point and get ten points across") illustrates this aptly (Tsui, 2007). However, as a result of Western hegemony in higher education and the attendant dominance of English, these traits are often viewed as not as important as Western norms and ideals, or worse as being in conflict. In this way, through the enactment of mainstream pedagogic approaches and 'diverse' assessment methods and rubrics, non-Western norms of learning are devalued and dismissed.

Silence is often (mis)used to cast aspersions on the motivations and abilities of international students. The withdrawn Asian student and other unfounded stereotypes abound (Chanock, 2010; Skinner et al, 2016; Zhou et al, 2005). New academics too are referred to remedial voice coaching classes in a bid to become comprehensible to English-speaking audiences. Research has shown that home students eschew students for whom English is a second language when it comes to forming peer learning groups for perceived cultural and linguistic reasons (Harrison & Peacock, 2007). In this sense, it is not just silence, but certain kinds of speech that are discriminated against. Is it any wonder then that some students prefer silence?

Some students face serious repercussions for speaking. As a citizen of a country where the freedom of speech is heavily curtailed, an international student or academic who speaks out risks career progression and even their life sometimes. Speech in this case becomes a highly fraught decision and privilege, something not many Western tutors or students are in a position to appreciate. In such situations, abandoning an argumentative, polemical style in favour of dispassionate discussion may be a more pragmatic option. This approach when adopted by lecturers and teachers tends to enable students to rise above taking entrenched positions on polarising issues (Gordon, 2019).

Disciplinary norms and department cultures also play a role in reifying oracy and exposition. Chanock explains how English for Academic Purposes programmes are deployed to help international students "'tool up'" and become au fait with the host country and home department conventions (2010, p. 549). (International teachers may similarly be encouraged to undertake an English for Teaching Purposes course.) While these kind of programmes and courses help international students and teachers, the focus is on the instrumental, often to the detriment of diversity and the adoption of World Englishes (Phillipson, 2009). This is a policy of assimilation that works to other international students and teachers and imposes a problematic level of consistency and false ideals. In the self-avowed global higher education institution, every teacher – whatever their background, culture, language, and preference – should be encouraged and provided with the space and time to evolve their own teaching and speaking style in line with their values, academic and otherwise.

Academic developers like me often unwittingly reinforce and perpetuate problematic practices by offering international teachers (and students) tips and tricks to acculturate to Anglo-Western norms rather than empowering them to own and advocate for their own approaches to speaking, writing, and learning. The onus lies with the audience too – with other students and teachers who must learn to appreciate and understand differing rhetorical styles, including silence and reticence, and what they bring to the discussion and learning. As has been suggested, academics and students should be provided with opportunities to develop greater critical awareness of language and communication styles to counter the asymmetries of power and pedagogy prevalent in Western higher education (Jaworski and Sachdev, 1999).

In my first blog post on silence, the note at the end of the post referred students to the school's wellbeing service if they were experiencing shyness or social anxiety.

> Note:
> (Students who are hesitant to participate on account of shyness or social anxiety can approach Student Wellbeing Services on campus)
>
> (Sequeira, 2020a)

More than two years later, the irony does not escape me: the note inadvertently pathologises silence in a post about the importance and benefits of silence. When will it become the norm for such self-referrals to be suggested to talkative students who tend to dominate a discussion because of their personality not their ideas?

Notes

1 www.timeshighereducation.com/cn/its-ok-to-be-shy/2015871.article
2 Anecdotal quote from an academic developer, 2017
3 https://blogs.darden.virginia.edu/brunerblog/2017/04/getting-the-best-out-of-the-quiet-student/
4 https://ryersonian.ca/a-silent-battle-participating-in-class-is-a-struggle-for-students-with-social-anxiety/

References

Amsler, S. (2011). From 'therapeutic' to political education: the centrality of affective sensibility in critical pedagogy. *Critical Studies in Education*, 52 (1), 47–63. https://doi.org/10.1080/17508487.2011.536512.

Angel, G. (n.d). UWE Bristol suicide prevention and response strategy. University of West England. www2.uwe.ac.uk/services/Marketing/about-us/pdf/Policies/UWE-Bristol-Suicide-prevention-and-response-strategy.pdf.

Bilmes, J. (1994). Constituting silence: life in the world of total meaning. *Semiotica*, 98. https://doi.org/10.1515/semi.1994.98.1-2.73.

Cain, S. (2012, February). *The power of introverts*. TED Conferences. www.ted.com/talks/susan_cain_the_power_of_introverts/transcript?language=en#t-5426.

Carpenter, S. K., Wilford, M. M., Kornell, N., and Mullaney, K. M. (2013). Appearances can be deceiving: instructor fluency increases perceptions of learning without increasing actual learning. *Psychonomic Bulletin & Review*, 20, 1350–1356. https://link.springer.com/article/10.3758/s13423-013-0442-z.

Chanock, K. (2010). The right to reticence. *Teaching in Higher Education*, 15(5), 543–552. https://doi.org/10.1080/13562517.2010.491907.

Ecclestone, K. (2004). From Friere to fear: the rise of therapeutic pedagogy in post-16 education. In J. Satterthwaite, E. Atkinson, & W. Martin (Eds.), *The disciplining of education: New languages of power and resistance* (1st ed., pp. 117–136). Stoke on Trent: Trentham Books.

Emler, N. (2001). *Self-esteem: The costs and causes of low self-worth*. York: Joseph Rowntree Foundation.

Flaherty, C. (2019, March 21). Death knell for trigger warnings? *Inside Higher Ed*. www.insidehighered.com/news/2019/03/21/new-study-says-trigger-warnings-are-use less-does-mean-they-should-be-abandoned.

Fung, D. (2017). *A connected curriculum for higher education*. London: UCL Press. http s://discovery.ucl.ac.uk/id/eprint/1558776/1/A-Connected-Curriculum-for-Higher-Educa tion.pdf.

Gordon, C. (Host). (2019, November 22). *Leave, remain, teach*. [Audio podcast]. LSE Higher Education Blog. https://blogs.lse.ac.uk/highereducation/2019/11/22/leave-remain-teach/.

Gourlay, L. (2015). Student engagement and the tyranny of participation. *Teaching in Higher Education*, 20 (4), 402–411. https://doi.org/10.1080/13562517.2015.1020784.

Harrison, N. and Peacock, N. (2007). *Understanding the UK student response to internationalisation*. UKCISA. www.ukcisa.org.uk/uploads/media/84/16025.pdf.

Hewitt, R. (2019). *Measuring well-being in higher education*. HEPI number Policy Note 13. www.hepi.ac.uk/2019/05/09/measuring-well-being-in-higher-education.

Jaworski, A. and Sachdev, I. (1999). Teachers' beliefs about students' talk and silence. In A. Jaworski, N. Coupland, and D. Galasinski (Eds.), *Metalanguage – social and ideological perspectives*. (1st ed., pp. 227–244). Berlin: Walter de Gruyter.

Kale, S. (2019, November 7). Faking it: could I go from being an introvert to an extrovert in one week? *The Guardian*. www.theguardian.com/global/2019/nov/07/fa king-it-could-i-go-from-being-an-introvert-to-an-extrovert-in-one-week-.

Kaufman, S. B. (2015, August 31). The difference between extrAversion and extrOver-sion. *Scientific American*. https://blogs.scientificamerican.com/beautiful-minds/the-difference-between-extraversion-and-extroversion.

Lexico.com. www.lexico.com/en/definition/extroversion.

Lightfoot, L. (2018, July 17). Universities outsource mental health services despite soaring demand. *The Guardian*. www.theguardian.com/education/2018/jul/17/uni versities-outsource-mental-health-services-despite-soaring-demand.

Lorenz-Spreen, P., Bjark, M.M., Hövel, P., and Lehmann, S. (2019, April 15). Accel-erating dynamics of collective attention. *Nature Communications*, 10, 1759. https://doi.org/10.1038/s41467-019-09311-w.

Macfarlane, B. (2011). Teaching, integrity and the development of professional responsibility: why we need pedagogical phronesis. In C. Sugrue and T. Solbrekke (Eds.), *Professional responsibility: New horizons of praxis*. (1st ed., pp. 72–85) Abingdon: Routledge.

Macfarlane, B. (2014, September 25). It's OK to be shy. *Times Higher Education*. www.tim eshighereducation.com/features/no-place-for-introverts-in-the-academy/2015836.article.

Macfarlane, B. (2017). *Freedom to learn: The threat to student academic freedom and why it needs to be reclaimed*. Abingdon: Routledge.

Malcolm, J. and Zukas, M. (2001). Bridging pedagogic gaps: conceptual discontinuities in higher education. *Teaching in Higher Education*, 6 (1), 33–42. https://doi.org/10.1080/13562510020029581.

McCarthy, M. (2002). Good listenership made plain: British and American non-minimal response tokens in everyday conversation. In R. Reppen, S. M. Fitzmaurice, and D. Biber (Eds.), *Using corpora to explore linguistic variation*. Amsterdam: John Benjamins.

Anonymous. (2020, 18 November). From the right numbers to the wrong outcomes. *LSE Higher Education Blog.* https://blogs.lse.ac.uk/highereducation/2020/11/18/from-the-right-numbers-to-the-wrong-outcomes/.

Ollin, R. (2008). Silent pedagogy and rethinking classroom practice: structuring teaching through silence rather than talk. *Cambridge Journal of Education,* 38 (2), 265–280. https://doi.org/10.1080/03057640802063528.

Pan, J. (2019) *Sorry I'm late, I didn't want to come: An introvert's year of living dangerously.* Kansas City, MO: Andrews McMeel.

Pate, D. (2020, January 13). The skills companies need most in 2020—and how to learn them. *LinkedIn: The Learning Blog.* https://learning.linkedin.com/blog/top-skills/the-skills-companies-need-most-in-2020and-how-to-learn-them.

Perrigo, B. (2019, December 13). 'Get Brexit Done': the 3 words that helped Boris Johnson win Britain's 2019 election. *Time.* https://time.com/5749478/get-brexit-done-slogan-uk-election/.

Phillipson, R. (2009). English in globalisation, a lingua franca or a lingua frankensteinia? *TESOL Quarterly,* 43 (2), 335–339. www.jstor.org/stable/27785012.

Rajan, A. (Presenter) and Hix, C. (Producer). (2019, 29 July). *How to break into the elite.* [Television broadcast]. BBC Two. www.bbc.co.uk/iplayer/episode/m000772n/how-to-break-into-the-elite.

Reda, M. (2009). *Between speaking and silence: A study of quiet students.* Albany, NY: SUNY Press.

Remedios, L.; Clarke, D., and Hawthorne, L. (2008). Framing collaborative behaviors: listening and speaking in problem-based learning. *Interdisciplinary Journal of Problem-Based Learning,* 2 (1). https://doi.org/10.7771/1541-5015.1050.

Rogers, C. R. and Farson, R. E. (1987). Active listening. In R. G. Newman, M. A. Danzinger, and M. Cohen (Eds.), *Communicating in business today.* Boston, MA: D. C. Heath and Company. https://wholebeinginstitute.com/wp-content/uploads/Rogers_Farson_Active-Listening.pdf.

Scott, S. (2006). The medicalisation of shyness: from social misfits to social fitness. *Sociology of Health and Illness,* 28 (2), 133–153. https://doi.org/10.1111/j.1467-9566.2006.00485.x.

Sequeira, L. (2020a). Silence in the classroom is not necessarily a problem. *The LSE Higher Education Blog.* https://blogs.lse.ac.uk/highereducation/2020/07/09/heresy-of-the-week-2-silence-in-the-classroom-is-not-necessarily-a-problem/.

Sequeira, L. (2020b). Heresy of the week – part 2: is there a place for trigger or content warnings in HE? *The Education Blog.* https://blogs.lse.ac.uk/highereducation/2019/10/10/part-2-heresy-of-the-week-part-2-is-there-a-place-for-trigger-or-content-warnings-in-he/.

Sequeira, L. (2020). The road less travelled. *The LSE Higher Education Blog.* https://blogs.lse.ac.uk/highereducation/2020/07/23/theroadlesstravelled/.

Skinner, V. J., Braunack-Mayer, A., and Winning, T. A. (2016). Another piece of the "silence in PBL" puzzle: students' explanations of dominance and quietness as complementary group roles. *The Interdisciplinary Journal of Problem-based Learning,* 10 (2). http://dx.doi.org/10.7771/1541-5015.1607.

Stentiford, L. and Koutsouris, G. (2020). What are inclusive pedagogies in higher education? A systematic scoping review. *Studies in Higher Education.* https://doi.org/10.1080/03075079.2020.1716322.

Szasz, T. (2003). *The myth of mental illness: Foundations of a theory of conduct* (revised edition). New York: Perennial.

Tsui, A. B. (2007). Linguistic paradoxes and cultural domination. *International Multilingual Research Journal*, 1 (2), 135–143https://doi-org.gate3.library.lse.ac.uk/10.1080/19313150701495496.

Turner, C. (2018, June 29). Universities may be fuelling the mental health crisis, leading psychiatrist warns. *The Telegraph*. www.telegraph.co.uk/education/2018/06/29/universities-may-fuelling-mental-health-crisis-leading-psychiatrist/.

Universities UK (n.d.). *Minding our future: starting a conversation about the support of student mental health*. www.universitiesuk.ac.uk/policy-and-analysis/reports/Documents/2018/minding-our-future-starting-conversation-student-mental-health.pdf.

Watts, R., Woolcock, N., Joiner, S. and Stannard, J. (2018, December 24). Times investigation: Universities spend millions but mental health emergency grows. *The Times*. www.thetimes.co.uk/article/times-investigation-universities-spend-millions-but-mental-health-crisis-only-grows-23xlnpz08.

Zhou, Y., Knoke, D. and Sakamoto, I. (2005). Rethinking silence in the classroom: Chinese students' experiences of sharing indigenous knowledge. *International Journal of Inclusive Education*, 9, 287–311. https://doi.org/10.1080/13603110500075180.

5 Global competencies and classroom interaction

Implications for student and staff training

Helen Spencer-Oatey and Daniel Dauber

Introduction

There is increasing awareness of the importance of fostering 'global competencies' among (*inter alia*) university graduates. For example, the British government's March 2019 International Education Strategy (Department for Education & Department for International Trade, 2019) refers to the need to "create a new generation of globally mobile, culturally agile citizens who can succeed in an increasingly globalised world" (p. 24). Yet it is not necessarily easy to know how this goal can be achieved. As Donald Pressley and Jo Beal mention in their foreword to a British Council (2013, p. 2) report, two elements are required: to better recognise what these 'global competencies' entail and to find effective ways of fostering them. This chapter addresses both of these issues.

What are global competencies?

From an academic point of view, there are numerous conceptualisations of intercultural competence in the literature (for reviews, see Spencer-Oatey & Franklin, 2009; Spitzberg & Changnon, 2009). Broadly speaking, the competency elements can be grouped into three interrelated categories, known as the ABC (Ward et al., 2001) of intercultural competence: affective, behavioural and cognitive. The affective aspects refer to the personal qualities (e.g. resilience, flexibility and spirit of adventure) needed for functioning effectively in unfamiliar contexts. The cognitive aspects refer to the knowledge and understanding needed (e.g. the history of a particular sociocultural group). The behavioural aspects refer to the skills (e.g. global communication skills, foreign language skills) needed for these contexts. Spencer-Oatey and Dauber (2020) dub these as intercultural vitality, intercultural understanding, and intercultural skilfulness respectively.

There have also been numerous studies of employer perspectives (e.g. CBI/ Pearson, 2017; QS Intelligence Unit, 2019; for an overview, see GlobalPeople, 2019), some of which have explored the skills gaps that employers perceive. For instance, the CBI/Pearson (2017, p. 93) study found that 47% of their respondents were not satisfied with graduates' foreign language skills, 39% of them were not satisfied with their level of international cultural awareness, and 32% of them were dissatisfied with their self-management and resilience. So clearly, there is a need for graduates to be more 'globally competent'. What role, then, can universities play in fostering 'global competencies' and how can they do this? This chapter focuses particularly on the contribution that classroom interaction can make to the process.

Factors that foster the development of global competencies

Several theorists (e.g. Mendenhall et al., 2017; Spencer-Oatey, 2018; Taylor, 1994) have argued that transformative learning (Mezirow, 1990) is fundamental to developing global competence. This learning process entails three elements: a trigger experience, careful reflection on that experience, and the acquisition of new perspectives. In other words, people need to move out of their comfort zones, reflect on and learn from those experiences, and apply that learning to future intercultural interactions. This notion has been incorporated into the University of Warwick's conceptualisation of Global Fitness (Spencer-Oatey & Dauber, 2020). The framework identifies three core interconnected elements: Global Fitness Environment, Global Fitness Engagement Routines, and Global Fitness Outcome Goals.

The environment (the university and its staff, in the case of the study reported in this chapter) needs to offer important affordances for growth; in other words, opportunities that can help trigger transformational learning experiences, guided support for help in interpreting those experiences, and a community of people who are open to each other. Students need to engage with these opportunities if they are to reap their benefits. This entails being sufficiently motivated to seek to develop global fitness, to move out of their comfort zones to experience differences, to mindfully reflect on their experiences, and to manage their stress levels so that their learning is not inhibited. The combination of the affordances of the global fitness environment with student engagement helps foster the global skills and attributes that employers are seeking.

In terms of the academic classroom, the importance of both the global fitness environment and global fitness engagement routines can be seen clearly. Recruitment policies can help provide a diverse student community. This student diversity (e.g. ethnic, linguistic, national, religious, socio-economic) and the differences in attitudes/beliefs, understandings and behaviours that may emerge from that diversity, can offer students (and staff) 'out-of-comfort-zone' experiences that are a pre-requisite for transformative learning. However, if students are to achieve that learning, they need to be sufficiently motivated to engage with those stretch opportunities and not simply interact with classmates whom they already know and feel comfortable with. They also need to reflect on those experiences so that they can gain new perspectives. We regard self-reflection ("Assessment of the way one has posed problems and of one's own meaning perspectives", Mezirow, 1990, p. xvi) to be a particularly important facet of reflection (see Mezirow, 1990 for other types of reflection which are also important for transformative learning). However, students typically need support in gaining meaningful insights into their experiences, and so 'guided support' by teaching staff also plays a vital role. Students' efforts need to be complemented by a supportive environment that encourages pro-active venturing and facilitates mindful reflection through careful management of the classroom. To achieve this, teachers need to aim to develop a 'safe space', where everyone's contribution is valued, and different viewpoints discussed openly and in an accepting manner.

How far, then, are classrooms offering these transformative learning opportunities that foster global fitness/intercultural competence? We developed the Global Education Profiler to explore these and related issues.

The study: Methodology[1]

The design of the Global Education Profiler

The Global Education Profiler (GEP) was designed to help staff (academic and professional services, including senior management) gain insights into internationalisation at their institution and to help both staff and students enhance their global fitness. The GEP (student version) probes five key constructs that are particularly relevant to internationalisation: Social Integration, Academic Integration, Global Opportunities and Support, Communication Skills, and Foreign Language Skills. In this chapter we focus on the construct Academic Integration (AI), which explores the interaction and cohesion of students from diverse backgrounds within classrooms and courses, both among themselves as well as with academic staff. This is highly valuable for nurturing students' growth in global fitness because, as explained above, personal engagement with diversity provides 'mindful venturing' opportunities, whereby students (and staff) can engage in 'out-of-the-comfort-zone' experiences that stimulate learning. Staff can (and need to) play a particularly important role in facilitating this engagement and with helping students mindfully reflect on their experiences. They may need support/training in this and the staff version of the GEP includes measures to probe this (not dealt with here for reasons of space).

Each construct in the GEP (student version) is probed with ten items that together capture the various facets of the particular construct. Students rate each of the ten items in two ways: 'Importance to me' and 'My actual experience'. The importance scale (IMP) reveals what is important to students – both the importance of the construct as a whole (AI, in this case), as well as the individual items that are particularly important to them. The higher the importance scores are, the greater are students' aspirations for a global education experience. This scale thus addresses the motivational/aspirational angle, which is a key foundational element for global fitness.

The experience scale (EXP) reveals what respondents perceive they are actually experiencing with respect to each construct. As explained above, experiences of difference through mindful venturing stimulate personal growth, and so high experience scores are another indicator of an enriching context. The higher the experience scores are, the greater are students' opportunities for and engagement with a global education experience.

When these two scales (IMP and EXP) are combined, with cut-off points half-way on each scale, they yield four quadrants that provide an overview picture of the diversity engagement context:

- high IMP and high EXP: a positive situation in that students experience the contextual elements that are important to them
- high IMP and low EXP: a problematic situation because students' expectations/desires are not met
- low IMP and high EXP: a positive context in terms of actual experiences, but people's aspirations are low
- low IMP and low EXP: the most problematic in terms of developing 'global graduates' because students not only attach low levels of importance to it but also experience it very little. This poses a double-layered challenge for higher education institutions, as they need to address not only motivational/aspirational aspects of their student community, but also their lack of engagement with opportunities for intercultural learning experiences

At the end of each set of items, students are given the opportunity to add any open comments they wish.

In relation to AI, the GEP thus provides information on each of the following questions:

- how important to students is academic integration?
- which are the most important elements/facets of academic integration for them?
- how far do students experience academic integration?
- how big a gap is there between students' aspirations and their experiences?
- where are the largest gaps?
- what reasons might there be for the above findings?

Participants

Students (home and international) at six English-speaking universities (three in the UK, one in the Republic of Ireland, one in Belgium and one in Germany) completed the GEP online. A wide range of nationalities were represented, but here we report on three regional groupings: home, European Economic Area (EEA), and Asian. This is because these were the largest student cohorts in the sample and the number of respondents which were not covered by these three clusters was marginal and statistically not useful. Home students were defined as students reporting their nationality to be the same as the country in which their university was located; for example, students of German nationality at a German university were classified as 'Home', while students of German nationality at a UK university were classified as 'EEA'. Asian students were defined by their nationality and classified as 'Asian' using the UN Country Classification System (United Nations, 2018). This resulted in a sample size of 2360 students who completed the survey in full. Of these, 1455 were home students, 265 were EEA students, and 640 were Asian students.

Analyses

Data were analysed quantitatively and qualitatively, using the programs R V.1.1.383 and MAXQDA, respectively. First reliability checks were carried out on the IMP and EXP scales for each of the constructs. They were found to be very high in all cases, including AI (Cronbach's alpha scores >0.85), confirming the reliability of the scales. In addition, exploratory as well as confirmatory factor analysis was run, which confirmed the robustness and distinctiveness of all GEP constructs.

After this, the following statistical analyses were carried out for respondents as a whole and by regional grouping: mean scores (by construct and by item for each scale), IMP/EXP gap scores (by construct and by item), IMP/EXP correlations (by construct), distribution of scores by quadrant, and full scatterplot of responses. The results relating to AI are reported below.

The open comments were analysed using the qualitative data analysis software package, MAXQDA. Data from the whole dataset were imported, and for the purposes of this study, the comments relating to AI were analysed. Multiple iterations of conventional content analysis in which coding categories are derived directly from the data (Hsieh & Shannon, 2005) were carried out. In other words, the comments were first coded 'bottom up' and then grouped into themes and sub-themes. After all the coding had been completed, the Code Matrix Browser function in MAXQDA was used to check how the number of codings per code were distributed across the three regional groupings, i.e. the co-occurrence of themes with a certain regional attribute. In all the tables that show coding frequencies (see Tables 5.5–5.7), MAXQDA's function 'count hits only once per document' was selected, so the results would not be distorted by a small number of respondents commenting frequently on a particular issue.

Findings

Quantitative findings: AI construct overall

The mean scores for AI, overall and by region, are shown in Table 5.1. As can be seen, the EXP scores (unsurprisingly) were consistently lower than the IMP scores, and for home students, the IMP and EXP scores were noticeably lower than for EEA and Asian respondents.

Table 5.1 Mean scores for AI, overall and by regional cluster (Spencer-Oatey & Dauber, 2019, p. 1048)

	Overall	Home	EEA	Asia
Importance	4.11	3.82	4.46	4.62
Experience	3.76	3.59	4.06	4.00

However, the mean figures cover up a large amount of variation, as can be seen from the percentage of scores falling into the different quadrants. For scatterplots of the results, please see Spencer-Oatey and Dauber (2019).

Several important points can be seen from this data:

- Within each regional grouping, there is a noticeable variation in viewpoints and experiences. This is particularly the case for home students
- Far fewer home students attribute (high) importance to AI than EEA and Asian students; looking at it from the reverse perspective, 35% (i.e. 11% + 24%) of home students regard AI as not (very) important
- Home students' experience of AI is (much) lower than that of EEA and Asian students; 47% (24% + 23%) report having a (very) low experience, compared with 27% for EEA students and 30% for Asian students
- The largest perceived gap between IMP and EXP is reported by Asian students

Our next step was to explore the individual items making up the AI construct, in order to gain more detailed insights.

Quantitative findings: Key AI items

First, we selected the four items that were given the highest importance ratings by the respondents (by region). The findings are given in Table 5.3.

Table 5.2 Percentage of scores falling into the different quadrants of the IMP/EXP matrix

	Home		EEA		Asia	
	(Very) Low Impor- tance	*(Very) High Impor- tance*	*(Very) Low Impor- tance*	*(Very) High Impor- tance*	*(Very) Low Impor- tance*	*(Very) High Impor- tance*
(Very) High Experience	11%	42%	6%	68%	3%	67%
(Very) Low Experience	24%	23%	8%	19%	8%	22%

Table 5.3 Respondents' top four items (out of 10) for importance (by region)

	Home	EEA	Asia
1	Participate comfortably in class	Participate comfortably in class	Participate comfortably in class
2	Interaction opportunities with staff	Confidence in seminar group members	Learn from working in groups
3	Confidence in seminar group members	Interaction opportunities with staff	Discussion of academic topics with diverse people
4	Learn from working in groups	Discussion of academic topics with diverse people	Interaction opportunities with staff

The most noticeable finding from this table is the degree of similarity among the respondent groupings. 'Participate comfortably in class' was given the highest importance ranking among all three regional groupings, and 'Interaction opportunities with staff' were also rated as high in importance by all three regional groupings. Furthermore, of the remaining two 'top four' items for each regional grouping, they were each shared by one other grouping, with the result that only five different items were ranked in the top four by the different groupings.

However, if we now look at the top four in terms of size of IMP/EXP gap, a very different picture emerges (see Table 5.4).

The data in Table 5.4 reveals the following insights:

• Feeling able to participate comfortably in class is of top importance to students from all three regional groupings, yet the gap between IMP and EXP for this item was one of the largest, indicating that students, irrespective of background, feel they are not experiencing it as much as they would like

Table 5.4 Top four items (out of 10) with the largest IMP/EXP gap (by region)

	Home	EEA	Asia
1	Participate comfortably in class	Interaction opportunities with staff	Discussion of academic topics with diverse people
2	Interaction opportunities with staff	Opportunities to give examples from my background	Participate comfortably in class
3	Opportunities to give examples from my background	Participate comfortably in class	Opportunities to do group projects
4	Learn from working in groups	Learn from working in groups	Opportunities to meet people from diverse backgrounds

- In addition to comfortable participation, home and EEA students feel the need for more opportunities for interaction with staff, for contributing examples from their own backgrounds, and they want to benefit more from working in groups
- Asian students, in addition to comfortable participation, want better opportunities to do more group projects, to meet people from diverse backgrounds, and to discuss academic topics with them

A common theme running through all these high IMP and high IMP/EXP gap items is the importance, and yet the limited experience students have, of working and interacting with others, especially those from different backgrounds. To try to gain more insights into possible reasons for these responses, we then explored the open comments. Our aim was to seek further insights into students' attitudes and experiences of culturally diverse classrooms in terms of mixing and discussing/working with students from diverse backgrounds, and into staff management of such matters.

Analysis of open comments

830 of the respondents made one or more comments on the survey and of these 519 individuals made a comment relevant to AI. Of these, 357 were home students, 53 were EEA students and 109 were Asian students (24.5%, 20% and 17%, respectively, of the respondent regional groupings). Table 5.5 shows the broad categories of comments. It is important to note that the frequencies of codes in the tables can only be compared within each of the regional clusters, not across them, because the sample size for each cluster varies. For example, 13 occurrences of a code might be considered a small number for the 'Home' category (total of 357 students, i.e. 4%), but for 'EEA' students it is a much larger proportion (total of 53 students, i.e. 25%).

For the purposes of this book chapter and in the light of the quantitative findings reported above, we focus on two code categories: 'Classroom mixing' and 'Classroom interaction/discussion'. Comments coded to 'Classroom mixing' referred to diversity in the classroom, how far students mixed with people from different cultural backgrounds, and the relevance of diversity to learning. Comments coded to 'Classroom interaction/discussion' referred more specifically to participation, interaction and discussion in the classroom, as well as staff behaviour in relation to this. In reporting our findings, and in view of the space

Code System	Region=Home	Region=EEA	Region=Asia
> General Evaluations/Comments	6	3	7
> General course design	2	1	7
> Classroom diversity	54	8	25
> Classroom Mixing	109	7	19
> Classroom interaction/discussion	53	13	21
> Group work	84	11	9
> Staff cultural background	33	5	6
> Staff behaviour/attitudes	16	5	15

Figure 5.1 Distribution of codes by region and by code categories (collapsed view)

limitations of this chapter, we focus on the comments that threw some light onto reasons for the low importance and low experience ratings reported above.

As can be seen from Table 5.6, while a good number of comments referred to mixing within the classroom as being valuable, with students identifying a number of benefits, the largest number of comments, especially those made by home students, referred to mixing in the classroom as not important. For some, it was just personally unimportant to them and they did not prioritise it, as the following open comments (OC) illustrate.

> OC1 The opportunities [for mixing] are usually there, I just don't really take them generally. [Home Male UG]

For other respondents it was irrelevant, especially for the academic context. They gave a variety of reasons, including 'everyone is the same', 'people from other cultures will have the same vision', 'classrooms are for academic purposes not cultural' and 'ability to discuss is key'.

Other students commented more explicitly on classroom participation, interaction and discussion; Figure 5.3 shows a semi-expanded view of the sub-codes and codings for this.

As can be seen from Figure 5.3, while there were a few comments about the benefits of classroom interaction, the vast majority of the comments referred

Code System	Region=Home	Region=EEA	Region=Asia
⌄ Classroom Mixing			
⌄ Extent of mixing			
> Good mixing	7		2
Not encouraged by dept	1	1	
Limited f2f	13	2	2
⌄ Attitudes to mix/mixing			
> Difficult	3		3
⌄ Not important			
> Not personally important	16	1	1
> Background irrelevant	33	1	2
Both advantages & disadvar			1
> Valuable	22	2	3
> Benefits of mixing	14		5

Figure 5.2 A semi-expanded view of the sub-codes and codes for 'Classroom mixing'

Code System	Region=Home	Region=EEA	Region=Asia
⌄ Classroom interaction/discussion			
⌄ Interaction good			
> Benefits of interaction	•	•	•
Lots of communication	•		
Other interaction opportunities			•
⌄ Interaction poor			
> Hindrances to interaction	•	•	•
Limited interaction	•	•	•
> No examples contributed	•	•	
What are seminars?			•
⌄ Staff management			
> Good management	•	•	•
> Poor management	•	•	•
Variation across staff	•	•	

Figure 5.3 Distribution of codings by region and by sub-code categories for 'Classroom mixing' (semi-expanded view)

to there being hindrances to interaction and that interaction was limited. Both home and Asian students mentioned language most often as a major hindrance to interaction. Many of the comments convey frustration and a sense of unfairness on the part of both home and EEA/Asian students, in that all parties felt the quality of their learning experience was being affected.

> OC2   I knew it would be hard to take part in classroom activities because of my less fluent English, but it is actually worse than I thought. Discussion is so fast that I hardly catch up with them. It gets even more difficult when native speakers are mumbling. Although we are studying International Relations, they don't seem to recognise that there are students whose mother tongue is not English. I often feel we are left out. [Asian Female PG]

However, the difficulties were not always ascribed to language and/or culture. Sometimes it was attributed to poor interpersonal relations and/or a general unwillingness to participate, leading to either silence prevailing or one or two people dominating.

> OC3   My experience of seminars has generally been that most people are too shy to talk, and the same couple of students contribute weekly... I think people are afraid to contribute as they fear getting the "answer" wrong. (That, or they have not adequately prepared for the seminar, which is even harder to change) [EEA Female UG]
>
> OC4   I have found that there is reasonably little encouragement for students to contribute in seminars, particularly those from different ethnic backgrounds. [Home Female UG]

Some students linked low levels of interaction with a range of personal traits, such as shyness, lack of confidence and fear of 'being wrong'. This situation can be confounded when people have different background knowledge:

> OC5   I often feel uncomfortable voicing opinions in a classroom, but this is nothing to do with culture or ethnicity. I am shy and have had previous negative experience elsewhere of my opinions being criticised and dismissed in group discussion. [Home Male UG]
>
> OC6   My background is different, therefore what may be common knowledge for British students/staff is not for me and the opposite way, which many do not recognise. I definitely think that if I bring an example in my lecture or classroom about my home country, it is not valued as much. It is mainly so because people don't have any knowledge about it and cannot relate to it, which is understandable. However, I sometimes wish it would be more valued and people would ask me to evaluate anything they don't understand. [EEA Male UG]

Several of the above comments also point to the important role that staff play, with their classroom management skills sometimes criticised.

> OC7 Class sizes are big and workshop leaders don't necessarily build relationships with students. [Home Female UG]
>
> OC8 In terms of feeling comfortable enough to participate my department are terrible at making students feel comfortable enough to do so. If anything, they make it worse by making you feel like you aren't clever enough to participate. [Home Male UG]

Discussion and implications

One of the key findings from our data is the very large variation among students, not just across different regional groupings (see Table 5.1) but importantly, also within each grouping (see Figures 5.3–5.5). This means that a 'one-size-fits-all' approach to promoting global competencies in the classroom is likely to be ineffective.

Consequently, it is vital to be aware that while some students regard learning from diversity as important, there are others who regard it as unimportant. This awareness is important because, although enhancing opportunities for engaging with diversity may be appreciated by those who regard it as important, those who think it is unimportant may simply disregard and ignore such attempts. To reach out to the latter, we need to understand why they regard it as unimportant, and the open comments suggest two core rationales: lack of personal interest and belief that it is irrelevant. Perhaps one way of handling these perspectives would be to hold focused discussions among students with varying viewpoints, so that those who regard it as less important may become more aware of the benefits of intercultural learning that others on their course perceive. It may also help them become more aware of other students' needs and desires in this regard and thereby encourage them not only to think of themselves but also to support others. Part of this will also entail learning about the types of difficulties students may experience in interacting with others and trying to participate (more) actively in class.

All this, of course, requires careful management by staff. The students' open comments identify a number of needs which staff need to pay attention to, including:

- build student confidence (e.g. OC3)
- foster a culture of mutual valuing among students and among staff with students (e.g. OC5, OC6, OC8)
- give students 'space' to share relevant experience/perspectives and value it (e.g. OC6)
- find ways of maximising student interaction, so that less confident and less fluent students feel more able to participate (e.g. OC2, OC3, OC4)

- help home students develop 'global communication skills' in which they can adjust their language to the needs of their interlocutors (e.g. OC2)
- help students to get to know each other and their staff through some personal sharing (e.g. OC7)

A key facet of these various points is the way that staff handle discussion and question and answer sessions in class. In line with the findings of Zhou, Knoke, and Sakamoto (2005), our findings indicate that it is often the dynamics within the classroom that can undermine confidence and discourage individuals or certain sections of the class from sharing their ideas and relevant expertise/background experience. This reluctance can derive from various elements of discourse management, such as different turn-taking practices and preferences (often exacerbated by language issues), as well as minimal effort to grasp what others wish to convey, sometimes stemming from a lack of interest in, or valuing (by both peers and staff) of, the ideas and experiences of others.

Needless to say, it is not easy to manage these multifaceted, interacting issues and yet they need to be addressed in order to maximise the quality of the student learning experience, not simply to help foster global competence but also to promote greater overall learning. Individuals may actually be unaware of their own behaviour, and the impact that it is having on others. So, an initial step could be to plan an activity that helps raise everyone's awareness of their interactional behaviour and how others perceive it. This has been experimented with at the University of Warwick and students have found it extremely enlightening. Some of the insights have been incorporated into an e-course, *Working in Diverse Groups* (GlobalPeople, 2018). This covers four main aspects of working together successfully in groups: communication patterns, trying out ideas, work patterns, and giving feedback (for more details, see Reissner-Roubicek & Spencer-Oatey, forthcoming). The e-course has an accompanying instructor guide that provides suggestions for classroom activities that can supplement the e-course, in terms of both lead-in and follow-up. It also gives additional background information on the four topic areas of the e-course, providing underpinning research insights, so that the instructor is better able to understand the rationale for the material and how it relates to relevant research.

The importance of supporting staff in the task of fostering global fitness is underlined by a recent internationalisation benchmarking project run by the Coimbra network of universities (Coimbra Group, 2019). Using the staff version of the GEP, with over 3000 staff respondents from across Europe, a significant gap emerged between (a) the importance that staff attribute to student and staff engagement (i.e. two constructs: student engagement in class and teacher engagement with students), and (b) staff confidence in handling such engagement. Despite this, there is often a motivational and priority issue for staff. Life is extremely busy, with numerous demands on staff time, and some may feel that such developmental support is unnecessary and beneath them. Clearly, any developmental support that is provided needs to be of very high quality, so that participants feel it has been extremely worthwhile, which in turn will encourage more staff to participate in the future.

Conclusion

Preparing students for living and working in a globalising world is a complex process that entails multiple, interacting facets. These various facets can be fostered (or hindered) in a range of contexts and in this chapter, we have focused on the context of the academic classroom. Classrooms with students from diverse backgrounds offer excellent 'stretch opportunities' for 'mindful venturing' and staff need to provide guided learning and support in order to facilitate students' engagement, reflection and learning from these opportunities. Data from a large-scale study of student perceptions of their classroom experiences indicate that much work still needs to be done, especially around enhancing the learning from intercultural interaction in the classroom. We recommend that more high-quality support resources, for both students and staff, are developed and that ongoing monitoring of their impact is carried out.

Note

1 For more details on the methodology, see Spencer-Oatey and Dauber (2019).

References

British Council. (2013). *Culture at Work. The Value of Intercultural Skills in the Workplace*. London: British Council. Available at www.britishcouncil.org/organisation/poli cy-insight-research/research/culture-work-intercultural-skills-workplace [Accessed 22 May 2020].

CBI/Pearson. (2017). *Helping the UK Thrive*. CBI/Pearson Education and Skills Survey. www.cbi.org.uk/media/1341/helping-the-uk-to-thrive-tess-2017.pdf [Accessed 22 May 2020]

Coimbra Group. (2019). Benchmarking for internationalisation. www.coimbra-group. eu/benchmarking-for-internationalization/ [Accessed 22 May 2020].

Department for Education, & Department for International Trade. (2019). *International Education Strategy: Global Potential, Global Growth*. London. www.gov.uk/governm ent/publications/international-education-strategy-global-potential-global-growth [Acce ssed 22 May 2020].

GlobalPeople. (2018). Working in Diverse Groups. https://warwick.ac.uk/fac/cross_fac/ globalpeople2/he_institutions/gpatuni/ [Accessed 22 May 2020].

GlobalPeople. (2019). Global Fitness for Work: Employer perspectives. https://warwick.ac. uk/fac/cross_fac/globalpeople2/companies/employersurveys/ [Accessed 22 May 2020].

Hsieh, H.-F., & Shannon, S. E. (2005). Three approaches to qualitative content analysis. *Qualitative Health Research*, 15(9), 1277–1288. https://doi.org/10.1177/ 1049732305276687.

Mendenhall, M. E., Weber, T. J., Arnardottir, A. A., & Oddou, G. R. (2017). Developing global leadership competencies: A process model. *Advances in Global Leadership*, 10, 117–146.

Mezirow, J. (Ed.) (1990). *Fostering Critical Reflection in Adulthood. A Guide to Transformative and Emancipatory Learning*. San Francisco, CA: Jossey-Bass Publishers.

QS Intelligence Unit. (2019). *The Global Skills Gap in the 21st Century*. www.qs.com/the-global-graduate-skills-gaps/ [Accessed 22 May 2020]

Reissner-Roubicek, S., & Spencer-Oatey, H. (forthcoming). Positive interaction in intercultural group work: Developmental strategies for success. In Z. Zhang, T. Grimshaw, & X. Shi (Eds.), *International Student Education in Tertiary Settings: Interrogating Programmes and Processes in Diverse Contexts*. Abingdon, Oxon, UK: Routledge.

Spencer-Oatey, H. (2018). Transformative learning for social integration: Overcoming the challenge of greetings. *Intercultural Education*, 29(2), 301–315. https://doi:10.1080/14675986.2018.1425828.

Spencer-Oatey, H., & Dauber, D. (2019). Internationalisation and student diversity: Opportunities for personal growth or numbers-only targets? *Higher Education*, 78, 1035–1058. https://doi.org/10.1007/s10734-019-00386-4.

Spencer-Oatey, H., & Dauber, D. (2020). *What is Global Fitness?* https://warwick.ac.uk/fac/cross_fac/globalpeople2/knowledgeexchange/frameworks/gp_building_global_fitness_200228v2.pdf [Accessed 22 May 2020].

Spencer-Oatey, H., & Franklin, P. (2009). *Intercultural Interaction: A Multidisciplinary Approach to Intercultural Communication*. Basingstoke: Palgrave Macmillan.

Spitzberg, B. H., & Changnon, G. (2009). Conceptualizing intercultural competence. In D. K. Deardorff (Ed.), *Sage Handbook of Intercultural Competence* (pp. 2–52). Thousand Oaks, CA: Sage.

Taylor, E. W. (1994). Intercultural competency: A transformative learning process. *Adult Education Quarterly*, 44(3), 154–174.

United Nations. (2018). Standard country or area codes for statistical use (M49). United Nations Statistics Division. https://unstats.un.org/unsd/methodology/m49/ [Accessed 22 May 2020]

Ward, C., Bochner, S., & Furnham, A. (2001). *The Psychology of Culture Shock* (2nd ed.). Cambridge: Cambridge University Press.

Zhou, Y. R., Knoke, D., & Sakamoto, I. (2005). Rethinking silence in the classroom: Chinese students' experiences of sharing indigenous knowledge. *International Journal of Inclusive Education*, 9(3), 287–311.

Part II

Classroom interaction and disciplinary contexts

6 Classroom interaction
Disciplinary contexts

Doris Dippold and Marion Heron

Introduction

From our experience of conducting workshops on classroom interaction with staff across the university, it is always very clear that university teachers' concerns and questions on the subject are shaped by their disciplines. Some staff mainly teach large lectures, and are keen to explore how they can best engage (all) students. Others teach small seminar groups and want to know how they can best scaffold learning through talk and interaction.

In this chapter, we will provide a snapshot of the main research trends of classroom interaction within disciplinary contexts. We posed ourselves the following questions to guide our summary of the extant literature:

- What specific discursive and interactional features does research on classroom interaction in disciplinary contexts focus on?
- To what extent does research on classroom interaction in disciplinary contexts discuss learning through talk and interaction?

Our analysis of the literature revealed four distinctive strands of research on classroom interaction in disciplinary settings:

- Strand 1: Interaction, learning and pedagogy in the second language classroom
- Strand 2: Negotiation of meaning through English as a lingua franca (ELF) in English-medium instruction (EMI) settings
- Strand 3: Discursive features and strategies in the disciplinary classroom and obstacles for second language learners
- Strand 4: Interaction and talk for learning in the disciplines

We will explore each of these in turn, quoting key representative texts in each strand.

Classroom interaction: The main strands of research

Research Strand 1: Interaction, learning and pedagogy in the second language classroom

The discipline with the richest body of research on classroom interaction in higher education (HE) is undoubtedly the second language classroom. The journal *Classroom Discourse*, for example, is dominated to a large extent by studies with a language learning focus, and browsing our own collections of papers and relevant searches on ERIC also revealed that the vast majority of papers on classroom interaction and classroom talk are published in journals with a language teaching focus such as *English for Specific Purposes, Journal of English for Academic Purposes*, and *TESOL Journal*.

The body of literature on second language classroom interaction is largely rooted in the communicative language teaching approach (CLT). In a CLT environment, the aim is to fulfil the communicative purpose of the activity, which requires students to interact with each other orally and through semi-structured tasks. This aligns with second language acquisition (SLA) theories such as Long's (1996) interaction hypothesis, and Swain's output hypothesis which suggest that interaction allows learners to negotiate meaning and to receive feedback (either explicit or implicit) on their output (Swain & Lapkin, 1995). Consequently, interaction with learners and teachers allows learners to develop their language competence.

Many monograph-length treatments of classroom interaction in a language learning context focus on the relationship between classroom interaction and pedagogy. For example, Sert's (2015) monograph on social interaction uses Conversation Analysis (CA) to "uncover key interactional and pedagogical practices" (p. 3) in the L2 classroom by examining both verbal and nonverbal features of teacher–student interaction. Similarly, Seedhouse (1997, 2004) has published extensively on the relationship between interaction and language pedagogy, such as on how repair contributes to error correction in the classroom (e.g. Seedhouse, 1997). This resonates with work by Walsh (2011, 2006) who identified typical features of second language classroom discourse (e.g teacher control of topic and management of the interaction, IRF pattern, question–answer routines, repair for feedback and error correction), and developed the notion of classroom interactional competence (CIC), which is defined as "teachers' and learners' ability to use interaction as a tool for mediating and assisting learning" (Walsh, 2006, p. 158) (see Chapter 2, this volume). Although Walsh's framework for Self-Evaluation of Teacher Talk (SETT) has been used in content- and language-integrated classrooms in school settings (Walsh & Urmenta, 2017), and despite its affordances for a broader context, it still has not yet been systematically applied to the analysis of HE classroom discourse in other disciplines.

In summary, the extensive body of research on classroom interaction in a second language learning context generally describes how learning and pedagogy are supported through talk and interaction. Methodologically, this research is supported by an interest in the micro-analysis of talk.

Research Strand 2: Negotiation of meaning through English as a lingua franca in EMI settings

Another large body of work on HE classroom interaction, emerging from the early 2000s, is research on English as a lingua franca (ELF). ELF research is methodologically driven by an analysis of naturally occurring classroom discourse and draws heavily on disciplinary classroom discourse in settings in which English is not a national language but used as a medium of instruction (EMI). This work constitutes somewhat of a hybrid: while it draws heavily on data gathered in various disciplinary settings beyond the language classroom, the focus of interest is the strategies used by students and teachers to communicate across different varieties of English, and not on disciplinary learning per se.

Given this focus, the classroom is merely a 'vehicle' for investigating ELF use. For example, in a monograph about academic English as used by non-native speakers in EMI settings, Mauranen (2012) shows little interest in the classroom, or in how language and interaction facilitate learning. The HE classroom is a convenient setting "because it is international, its domain spans the globe, and it has settled on English as its common language" (Mauranen, 2012, p. 1).

Examples of ELF studies in EMI settings include Smit's (2010) longitudinal study on ELF in classroom discourse, which follows a Master's course in hospitality. It shows that the group of students formed their own community of practice in which directness and explicitness were acceptable. Knapp (2011) discusses an example of conflict in an engineering classroom at a German university, and Björkman (2011, 2014) investigates pragmatic strategies to achieve communicative effectiveness, convey meaning and prevent communicative disturbance at a Swedish technical university.

In all cases, the discipline(s) in which these investigations are conducted fade into the background whereas ways of achieving explicitness (of course content) and negotiation of meaning through strategies such as confirmation checks, word replacement and repair strategies are foregrounded. For example, Hynninen (2011) focuses on mediation in classroom discourse, in which one participant rephrases the turn by another participant which had been addressed to a third party. The methodology section shows no interest in the discipline as such, simply stating that "the data used in the analysis come from one English-medium Master's level seminar course arranged at the University of Helsinki in 2008" (p. 968).

In summary, ELF research is centred around the premise that, in a classroom in which learners speak different varieties of English, they need to use strategies to negotiate meaning. Although successful negotiation of meaning may, in turn, create the right conditions for learning to happen, there is no distinct focus on how disciplinary learning is or could be scaffolded through ELF talk.

Research Strand 3: Discursive features and strategies in the disciplinary classroom and obstacles for second language learners

A third tranche of studies which take their data from disciplinary contexts primarily evaluates the use and purpose of specific discursive features and strategies in the HE classroom. Data are primarily, but not exclusively, gleaned from Anglophone HE settings, with a range of disciplines featured. These studies are often undertaken to inform English for Academic Purposes (EAP) provision.

For example, recognising the possibility of using analysis of classroom discourse for teacher training, Basturkmen (2018) investigated how accounting teachers help students who are non-native speakers with the development of specialised vocabulary. They found that teachers often transition from content to language support, for example to highlight specialised vocabulary. Northcott (2001) explored different kinds of interactive styles in MBA lectures used by more and less experienced teachers. She suggests that further explorations of this kind can help EAP professionals as well as subject teachers make sense of the communicative demands placed on teachers and students. Dafouz, Hüttner and Smit (2018) discuss how teachers in a financial accounting and a consumer behaviour class in a Spanish EMI setting use language-related episodes to clarify meaning and support vocabulary development.

These examples show that this strand of research has a distinct focus on language and development in disciplinary settings, which is also evident in research which highlights particular discourse features, e.g. 'just' (Grant, 2011), definitions (Flowerdew, 1992), laughter (Nesi, 2012), highlighting devices (Deroey & Taverniers, 2012), and 'we' (Fortanet, 2004). For example, Grant's (2011) investigation of the frequency and function of 'just' in lecture discourse in four disciplines found differences between lecturer and student use of the discourse marker. Using this, he suggests that students taking EAP classes should be taught the function of 'just'. Deroey and Taverniers (2012), investigating signposting devices which highlight important or relevant features of lecture discourse, identified a gap between those commonly used in lectures and those presented in EAP textbooks, which lead them to suggest that students may require further support to recognise these markers.

Another group of studies in this tradition explicitly compares discourse in disciplinary lectures or seminars and EAP classes. For example, Lee and Subtirelu (2015) conducted a corpus-based comparison of 18 EAP lessons and 18 university lectures and found that EAP teachers made use of metadiscourse to negotiate classroom interaction, whereas university disciplinary teachers use it to establish a relationship between ideas. Using these results, they suggest that teachers and EAP teachers need to engage in reciprocal learning about how to use metadiscourse effectively. Differences between the communicative demands and practices in EAP classes and in disciplinary HE classes were also mentioned in other studies. Dippold (2014) identified and compared feedback practices in an HE accounting class and an EAP class and questioned whether EAP classrooms adequately prepare students for disciplinary study. Furthermore, Basturkmen (2002), Thompson (2003), Shaw, Carey and Mair (2008) and Rappa and Tang (2018) noted differences between EAP textbook models of features of classroom discourse and those observed in disciplinary class sessions.

To summarise, studies in this research strand investigate the form and function of various discursive features, sometimes in comparison with EAP and disciplinary classrooms, and highlight the possible obstacles faced by non-native speakers in accessing and taking part in classroom interaction in the disciplines. In doing so, they allow authors to make suggestions for how to use the results for new pedagogical approaches in either teacher or student development and inform EAP support.

Research Strand 4: Interaction and talk for learning in the disciplines

Within three strands of research discussed earlier, only Strand 1 focusing on interaction in the second language classroom discusses issues of how talk and interaction support learning, resonating a sociocultural approach to learning which proposes that learning is scaffolded through educational talk (see Alexander, 2004; Mercer & Howe, 2012;). This focus has, so far, not yet systematically transferred to other disciplines, in particular in HE contexts. There are however a few notable exceptions.

For example, Hardman (2016), analysing UK university classes in engineering management and in accounting and finance, identified key teacher moves and student responses, finding that "the line of enquiry was often prematurely curtailed, preventing the chaining of tutor questions and student responses into an extended discourse to promote higher order thinking" (p. 73). Heron (2018) used episodes of classroom talk in combination with stimulated recall interviews to explore how HE teachers in liberal arts, accounting and sociology dealt with conflicts between disciplinary aims, their own values and contextual constraints to shape their strategies for seminar interaction.

However, these studies in HE settings are the exception rather than the rule, and the majority of research in this tradition stems from school settings. The insights gained from these studies could suggest implications for HE. For example, Chin (2006) and Chin and Osborne (2008) describe secondary school science students' questions as a "potential resource for teaching and learning science" (p. 1) and later summarise their findings by saying that "students' questions can help students to monitor their own learning, explore and scaffold their ideas, steer thinking in specific directions, and advance their understanding of scientific concepts and phenomena" (p. 34). From this, they conclude with implications for teaching and teacher training. Similarly, Tang (2017) examines the role of metadiscourse in the construction of scientific knowledge.

Other studies in school settings whose insights have potential relevance for HE are concerned with the development of discipline-specific discourse patterns. For example, Larsson (2018) presents a longitudinal study of the development of scientific discourse at a Swedish school, concluding that the "gradual building of knowledge and language in these contexts may... be conceptualized as a waving pattern or as a recurrent movement between and within discourse" (p. 73). Similarly, Sfard (2007) report on how students acquire the discourse of negative numbers, and Forey and Cheung (2019) describe how explicitly teaching the language of Physical Education has benefits for learning discipline-specific terminology, which positively impacted on the students' writing. Teachers also benefited in that they were able to use language to clarify the requirements of a task and provide an assessment and feedback tool.

In summary, this final strand of discourse focuses explicitly on classroom talk and interaction for disciplinary learning. However, data so far stem primarily from school settings, with research in HE only just emerging.

Conclusion

As our review has shown, there is already a rich body of research on classroom interaction and talk in disciplinary contexts in HE, but disciplinary knowledge construction is rarely the focus. Different strands of research support different conceptualisations of language and interaction in the classroom. These include a focus on negotiation of meaning (ELF in EMI settings) on the one hand, and the discursive and interactional features of classroom talk and how they might support or constrain non-native speakers on the other. Issues of how classroom talk supports pedagogy are currently primarily discussed in the literature on the second language classroom, and in studies emerging from school settings. However, there is also a small body of literature on disciplinary learning through classroom talk in HE.

Researcher demographics may be a reason for the current under-representation of a wider variety of disciplinary contexts in research on classroom interaction in HE. Researchers with an interest in classroom interaction and talk are likely to have a background in linguistics, which, in a typical career trajectory, is likely to include employment in language teaching, EAP or learning development. Given the proliferation of EMI classrooms and the growing international student numbers in Anglophone countries, these trajectories are mirrored in the theoretical and practical concerns of the HE-centred research papers on classroom interaction, such as interaction in the L2 classroom, use of English as an academic lingua franca and issues of negotiation of meaning, as well as language use and EAP learner support. In contrast, internationalisation is not a matter of concern in school classroom research, which means that there is more scope to focus on language as a vehicle for disciplinary learning.

In summary, given the patterns observed, we feel that there is considerable scope still to develop inquiries into interaction and discourse as a vehicle for learning in the disciplines. Linguists collaborating with disciplinary experts on an analysis of classroom language has the potential also to significantly contribute to mainstream research in HE which, so far, has not yet recognised the potential of pedagogies which are based on an analysis of language, discourse and interaction in the classroom.

References

Alexander, R. (2004). *Dialogic teaching*. York: Dialogos.

Basturkmen, H. (2002). Negotiating meaning in seminar-type discussion and EAP. *English for Specific Purposes*, 21(3), 233–242. https://doi.org/10.1016/S0889-4906 (01)00024-2.

Basturkmen, H. (2018). Dealing with language issues during subject teaching in EMI: the perspectives of two accounting lecturers. *TESOL Quarterly*, 52(3), 692–700. https://doi.org/10.1002/tesq.460.

Björkman, B. (2011). Pragmatic strategies in English as an academic lingua franca: ways of achieving communicative effectiveness. *Journal of Pragmatics*, 43(4), 950–964. https://doi.org/10.1016/j.pragma.2010.07.033.

Björkman, B. (2014). An analysis of polyadic English as a lingua franca (ELF) speech: a communicative strategies framework. *Journal of Pragmatics*, 66, 122–138. https://doi.org/10.1016/j.pragma.2014.03.001.

Chin, C. (2006). Classroom interaction in science: teacher questioning and feedback to students' responses. *International Journal of Science Education*, 28(11), 1315–1346. https://doi.org/10.1080/09500690600621100.

Chin, C., & Osborne, J. (2008). Students' questions: a potential resource for teaching and learning science. *Studies in Science Education*, 44(1), 1–39. https://doi.org/10.1080/03057260701828101.

Dafouz, E., Hüttner, J., & Smit, U. (2018). New contexts, new challenges for TESOL: understanding disciplinary reasoning in oral interactions in english-medium instruction. *TESOL Quarterly*, 52(3), 540–563. https://doi.org/10.1002/tesq.459.

Deroey, K., & Taverniers, M. (2012). Just remember this: lexicogrammatical relevance markers in lectures. *English for Specific Purposes*, 31(4), 221–233. https://doi.org/10.1016/j.esp.2012.05.001.

Dippold, D. (2014). "That's wrong": repair and rapport in culturally diverse higher education classrooms. *The Modern Language Journal*, 98(1), 402–416. https://doi.org/10.1111/j.1540-4781.2014.12061.x.

Flowerdew, J. (1992). Definitions in science lectures. *Applied Linguistics*, 13(2), 202–221. https://doi.org/10.1093/applin/13.2.202.

Forey, G., & Cheung, L. (2019). The benefits of explicit teaching of language for curriculum learning in the physical education classroom. *English for Specific Purposes*, 54, 91–109. https://doi.org/10.1016/j.esp.2019.01.001.

Fortanet, I. (2004). The use of "we" in university lectures: reference and function. *English for Specific Purposes*, 23(1), 45–66. https://doi.org/10.1016/S0889-4906(03)00018-8.

Grant, L. E. (2011). The frequency and functions of just in British academic spoken English. *Journal of English for Academic Purposes*, 10(3), 183–197. https://doi.org/10.1016/j.jeap.2011.05.006.

Hardman, J. (2016). Tutor-student interaction in seminar teaching: implications for professional development. *Active Learning in Higher Education*, 17(1), 63–76. https://journals.sagepub.com/doi/abs/10.1177/1469787415616728.

Heron, M. (2018). Dialogic stance in higher education seminars. *Language and Education*, 32(2), 111–126. https://doi.org/10.1080/09500782.2017.1417425.

Hynninen, N. (2011). The practice of 'mediation' in English as a lingua franca interaction. *Journal of Pragmatics*, 43(3), 965–977. https://doi.org/10.1016/j.pragma.2010.07.034.

Knapp, A. (2011). Using English as a lingua franca for (mis-)managing conflict in an international university context: an example from a course in engineering. *Journal of Pragmatics*, 43(4), 978–990. https://doi.org/10.1016/j.pragma.2010.08.008.

Larsson, N. (2018). "We're talking about mobility:" discourse strategies for promoting disciplinary knowledge and language in educational contexts. *Linguistics and Education*, 48, 61–75. https://doi.org/10.1016/j.linged.2018.10.001.

Lee, J., & Subtirelu, N. (2015). Metadiscourse in the classroom: a comparative analysis of EAP lessons and university lectures. *English for Specific Purposes*, 37(1), 52–62. https://doi.org/10.1016/j.esp.2014.06.005.

Long, M. (1996). The role of the linguistic environment in second language acquisition. In W. Ritchie & T. Bhatia (Eds.), *Handbook of second language acquisition* (pp. 413–468). San Diego: Academic Press.

Mauranen, A. (2012). *Exploring ELF: academic English shaped by non-native speakers.* Cambridge: Cambridge University Press.

Mercer, N., & Howe, C. (2012). Explaining the dialogic processes of teaching and learning: the value and potential of sociocultural theory. *Learning, Culture and Social Interaction*, 1(1), 12–21. https://doi.org/10.1016/j.lcsi.2012.03.001.

Nesi, H. (2012). Laughter in university lectures. *Journal of English for Academic Purposes*, 11(2), 79–89. https://doi.org/10.1016/j.jeap.2011.12.003.

Northcott, J. (2001). Towards an ethnography of the MBA classroom: a consideration of the role of interactive lecturing styles within the context of one MBA programme. *English for Specific Purposes*, 20(1), 15–37. https://doi.org/10.1016/S0889-4906(99)00016-2.

Rappa, N. A., & Tang, K. S. (2018). Integrating disciplinary-specific genre structure in discourse strategies to support disciplinary literacy. *Linguistics and Education*, 43, 1–12. https://doi.org/10.1016/j.linged.2017.12.003.

Seedhouse, P. (1997). The case of the missing "No": the relationship between pedagogy and interaction. *Language Learning*, 47(3), 547–583. https://doi.org/10.1111/0023-8333.00019.

Seedhouse, P. (2004). *The interactional architecture of the language classroom: a conversation analysis perspective.* Malden: Blackwell.

Sert, O. (2015). *Social interaction and L2 classroom discourse.* Edinburgh: Edinburgh University Press.

Sfard, A. (2007). When the rules of discourse change, but nobody tells you: making sense of mathematics learning from a commognitive standpoint. *Journal of the Learning Sciences*, 16(4), 565–613. https://doi.org/10.1080/10508400701525253.

Shaw, L., Carey, P., & Mair, M. (2008). Studying interaction in undergraduate tutorials: results from a small-scale evaluation. *Teaching in Higher Education*, 13(6), 703–714. https://doi.org/10.1080/13562510802525437.

Smit, U. (2010). *English as a lingua franca in higher education: a longitudinal study of classroom discourse.* Berlin/New York: De Gruyter Mouton.

Swain, M., & Lapkin, S. (1995). Problems in output and the cognitive processes they generate: a step towards second language learning. *Applied Linguistics*, 16, 371–391. https://doi.org/10.1093/applin/16.3.371.

Tang, K.-S. (2017). Analyzing teachers' use of metadiscourse: the missing element in classroom discourse analysis. *Science Education*, 101(4), 548–583. https://doi.org/10.1002/sce.21275.

Thompson, S. E. (2003). Text-structuring metadiscourse, intonation and the signalling of organisation in academic lectures. *Journal of English for Academic Purposes*, 2(1), 5–20. https://doi.org/10.1016/S1475-1585(02)00036-X.

Walsh, S. (2006). *Investigating classroom discourse*. London: Routledge.

Walsh, S. (2011). *Exploring classroom discourse: language in action*. London: Routledge.

Walsh, S., & Urmenta, C. (2017). Classroom interactional competence in language and content integrated learning. In A. Llinares & T. Morton (Eds.), *Applied linguistics perspectives on CLIL* (pp. 183–200).

7 Scaffolding peer interaction within a language-and-content integrated business curriculum

A case study in a western Canadian university

Bong-gi Sohn and Valia Spiliotopoulos

Introduction

In the last 15–20 years, Canadian higher education has embraced the educational trend of internationalisation in higher education, and there are an increasing number of students who have recently immigrated to Canada, especially from the Pacific Rim (Statistics Canada, 2016). According to student data from Immigration, Refugees, and Citizenship Canada (IRCC), there has been an increase of 73% in the number of international students with Canadian study permits in the last five years (ICEF, 2019). Most colleges and universities in western Canada welcome international and multilingual students from all over the world, and the current student demographic represents a high degree of linguistic and cultural diversity (Agosti & Bernat, 2018).

The context for this study is in a primarily undergraduate (comprehensive) university in Canada's western province. This university was founded in 1965, and has 35,000 undergraduate students, 20% of whom are international students (Institutional Research and Planning, 2020). The results from institutional self-report data show that 25% of students enrolled in credit-bearing programmes are learning in their second language (L2) with varying levels of linguistic proficiency and academic literacy skills. In this university, there are diverse multilingual and multicultural students including recent immigrants, so-called generation 1.5, and Canadian-born students who come from multilingual families or English-speaking families, and international students who enter the university with a minimum of IELTS 6.5. Nonetheless, some faculties in various disciplines have not adapted their curriculum or instruction to respond to this multilingual diversity; as such, there is a pressing need to respond, especially in the area of improving students' oral language through interaction between Canadian-born, English-speaking learners and those learning in a second language. In the case addressed by this chapter, business faculty, and administrators collaborated with applied linguists to redesign the curriculum and instructional strategies of a disciplinary course by foregrounding language, business discourse, and interactive activities to adequately respond to multilingual students' needs and address curricular expectations.

In this chapter, we first address the relevant research literature to contextualise the challenges faced in the faculty of business. We then describe the new activities in the co-designed undergraduate business course, which now offers a range of communicative, student-centred activities. As a part of quality assurance, we document the implementation of a new approach to curriculum and instruction, and focus on student peer discussions within their first group assignment. Using Goffman's (1981) participation framework, we illustrate how some multilingual students are often marginalised in their group discussions, and we discuss pedagogical implications from our findings.

Literature review

Linguistic diversity in Canadian higher education

Within the Canadian context, there is a history and policy of additive bilingualism since 1969 (French/English; Burnaby, 2008); however, more recently, we have seen a shift from bilingualism to plurilingualism, recognising Canada's broader linguistic and cultural diversity due to immigration, the recognition of First Nations languages and cultures, and internationalisation in education (Dagenais, 2013). Trends have slowly shifted from excluding the use of one's mother tongue (which is often not an official language) in the classroom, to strategically including the home or community language in the classroom (Smythe & Toohey, 2009), although practising inclusive multilingualism is not always easy (Haque, 2012). Scholars are challenging the notion that learners in educational settings should be recognised for their level of competence in English only; they are advocating for an appreciation of their plurilingual competence (Coste, Moore, & Zarate, 2009) and encouraging our educational systems to celebrate the development of a repertoire of various languages and different forms of knowledge in ways that are not separate or compartmentalised. To perpetuate a monolingual, anglophone bias in our increasingly globalised institutions does not align with inclusion and diversity initiatives. Given the increasing cultural and linguistic diversity in education, "the reality of multicultural and multilingual classrooms is not about to change" (Murray, 2016, p. 44). To that end, these trends and different lenses have been put forth to recognise the diversity, and to challenge prevailing monolingual discourses.

Despite the progressive discourses and practices of plurilingual approaches, especially amongst the applied linguistics community, the expectations of many mainstream educators, especially in the higher education context, involve achieving both communicative competence in English and within the disciplinary discourse. This includes the development of receptive skills as well as expressive skills, through interaction – a skill that is increasingly regarded as foundational (Council of Europe, 2001). The reality of the mainstream anglophone university classroom in the content areas is that some recently arrived multilingual or international university students struggle to engage with English-dominant students, and the traditional 'lecture'-style learning environment provides minimal opportunities to practice and measure interactive oral communication skills (Murray, 2016).

Although business faculty and administrators demonstrated some resistance to plurilingual pedagogies, the faculty addressed the growing linguistic diversity in their classrooms. For example, one of the perceived challenges is student grouping, which tends to be segregated between English-dominant and multilingual students. Another challenge reported through their programme needs analysis is that all business undergraduate students – whether they are English-dominant or not – need to learn disciplinary concepts and vocabulary, and use them effectively in their interactive business contexts. Finally, the business faculty noted the importance of meeting the learning outcomes articulated for accreditation purposes. One of those outcomes was communicative competence, and the faculty were supportive of providing students with developmental support in business communication skills early on and throughout the programme. Rather than viewing multilingual students as a 'problem', this chapter focuses on how faculty can modify and adapt curriculum and instruction within a discipline-specific learning environment to increase student opportunities for interaction with their peers and instructors, so that the classroom becomes a mutually respectful and engaging space for both English-dominant and multilingual students.

Disciplinary discourse development through content and language integration

In order to support the development of recently arrived international/ multilingual students' communicative competence in the target language, as well as English-dominant students' skills in interacting with international/multilingual students in their classroom, the authors (applied linguists) had the opportunity to collaborate with business faculty to develop new models of support by redesigning curriculum, assessment, and instruction, and thereby sharing the responsibility for supporting international/English as an additional language (EAL) learners. With the growing linguistic diversity in mainstream university classrooms, there are increasing needs for curricular innovation, which nurtures students' discipline-specific language and literacy competences and departs from a traditional lecture style to an interactive classroom.

Various Content-Language Integrated Learning (CLIL) models of support have been put forth to develop disciplinary discourse and communication (Figure 7.1).

In contrast to 'adjunct' approaches to CLIL that are 'bolted on', integrated and embedded approaches are often characterised as 'built-in' because the academic language and literacy are taught seamlessly alongside the content (Fenton-Smith & Humphreys, 2015). Integrated and embedded approaches have received considerable attention in the literature and are widely regarded

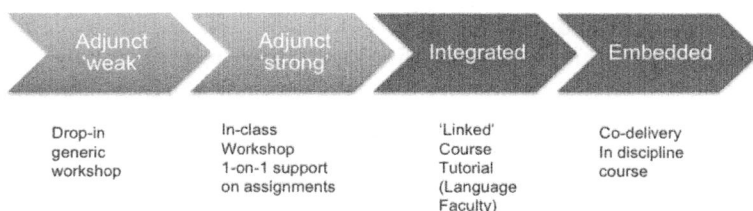

Adjunct 'weak'	Adjunct 'strong'	Integrated	Embedded
Drop-in generic workshop	In-class Workshop 1-on-1 support on assignments	'Linked' Course Tutorial (Language Faculty)	Co-delivery In discipline course

Figure 7.1 Models of Content-Language Integrated Learning (CLIL)
Adapted from Fenton-Smith and Humphreys (2015)

as the most effective way of connecting language and content (Coyle, Hood, & Marsh, 2010; Lin, 2016).

Incorporating the stronger CLIL model, the current study took place in a mainstream business course where recent immigrants, international students, and generation 1.5 and Canadian-born students are enrolled in the same class. Given the pilot, experimental status of the course redesign and resource limitations, since fall 2017 some business courses have adopted variations of an 'integrated' model. However, all sections of the course integrated language learning with content in the curriculum by foregrounding the relevant lexical, grammatical, and genre-based features of business discourse through intensive practice of the expressive linguistic skills of writing and speaking in most lessons. This study focused on the speaking skills practised through interactional discourses within interactive activities (Heron, 2019) that supported students in engaging in business discourse (Bargiela-Chiappini, Nickerson, & Planken, 2013).

Research context: Mainstreamed multilingual students in an anglophone university in western Canada

The context for this study was a second-year undergraduate writing and speaking intensive course that is required for all students in the business school. Since a 2017 fall course pilot, there have been five to six course sections in each term with a maximum of 45 students in each section. The student demographics in this course are unique as they represent the hyper-diversity of the Canadian classroom context. Within the domestic students, there are students who are native-born in Canada whose parents use English as their first language or another language that is non-official. There are also recent immigrant students who arrived in Canada in high school and then transferred to university. About 28% of the undergraduate students are categorised as international students who recently entered Canada for study purposes. The ethnolinguistic diversity of students includes China, Hong Kong, India, South Korea, USA, Pakistan, Iran, Taiwan, Mexico, France, Germany, and so on (Institutional Research and Planning, 2020). The undergraduate course is a prerequisite for all business school students where multilingual students participate alongside native speakers of English who were Canadian or American-born.

The newly created course aims to highlight discourse and linguistic features of business content and communication, and make an explicit connection to language and critical thought. For example, students learn comparative language to examine and analyse stakeholder and shareholder differences and similarities. Students learn analytic skills and language that are related to business, and explicitly learn to develop their critical thinking in business by using the rhetorical appeals of 'ethos (emotion)', 'pathos (authority)' and 'logos (logic)'. In doing so, the course highlights key vocabulary and expressions that are used in business settings. The course also aims to incorporate more dialogue and small-group activities and projects so that students can increase their expressive skills and experiment with plurilingual discourses.

The peer discussions have been one of the key components of the assignments that students complete over the term, which is 25% of their total grade (50% of the grade is for written assignment and 25% for the final exam). In the 13 weeks of instruction, there are three group assignments. In each assignment, students are randomly assigned into groups of four to five and these groups change in every assignment; as such, each group has both native and non-native English-speaking students. In week 6, students are introduced to the first peer discussion assignment (7% of the final grade), which is the focus of this study.

In an effort to better understand how the interactive activities designed in class supported students with the development of business discourse and oral communication skills, the following research questions were posed using discourse/conversation analysis (Goffman, 1974, 1981; Sacks et al, 1974; Ten Have, 2007) as a framework:

1   How do students engage in peer interaction in university classroom contexts within business programmes? In particular, in what ways does the peer interaction facilitate multilingual students' group participation within the university business classroom?
2   How do opportunities for peer interaction in the classroom at the curricular core impact student language/communication development and socialisation?
3   What are the implications for instructional design, delivery, and assessment?

Methodology: An ethnographic case study

This study was part of a quality assurance process that examined an undergraduate business course co-designed and co-developed by the business faculty who collaboratively worked alongside faculty in language and literacy education.[1] To that end, we gathered student self-reported data on the impact of the course, achievement data on student oral and written performance based on criterion-referenced rubrics, and pedagogical documentation of student activities (video footage of student interactions). This study uses ethnographic case study (Creswell, 2007; Duff, 2008) as a research methodology and it represents one pilot project within the four-year longitudinal research study in disciplinary settings where language faculty collaborated with content faculty. Both authors are practitioner-researchers as they had taught and helped design the course.

This study was initiated in order to further examine the impact of the interactive activities in the newly designed business course in response to university-wide concerns about the importance of continuing to develop the communication skills of undergraduate and graduate students. To do so, we gathered student materials that were part of the course requirements. In particular, we focused on the first group assignment, closely looking at the 15-minute, students' self-videotaped peer discussion. In this assignment, students were assigned into groups of four or five (ten groups in the course) and were asked to provide a video recording consisting of a three-minute pitch and 15 minutes of their group discussion, which was approximately an hour long. The 15-minute discussion was organised based on identifying the most compelling arguments that the students would use in the three-minute pitch and how they would organise it. Students were given a task where they needed to persuade an imaginary business person, in this case from Amazon, to build their new headquarters in a Canadian city (Pseudonym: Beautiful City). To convince their audience, students were required to provide three persuasive elements: emotional, logical, and authoritative appeals.

Before students began their assignment, they were given the assessment rubric and told that only their three-minute pitch would count for their grade, while their self-selected 15-minute video-taped group discussion would be used to encourage student interaction, and to ensure course quality. By asking students to record 15 minutes of their group discussion without a grade, we expected the activity to be low-stakes and aimed to further nurture the peer interaction. Students were asked to submit both videos (three-minute business pitch and 15-minute group discussion) by the end of the instructional day.

Analysis: Peer interaction in an undergraduate business course

While reviewing the self-video-taped 15-minute footage, we observed that international students, especially of East Asian descent, were not fully part of the group discussion. After reviewing the videos, we later acknowledged that the assignment was rather intimidating as these multilingual students were asked to collaborate, discuss, and engage with native speakers of English as their first group assignment when they had not yet developed a strong rapport with each other. Video taping both the process and product of their assignment was likely intimidating as students knew that the footage would be reviewed by the instructors. Because of these issues and challenges, it was worth examining in more depth why certain particular ethnolinguistic groups were marginalised in the peer discussion setting. To that end, we decided to closely explore peer interaction through conversation analysis and Goffman's participation framework. Our primary analytic focuses are: (1) how peer interaction shapes group participation and engagement and (2) how students position and co-construct their emergent roles through talk.

To do so, we first looked at the entire 15-minute videos that students submitted. We treated the students' assigned group assignment as a type of institutional talk (Heritage, 2005), as opposed to a naturally occurring interaction. This means that to complete an institutional activity – in this case, a three-minute pitch – students reconfigured the organisation of ordinary conversation so that it oriented to the specific institutional purposes of the event. The purpose of the 15-minute discussion was to plan their three-minute pitch. The overall organisational pattern of peer discussion generally consisted of three parts. In the first one to two minutes, students examined the grading rubric for the three-minute pitch in order to understand what is required for the assignment. Between 3 and 13 minutes, students brainstormed and researched why Beautiful City is an attractive place for establishing Amazon's second headquarters. In the last portion of the video (14–15 minutes), students discussed how they were going to organise their three-minute pitch.

With this in mind, we focused on the 15-minute video-recorded talks and looked at how the turn-taking of each group was organised. Amongst the ten videos that we received, we noticed how there was unequal participation in most groups; however, we found that two groups in particular faced more pronounced issues than others in the group discussion and they are the focal part of our study (Table 7.1).

In Group 9, students did not assign speaker roles, but randomly participated and provided their ideas. In doing so, we found that the Asian female student was silenced, despite the fact that she was moving and leaning her body forward a number of times, which may have indicated her attempts to speak up in the group discussion. On the other hand, in group 10, one White male student assigned one Asian male student to become a fact checker in the middle of their group discussion. Although this role assignment might have come from the White male student's goodwill to include the relatively quieter Asian male student, this ended up excluding the Asian student both verbally and spatially. This needed further examination in order to better grasp what was happening and how students created their social roles in this particular classroom discourse setting.

We found Goffman's discussion on social interaction notably useful for understanding business classroom discourse in these multilingual peer interaction incidents (Goodwin & Goodwin, 2004). In particular, Goffman's work on participation in the dyadic (speaker–hearer) model of communication was

Table 7.1 Student demographics

Group 9	One East-European male with a baseball cap (EBM), one Portuguese-Canadian male (PM), one Indo-Canadian female (IF), one Asian female (AF)
Group 10	One White male student with a baseball cap (WBM), one White male student with a cardigan (WCM), one White female student (WF), one Asian male with glasses (AGM)

helpful in understanding the complexities of speaker and listener identities. His classification of the speaker and hearer affords a close analysis of how the participants take up different aspects of the hearer and speaker in producing talk, whereby the speaker is comprised of (1) an animator, an actual person who produces an utterance; (2) an author who originates beliefs of an utterance and composes the utterance through which those beliefs are expressed; and (3) a principal who is committed to the words and responsible for the message. The listener roles are divided into (1) ratified hearers (addressed and unaddressed recipients) and (2) unratified hearers (bystanders, overhearers, and eavesdroppers; please see the examples in the Findings). By detailing speaker-listener roles, Goffman's participation framework outlines how a particular participation is constituted by a particular production format and participation status (Goffman, 1981). Complementing Goffman's idea, we analysed turn-taking sequences (Sacks, Schegloff, & Jefferson, 1974) as this allowed us to examine how the students orient to each other within moment-by-moment interaction.

Findings

The first segment we analysed is derived from Group 9, between 10 minutes 11 seconds to 10 minutes and 42 seconds. Students were looking at the assignment guidelines, and started discussing how to use logos, ethos, and pathos in order to convince Amazon to establish its new headquarters in Beautiful City. They were sitting in two rows of two, side by side where a male student with a baseball cap (EBM) sat next to the Asian female student (AF) and faced the Portuguese-Canadian male student (PM). The Indo-Canadian female (IF) student was facing the Asian student. IF and AF shared one computer on their side, while EBM jotted down the ideas that the group discussed. Figure 7.2 represents how students were physically positioned during the group interaction, and the transcript in Figure 7.3 presents the verbal and non-verbal interaction.

Figure 7.2 Student seating positions in Group 9

```
1    EBM?:   (looking down) ∘pathos?∘ (frowning and turning his head)
2    PM:     and then (.) pathos we can go with the-uh:
3    AF:     (looking at PM)
4    PM:     the culture that we have here. (looking at EBM)
5            right↑?
6    EBM:    (slightly nodding)
7    PM:     like we: very open [h.          welcoming=
8    EBM:                       [(looking at PM)    =yeah (nodding)
9    AF:                        [(looking at PM). ∘welcoming∘
10   IF:                        [(looks down and nodding)
11   PM:     cul[ture super diverse with bunch different neigh-
12   EBM:       [(nodding)right (nodding)
13   IF:       [(looking down and nodding)
14   AF:     ∘culture super diverse∘
15   PM:     er different ethnic diversities=
16   EBM:    =yeah
17   AF:     (nodding her head)
18   PM:     ↓yeah
19   EBM:    yea↑h that's- that's good.
20   AF:     (rolling her eyes left and right)
21   IF:     (turning to her left, looking at her computer)
22           (6.0)
23   EBM:    (looks at AF) anything else you could add? ↓er (looks at the
24           bottom)
25   AF:     (looks at EBM) ∘um∘
26   PM:     (looks at AF)
27   IF:     (continues to look at her computer)
28           (2.0)
29   EBM:    (looks at the bottom) ∘not really?∘
30   PM:     (smile, turns his head down)
31   AF:     (bites her lips)
32           (7.0) (PM look at the bottom, EBM writes something. IF looks at
33           the computer screen on her left)
```

Figure 7.3 Group 9 "Anything else you could add?" transcript

The first part of the segment involves students discussing examples related to pathos. Then, the East-European male with a ballcap (EBM) turned to the Asian female student (AF), asking whether she had anything to add.

When EBM posed a question with a rising tone, he was also frowning and turning his head, which called for a next response sequence (line 1). The Portuguese-Canadian male student (PM) responded by explaining what counts as an emotional appeal (pathos). As PM explained what could potentially count as pathos (line 2, 4, 7, 11, 15), EBM provided preferred responses (line 6, 8, 12, yeah, right) which facilitated PM's elaboration. Similarly, as soon as PM responded, AF looked at him (line 3) and nodded, which served to co-facilitate the PM's responses, as did the Indo-Canadian female student (IF, line 10). Through these interactions, EBM, AF, IF, and PM were collaboratively supporting a 'discussion-generator footing' (Goffman, 1981), meaning that their responses and gestures promoted the continuation of the discussion. However, it is important to note that in line 9 and 14, AF quietly repeated what PM said. No one noted her iterations, nor that it was a repetition of what PM had said. Therefore, AF's principal was a 'repeater' as she re-affirmed to herself what was said by PM. Although AF was attentive to the speakers and sensitive to what was said, by not providing a different utterance that productively developed the discussion, she risked being excluded from the group discussion frame.

Once this discussion footing was completed, (line 1–19), AF and IF provided different positions: by looking left and right, AF worked as a quiet addresser, seeking the next speakers. IF, on the other hand, turned her body, sat in an opposite direction from others, and looked at her computer, all of which indicated her working towards becoming author and animator for the next sequence. However, despite these actions in this segment, ongoing footage demonstrated that IF continued to look at her computer and only participated verbally when she provided information. Although IF was somewhat engaged in the group interaction process as an 'author', AF continued to be excluded without a clear role even though she made efforts to engage through eye contact. She was neither 'animator' nor 'author', but an unaddressed hearer in the group interaction.

In line 21, EBM turned his head to AF and asked her whether there was anything that she would like to add. However, soon after he completed his question formation, he turned his head down to his desk. Such a physical movement did not work as a preferred question formation, but suggested that he was not expecting AF to respond. Right after EBM's iteration, PM looked at AF, which positioned AF as a potential respondent to the question that EBM had raised. She responded with a quiet 'um' and remained silent for 2 seconds, which did not work as a preferred response for EBM's question. In line 25, EBM quietly iterated 'not really', affirming AF's dispreferred discussion contribution. PM turned his head down in line 29, collaboratively advancing what was accomplished through EBM and AF's interaction. In line 27, she bit her lips, showing negative sentiment to the previous sequences that happened. Yet, she or other students did not facilitate her group discussion participation, but remained silent (line 28).

Therefore, in this segment, while the Asian female student attentively listened and silently reiterated what another person had said, this was not heard or taken up as full participation in her group. When she was assigned to become an author in an unwelcoming context, she provided a short iteration of 'um' followed by silence, co-treating her as a non-participant in the group discussion.

Group 10: "Do fact-checking": accidental marginalisation

The second group was another example of unintended marginalisation of a multilingual student in an interactive group activity. In examining the spatial organisation of the group throughout the video, we noticed that in the first half of the segment, students are sitting and sharing ideas in a circle, while in the second half of the second, some students are standing up on the whiteboard, brainstorming ideas. At the halfway point of the segment, WBM assigned the Asian male student with glasses (AGM) to become a fact checker.

The interactional segment that we focused on is between 12 minutes 13 seconds and 12 minutes 40 seconds where three students stood next to the whiteboard and AGM sat at a desk with a computer (Figure 7.4).

Figure 7.4 Student positions in Group 10

WBM asks AGM to look for Beautiful City's international population. The other White male student with a cardigan (WCM) looked at another White female student (WF) writing on the board.

While AGM was looking at the others from a distance (line 1), WF listed ideas that highlighted the city as an optimal place to grow a business, and then animated a question. WCM overlapped WF's question that she raised.

```
1    AGM:  (looking at the others)
2    WF:   (writing on the board)culture. greener city. ah: wha[t else culture
3          (looking at WCM)?
4    WCM:                                                    [west coast
5    WF:   >there you go< (writing on the board) westcoast vibe.=
6    WBM:  =(pointing to the board) diverse culture. (looking WCM and WF
7          interchangeably) one of the most international cities in the world=
8    WF:   =right.(writing on the board) international
9    AGM:  (pulling himself to the right to look at the whiteboard)
10   WBM:  (turning and walking towards AGM)I write something about er-(turning
11         his head to WF then AGM)
12   WCM:  (turning towards AGM and looking down to the table)
13   WBM:  our percentage of- (pointing AGM's computer) Beautiful City in
14         international population. um could we see Beautiful City
15         international population is?
16   AGM:  (typing in his computer)
17   WCM:  (looking towards AGM and tightly closing his lips)
18   WF:   ok.(finishing writing)
19   WCM:  (turning to the whiteboard and skimming what's written)
20   WBM:  (looking AGM's screen)(bending over to AGM) you can find the number
21         of Beautiful City actual population that'll be great.(turning to the
22         whiteboard)
23   WF:   (looking at the board)I wish we can have different colors=
24   WCM:  (looking at the board)=yeah=
25   WF:   =yeah
```

Figure 7.5 Group 10 "What else culture?" transcript

As such, between lines 2 and 8, the three White students looked at each other, wrote on the whiteboard, and made overlaps and latched utterances, creating quick turn-taking sequences. Through their collaborative body movement and verbal co-constructions, the three White students were collectively participating as discussion tellers, discussion holders, and discussion makers. In the meantime, AGM sat on a chair and looked at the whiteboard and at others, while no one acknowledged his presence, creating AGM as an unaddressed hearer.

In line 9, AGM pulled his body to the right and looked at the whiteboard, which demonstrates his attempt to participate in this discussion-generator footing that is solely occupied by the three White students. WBM turned and walked to AGM as he was generating his idea to the other White students (line 10 and 11). Then, WBM pointed at AGM's computer screen, saying "Beautiful City in international population" with a falling tone, providing an incomplete imperative account that assigned AM to become an author. Yet, this abrupt completion might be incomprehensible to his addressee. WBM self-repaired his utterance and requested AGM to search the information for the group (line 14 and 15). AGM reached out to his computer, showing his preferred participation with his body language. In line 20 and 21, WBM continued to look at what AGM did, bent over, and requested a new assignment (search the population of Beautiful City), which was different from his initial request. Then, in line 22, he turned to the whiteboard where the other two White students were. Through these actions and utterances, it is possible to understand that WBM was a facilitator/animator/principal to help AGM to become both discussion teller and discussion maker by providing supplementary information to the White students' discussion, yet in an assertive inattentive manner. In addition, WBM's continuous physical turning to the whiteboard demonstrates his attempts to participate in the other two White students' discussion, which became the main stage (Goffman, 1974) of their group discussion.

From students' body language and their physical position in the group, we can clearly see that three students became collaborative and collective discussion makers, holders, and tellers, and one was excluded from the main interaction. The female student recorded, animated, and stayed in the White student group discussion. Two White male students provided the direction for the discussion and suggested the ideas amongst themselves. The Asian student was assigned to be a fact checker of a confusing task that supplements the main discussion frame. Additionally, his assigned role spatially marginalised him from the rest, and thereby exacerbated his exclusion from his peers.

Discussion: Implications for teaching and research

The findings of this study point to the challenges and opportunities of implementing communicative interactive activities in mainstream courses where students who are developing proficiency in English are integrated with domestic or so-called 'native' or highly fluent speakers of English. We framed our study by drawing on Goffman's participation framework within a disciplinary course that was redesigned to foreground language and content-integrated activities. Interestingly, although our intent was to increase opportunities for interaction both through group discussion and tasks, and to do this in a way that integrates speakers from different language backgrounds, an unintended consequence was that some of the recently arrived international university students became marginalised and did not participate to the extent that the participant-researchers would have hoped. The response to the first research question would suggest that although business students from different language and cultural backgrounds aim to collaborate and interact, there is still, in some instances, based on the group behaviours observed, a lack of participation by students with developing English proficiency, and exclusion by the more proficient speakers of English. It was clear that in some groups, students were not able to engage, and the opportunities provided for interaction and socialisation did not always facilitate multilingual students' group participation amongst their anglophone peers.

Such findings suggest a number of pedagogical implications. First, the study reinforces the importance of highlighting the classroom diversity where *all* students are in need of acquiring multilingual sensitivity (Dippold, 2015). To do so, it is important to create a pedagogical space that cultivates students' identities as brave, agentive, and confident learners and users of the English language and other languages. In this business classroom, curriculum and instructional redesign could further enhance student interactions by creating an opportunity for students to self-reflect by observing their video of the team interaction. It is also possible to allocate in-class time for a self-assessment of the peer interaction. This would further support critical thinking skills and intercultural competency in business and help them to engage in more inclusive and respectful peer interactions.

Additionally, the findings recommend explicit recognition of diversity in the classroom through materials redesign and explicit instruction. By more explicitly acknowledging the multilingual diversity of the student population, both English-dominant and multilingual/international students can become more agentive and active, and could represent plurilingual negotiation as participatory and enjoyable. By mobilising multilingual students' social and cultural resources, students' competent and agentive classroom participation can be effectively achieved. For example, we found that the case involving an American company – Amazon – was not addressing the international, multilingual, and multicultural profile and interests of the student body. Perhaps a case from a different, non-anglophone geographic context could have been selected to internationalise the curriculum and better engage and include students.

Finally, our general observation of all the groups, but more specifically, the findings from observations of the two student groups described in this study suggests a need for explicit instruction of discourse skills to not only the multilingual/international students but to all students, particularly in response to the rapidly growing linguistic diversity in the classroom. It is because 'native-ness' of native speakers of English cannot be the default of good international business English communication. To do so, we recommend instructors facilitate students' multilingual awareness and foreground a mutually respectful communicative framing and schema within the classroom community. In other student videos, we found that students employed a number of communicative strategies (such as monitoring and identifying cues) to engage in effective communication (see Appendix). Explicit teaching of discourse skills in a multilingual business classroom, therefore, would be even more important given the increasingly globalised business context. By deliberately negotiating intercultural communication in a disciplinary setting, students will be more equipped for the multilingual and multicultural business communication where the monolingual norm is no longer dominant.

These recommendations can further be explored through ongoing research. The current study reflects upon peer interaction in an undergraduate business programme in an anglo-dominant university, demonstrating how language was used amongst peers in a small-group discussion that created unexpected outcomes and identities in some cases. However, it is important to acknowledge that there are successful examples of peer engagement where multilingual students effectively manoeuvre their challenging circumstances. Although it is important to examine the factors that support successful interactions, the researchers felt the ethical need to first examine how and why some interactions led to marginalisation. Although it is beyond the scope of the chapter to focus on successful peer interactions, we have observed positive, respectful processes as the students develop their communicative repertoires in their business classroom as they complete various group assignments. In addition, what we learned from this study is to inform students how to engage with others with more explicit models of peer interaction (see Appendix). Therefore, systematically examining such discourse cases would shed light on how students negotiate their speaker and listener roles, thereby developing their multilingual sensitivity in the linguistically diverse disciplinary situation.

Conclusion

Our data and suggestions for practice and research point to the fact that, especially in anglo-dominant contexts, there is progress to be made in effectuating an institutional culture shift from linguistic 'difference as deficit' to 'difference as resource'. Faculty in mainstream 'content' classrooms should explicitly create awareness about the linguistic and cultural diversity in the classroom, and promote inclusive behaviours and communication. This does not suggest that there should not be any standards around communicating in the target language and the language of instruction that many international and recent immigrant students have chosen to learn in. Faculty should continue to model disciplinary discourse and effective communication, and create opportunities that encourage all learners to become members and engage in the discourse of their discipline for student success, while foregrounding the richness of the diverse context.

Acknowledgement

This research was supported by the Centre for English Language Learning, Teaching and Research, funded by the Vice-President Academic's Office and the Faculty of Education at Simon Fraser University. We would like to express our special thanks to Doris Dippold and Marion Heron for their helpful comments and dedicated feedback in writing this chapter.

Note

1   This study received a Research Ethics Board approval (Certificate number: 2018s0323).

Appendix

These are the extracts from transcribed conversation from peer group discussion in the 2017 pilot study.

- Identifying cues and inferring
    - "That's a great idea"
    - "Are you taking notes?"

- Turn-taking (Taking the floor)
    - "Sorry... go ahead"
    - "I also think that..."

- Co-operating
    - "I agree, but should we consider...; ...shouldn't we..."
    - "Do you mind checking that?"

- Asking for clarification
    - "Like what do you mean...?"
    - Avoid "and stuff like that..." "this" "it"
    - "We might have to double-check that fact"
    - "I feel that..."

- Questioning/answering sequences
    - "Do you think we have to mention the cons?"
    - "Do you think we have to mention the tools explicitly?"
    - "How can we organise this effectively? Coherently?"

- Planning
    - "So how many minutes do we have?... We should allocate 10 min. to X"
    - "Let's make sure we address all the criteria/tools"
    - "Going on from that..."

- Compensating/monitoring and repair

  - "What I meant was..."
  - I'm sorry... now I understand..."

References

Agosti, C. I., & Bernat, E. (Eds.). (2018). *University pathway programs: Local responses within a growing global trend.* Cham, Switzerland: Springer.

Bargiela-Chiappini, F., Nickerson, C., & Planken, B. (2013). *Business discourse* (2nd ed.). New York: Palgrave Macmillan.

Burnaby, B. (2008). Language policy and education in Canada. In S. May & N. H. Hornberger (Eds.), *Encyclopedia of language and education: Vol. 1. Language policy and political issues in education* (2nd ed., pp. 331–341). New York: Springer.

Council of Europe. (2001). *Common European Framework of Reference for Languages: Learning, teaching, assessment.* Cambridge: Cambridge University Press.

Coste, D., Moore, D., & Zarate, G. (2009). *Plurilingual and pluricultural competence.* Strasbourg, France: Council of Europe.

Coyle, D., Hood, P., & Marsh, D. (2010). *Content and language integrated learning.* Cambridge: Cambridge University Press.

Creswell, J. W. (2007). *Qualitative inquiry and research design: Choosing among five approaches* (2nd ed.). Thousand Oaks, CA: Sage.

Dagenais, D. (2013). Multilingualism in Canada: Policy and education in applied linguistics research. *Annual Review of Applied Linguistics*, 33, 286–301. doi:10.1017/S0267190513000056.

Dippold, D. (2015). *Classroom interaction: The internationalised Anglophone university.* Basingstoke: Palgrave.

Duff, P. A. (2008). *Case study research in applied linguistics.* New York: Lawrence Erlbaum.

Fenton-Smith, B., & Humphreys, P. (2015). Language specialists' views on academic language and learning support mechanisms for EAL postgraduate coursework students: The case for adjunct tutorials. *Journal of English for Academic Purposes*, 20, 40–55. doi:10.1016/j.jeap.2015.05.001.

Goffman, E. (1974). *Frame analysis: An essay on the organisation of experience.* New York: Harper & Row.

Goffman, E. (1981). *Forms of talk.* Philadelphia, PA: University of Pennsylvania Press.

Goodwin, C., & Goodwin, M. H. (2004). Participation. In A. Duranti (Ed.), *A companion to linguistic anthropology* (pp. 222–244). Malden, MA: Blackwell.

Haque, E. (2012). *Multiculturalism within a bilingual framework: Language, race, and belonging in Canada.* Toronto, ON: University of Toronto Press.

Heritage, J. (2005). Conversation analysis and institutional talk. In K. L. Fitch & R. E. Sanders (Eds.), *Handbook of language and social interaction* (pp. 103–148). Mahwah, NJ: Lawrence Erlbaum.

Heron, M. (2019). Pedagogic practices to support international students in seminar discussions. *Higher Education Research & Development*, 38(2), 266–279. doi:10.1080/07294360.2018.1512954.

ICEF (2019). Canada's foreign student enrolment took another big jump in 2018. *ICEF Monitor.* Retrieved from https://monitor.icef.com/2019/02/canadas-foreign-student-enrolment-took-another-big-jump-2018/

Institutional Research and Planning. (2020). *Fall international student report.* 'Plurilingual' University, Canada.

Lin, A. M. Y. (2016). *Language across the curriculum & CLIL in English as an additional language (EAL) contexts: Theory and practice.* Singapore: Springer.

Murray, N. (2016). *Standards of English in higher education: Issues, challenges and strategies.* Cambridge: Cambridge University Press.

Sacks, H., Schegloff, E. A., & Jefferson, G. (1974). A simplest systematics for the organisation of turn-taking for conversation. *Language,* 50. 696–735.

Smythe, S., & Toohey, K. (2009). Investigating sociohistorical contexts and practices through a community scan: A Canadian Punjabi–Sikh example. *Language and Education,* 23(1), 37–57. doi:10.1080/09500780802152887.

Statistics Canada. (2016). *International students in Canadian Universities, 2004–2005 to 2013–2014* (Report No. 81–599-X – No. 11). Retrieved from www150.statcan.gc.ca/n1/pub/81-599-x/81-599-x2016011-eng.htm.

Ten Have, P. (2007). *Doing conversation analysis: A practical guide* (2nd ed.). Thousand Oaks, CA: Sage.

8 Challenges faced by transnational education students in advanced STEM practical classes

Philippa Cranwell, Daguo Li, Elizabeth M. Page, Karin Whiteside and Aaron Woodcock

Introduction

A transnational education (TNE) student is defined as a student "studying a higher education degree programme leading to a UK qualification in a country other than the one in which the awarding institution is located. This includes joint, double or dual awards" (HE Global report, 2016). In recent years, the number of students studying on transnational degree programmes has increased significantly. In 2012–13 there were 598,925 students studying on transnational courses (undergraduate and postgraduate), which rose to 701,010 by 2015–16 (Universities UK International report, 2018). The majority of TNE students at undergraduate level were from Asia (41%), with Malaysia and China having the most students enrolled on undergraduate programmes (44,690 and 23,615 students, respectively). In Malaysia and China, a significant number of students study for their qualification wholly overseas. During a TNE programme, course delivery may be through one, or a combination of, three main modes (HE Global report, 2016):

- Distance/online learning, either with or without local support.
- Local delivery partnerships, e.g. franchised delivery, joint and dual degrees, twinning arrangements, validation and quality arrangements.
- Physical presence, e.g. branch campus, study centre or 'flying faculty'.

Within chemistry, there has been a rapid growth in the number of TNE providers, particularly between the UK and China. Delivery of these programmes is usually through a model where students study for two, three or four years in China and, if the programme allows, transfer to the UK for their final year. These models are referred to as 2+2, 3+1 or 4+0, respectively, with the former number referring to the number of years the student spends in China and the latter the number of years the student spends in the UK. In this study, students were studying on a 3+1 BSc Applied Chemistry programme, with content in China delivered by local staff interspersed with short visits from UK-based academics using the 'flying faculty' model (Smith, 2014).

In the programme discussed, the first year of study in China is very general. The second and third years in China are aligned with the UK institution's chemistry curriculum and are taught in English by faculty members in China. During the students' second and third years of study, there are two visits from the UK faculty staff per year, each lasting for a fortnight. During these visits, some subject-specific teaching by the UK faculty member takes place. While in China, students study both general academic English and Chemistry-specific academic English. In order to transfer to the UK, students need to meet a pre-determined academic threshold in years two and three, and a specific IELTS score. Once in the UK, the Chinese students are fully integrated with the UK-based students and share lectures, tutorials and practical classes. The assessment of core chemistry knowledge in this year is identical to that of the domestic students. The TNE students also have additional assessments relating to the English language module and a bespoke key skills module, each contributing 10 credits (5 ECTS credits) in place of some optional chemistry content. Overall, the year in the UK contributes two-thirds of the credit towards the TNE students' final degree classification, in line with the UK-based student cohort. Students attain two BSc degree qualifications, one from each institution.

Integration of international students into the domestic cohort

There has been some investigation of the integration of international students into a domestic cohort, either as international students studying their whole degree in another country, or as part of a bespoke programme with one year of study abroad embedded (Cranwell et al., 2019; Smith & Khawaja, 2011; Ward, Masgoret & Gezentsvey, 2009). Whatever the mode of study for these students, there are large numbers of reported pressures on them. For example, TNE students are expected to study and achieve good grades in an unfamiliar academic culture, often in their non-native language, as well as interact with those in their host country and make friends with home students on campus (Hou & McDowell 2014). Lee and Rice (2007) showed that in the United States, students from Western cultures and English-speaking countries integrated into the host society much more efficiently and were discriminated against less than those students from other societies. True integration into the host culture or society, particularly by Chinese students, is unusual, and one reason for this may be due to the fact that student mobility is seen as temporary; many students study in the host country for only one year (Li & Pitkänen, 2018). The extent of integration of students will also likely depend upon the degree programme that the students study, and the relative size of the host and international cohort. Some programmes comprise mainly international students, for example Master's programmes in business, whereas others do not. Subject "norms" and international composition of the cohort has a bearing upon the integration and cohesion of the cohorts.

Practical classes in the UK

Many studies into how students undertake learning within the science laboratory have been conducted, and numerous reviews have been published since the 1960s (Hofstein & Lunetta, 1982, 2004; Lazarowitz & Tamir, 1994; Lunetta, Hofstein & Clough, 2007; Ramsay & Howe, 1969a, 1969b; Tobin, 1990). However, there have been fewer studies into the interactions between laboratory users (Lang, Wong & Fraser, 2005), and, to the best of our knowledge, no studies into the interaction and integration of TNE students with other laboratory users. A practical class within a chemistry laboratory comprising a mixed cohort of international and domestic students, with associated teaching staff, provides opportunities for a multitude of oral interactions between laboratory users.

In the programme in this study, upon transfer to the UK the TNE students experience a laboratory class module that is significantly different to that in China. The module contributes 20 credits (10 ECTS credits) to the TNE students' final-year grade. There are around 50 students present per session and each session is nine hours in duration. In this time, students complete advanced-level experiments and collect data. There is not usually time to analyse data during the session. Both TNE and UK students work in pairs to complete the same experiments and the pairs are physically interspersed with each other. The assessment of the TNE students comprises ten short online tests before each session that each contributes 1% to the overall grade, and three full scientific reports, each contributing 30% to the final overall grade. The class is supervised by one member of academic staff along with a native Chinese-speaking International Support Tutor (IST). The IST's role is to support students academically and pastorally both before and after transfer to the UK, and also provide extra-curricular support to students throughout the programme. While in the laboratory, there are numerous people that students can consult for advice and reassurance: the IST, academic staff, teaching assistants (TAs), technicians, UK students or their partners. Although manuals outlining fundamental instructions and processes necessary for the experiment are issued, these require further interpretation to allow full comprehension of specific instructions as they are written in a highly technical register. Due to the UK and TNE student pairs working side-by-side, the opportunities for cross-cultural communication are numerous. The environment contrasts with that experienced in China where a laboratory session, conducted solely in Chinese, may be two hours in duration, supervised by a single Chinese member of staff who demonstrates techniques at the start and provides written recipe-style instructions.

Within this chapter, trends identified in TNE students' self-reported classroom experience and perception of classroom interaction in a chemistry laboratory within a TNE chemistry programme after transfer to the UK are discussed. Although this study considers the integration of Chinese students into a chemistry programme and their subsequent interaction with the UK-based cohort, it is anticipated that several of the issues identified and observations made herein are applicable to other STEM subjects, and subjects with a large practical element involving experiential learning, such as art or film studies. Our preliminary findings are outlined below.

Materials and methods

When collecting data for this project, a mixed-methods approach (Bergman, 2008; Hesse-Biber, 2010; Johnson & Onwuegbuzie, 2004) was used with three modes of data collection: questionnaires, individual interviews with selected participants, and observation/video recording of practical classes by the researchers. The data were collected after the TNE students had been studying in the UK for three months. During the practical sessions, all students were arranged into three groups of approximately 16 students that comprised five UK student pairs and three TNE student pairs. This research received Research Ethics Board approval from the International Study and Language Institute at the University of Reading.

Questionnaires

The questionnaires were written in English and translated into Chinese, and were designed to investigate the key interactions of the TNE students with other laboratory users from a TNE student perspective. Participants answered the questionnaires in Chinese. The questionnaires comprised a selection of open and closed questions, and Likert-style items to allow collection of data that could be both statistically analysed for significance and assessed and coded by adopting an inductive qualitative content analysis approach, where written or oral materials were grouped/classified into categories of similar meanings (Cho & Lee, 2014; Elo & Kyngäs, 2008; Moretti et al., 2011). Answers to the open questions were translated back into English for analysis. Statistical analysis was completed using SPSS.

Interviews

The semi-structured interviews were conducted in Chinese. Ten interviews were undertaken. The transcripts were translated *verbatim* into English by a native Chinese speaker and the responses thematically coded by the researchers by looking for both salient and recurring themes among students. The guide interview questions are included in the Appendix.

Laboratory observations

The participants were observed during one physical chemistry practical session at three different points by the researchers, and notes were taken according to key interactions between laboratory participants. These points were at differing times throughout the practical work: the beginning of the session when students were setting up their experiment(s); the middle of the session when experimental data were being collected; and the end of the session when experimental results were being analysed. The material collected during the laboratory sessions were reviewed. Key observations were noted and triangulated with the results from the interviews and questionnaires as described in the following section.

Challenges faced during data collection

The main challenge with this investigation was accurately capturing the interactions of the TNE students with the other laboratory users. The laboratory is an extremely busy environment and the frequency of interactions is high. In addition, the laboratory environment can be quite noisy both due to conversations between laboratory users and the use of the fume-hood air extraction system, so accurately hearing the exchanges and documenting them was occasionally difficult.

Results

When in the UK laboratory, all students work in pairs. The UK students already had established laboratory partners from previous years; therefore, it was decided by academic staff that pairings would be UK student–UK student and TNE student–TNE student. The pairings were assigned in the first laboratory session of the year. Upon analysis of interview data, it was seen that the lack of forced integration may have been a hinderance to interaction between cohorts. The TNE students commented on the lack of mixed pairings as a negative, and one student stated that they would have preferred to have been paired with a UK-based student because of the benefits of integration with the local students:

INTERVIEWER: When you were experimenting [in the UK], you were grouped up with another [TNE] student. Are you happy with this? Do you want to group up with some students from other countries?
STUDENT: In fact, I still hope to be in a group with foreign students… In fact, I really want to communicate with foreign students.

And

INTERVIEWER: If you can make your own choice, you will choose to be with a [TNE] student or…?
STUDENT: Probably with local students. Because I came here to learn more from them and integrate into the lives here.

Analysis of the questionnaire data showed that 76.9% of the TNE students believed that there were barriers to communication with the UK-based students[1] and that there was a great deal of interaction between TNE students, but less between the TNE students and UK students.[2, 3] This suggests that, in line with the findings of Li and Pitkänen (2018), significant interaction with UK-based students was not occurring. When asked to clarify the barriers faced, students cited speaking and listening as major issues. Time pressure to complete experiments, for both TNE and UK students, and therefore satisfy the assessments was also mentioned numerous times.

STUDENT: There are many terminologies that we could not pronounce. Or I am afraid of not being understood even after I pronounced it. Everyone is doing experiments and it is impossible to read the words slowly. Others need to do their experiments, too.

And

INTERVIEWER: Have you ever tried to communicate with other foreign students outside of your group?
STUDENT: I have tried to communicate. But my listening is not very good, and they speak too fast, so that I can't get used to it. Once he/she talked to me and he/she spoke two sentences, I could not understand either of them, this was quite embarrassing.
INTERVIEWER: Language barrier?
STUDENT: The language barrier is still quite big.

And

INTERVIEWER: Have you taken the initiative to communicate with other British students or foreign students outside the group?
STUDENT: Yes, but quite few times.
INTERVIEWER: Is it because you were busy with the experiment or…?
STUDENT: Should be busy with experimenting.
INTERVIEWER: Do you feel foreign students from other groups ever take the initiative to communicate with you?
STUDENT: Not really. They were focusing on their experiments.

Technical vocabulary was also difficult, particularly the specific vocabulary required within a practical class due to students' unfamiliarity with the words.

INTERVIEWER: Is there any challenge [in the practical class]?
STUDENT: As for challenges, they are mostly in terms of communication.
INTERVIEWER: Like what?
STUDENT: We couldn't express accurately our opinions. Sometimes the British students are also very confused with what we've said.
INTERVIEWER: The expression is unclear? Is it the vocabulary problem still?

STUDENT: Yes, vocabulary problems, terminology. Now we know some of the basic chemistry terms, but we still have difficulties of combining them together.

When communication did occur, it was usually related to experimental techniques rather than day-to-day chatting:

INTERVIEWER: Do you have any initiative to communicate with foreign students?
STUDENT: When we do experiments, we ask each other about yields, etc. Because if we have not done this experiment before, we are not sure if we are doing it well or not. We just compare slightly with each other. They also ask about how to use the instrument, etc.

Student responses showed that the language of communication between TNE students during the practical sessions was "mostly Chinese with some English" (85% students, n = 13), with some students (15%, n = 13) consistently speaking to their TNE classmates in Chinese only.[4] When the reasons for predominantly using Chinese were probed, it was discovered it was for ease and to avoid miscommunication. In addition, students perceived the main goal of practical work to be completion of the credit-bearing experiment rather than improvement of English language skills, which could be learnt after class. For example, one student stated:

INTERVIEWER: Does [talking Chinese] affect your language improvements? Your English improvements?
STUDENT: I think it is affected. But after all, I regard finishing experiments as my main goal. I could learn the language after lab class in other activities.

Unsurprisingly, questionnaire data revealed that interactions between TNE students and UK-based staff were likely to be in English with 61.5% students using "mostly English with some Chinese" and 30.8% using "English only".[5] Concerningly, one student "never" talked to UK-based staff.[6] It was noted during observations that the TNE students mainly interacted with the IST rather than approach the English-speaking UK-based academic staff or TAs. In addition, it was noticed that the TNE students asked the IST questions in Chinese and the IST answered in English. When asked about this in interviews, one student said that although the IST answered in English, the speed at which the IST spoke was more manageable for students:

INTERVIEWER: [The IST] usually explains to you in English. But it seems like you normally reply in Chinese?
STUDENT: We don't answer much, it's mainly listening to him/her, and we can understand it. Because he/she asks us if we understood or not if it's something quite difficult. Also, s/he doesn't speak fast.

English was used by the TNE students if they were using vocabulary that they had learnt while in the UK, such as when using chemical names or discussing reaction phenomena.

INTERVIEWER: Do you communicate a lot with your experimental partner?
STUDENT: It's quite a lot. We exchange our ideas of division of labour.
INTERVIEWER: Was it in Chinese or English when you communicating with each other?
STUDENT: Most of the time we use Chinese, sometimes in English.
INTERVIEWER: Under what circumstances is English used?
STUDENT: The names of some compounds, because we do not understand them in Chinese anyway, so we use English.
INTERVIEWER: Are they newly learnt compounds?
STUDENT: Yes, newly learnt.

The TNE students had mixed views over how useful their interactions with other laboratory users were in terms of learning practical chemistry techniques. Interactions with other TNE students, UK-based staff, the TAs and technicians were all seen to be useful, as shown by statistical analysis of the questionnaire data.[7],[8],[9] Interactions with the UK-based students were only seen as "quite" useful[10] and did not occur regularly.

Discussion

TNE students working in UK teaching laboratories for the first time face a number of challenges. Their interaction with the UK-based cohort has been studied through analysis of TNE students' reported experiences and perceptions using questionnaire data and individual interviews.

A very real obstacle limiting interaction between the TNE students and other laboratory users is the high stakes of the assessment linked to successful completion of the experiments. The advanced practical course is a 20-credit Level 6 module, assessed entirely on the basis of laboratory reports and reaction outcomes. As noted earlier, the TNE students perceive the main goal of the laboratory work to be gaining associated credit; English language improvement, gained by communicating with other laboratory users, is secondary. In addition, the TNE students acknowledge that the UK students are also working to obtain a good mark and that by conversing with and requesting help from the UK students they may be slowing them down and causing them to sacrifice credit. This is likely compounded by the limited English language skills of the TNE students, resulting in prolonged oral interactions as both groups of students strive to make themselves understood. Without considerable adjustments to assessment design to lower the perceived and real risk of impact to credit outcomes, it is difficult for chemistry educators to rationalise 'engineering' greater cross-national grouping within laboratory sessions.

Despite the unfamiliar physical environment and differences in working practices, there is a desire from the TNE students to interact with the UK-based students. We believe that another major barrier to achieving successful interaction and integration was instigated in the first laboratory session that students attended, where they were divided into pairs. Integration between cohorts was not encouraged (i.e. by mixed-cohort pairings) and may have actually encouraged the lack of interaction over the course because there was little impetus for students to interact.

A final substantial challenge stems from the TNE students' perceived competence in using the English language. Although all students have to meet the university's required IELTS grades in English for enrolment, this is not necessarily adequate to prepare them to fully communicate with other laboratory occupants as it does not measure discipline-specific language and literacy. Results from the questionnaires, interviews and observations show that after transfer to the UK the TNE students tend to rely on each other rather than an academic member of staff or other laboratory occupants. This is because they find it easier to communicate in Chinese rather than English due to lack of confidence in the English language, the speed of discourse they encounter, and the subject-specific vocabulary required. Other challenges to interaction between the TNE students and other laboratory users identified include: the laboratory environment being very loud so hearing and explaining issues is difficult, the fast pace at which interactions with other interlocuters occur, and the high-stakes credit linked to the assessment of the practical work completed. It is possible that because all laboratory users are under pressure to complete the experiments and gain academic credit, there may be lower tolerance towards less-proficient English language users and vice versa; however, this was not investigated further.

Impact on student learning

The TNE students' lack of confidence in technical, subject-specific language upon transfer to the UK has been shown to be a barrier for student interaction, and therefore student integration, in practical classes. Limited levels of integration and interaction during lectures or other teaching events will also undoubtedly have an impact upon student learning and could lead to a lack of understanding of a topic with a resulting impact upon student attainment. The risk is intensified for these students as they transfer to the UK for their final year of study, which is particularly demanding and contributes a large proportion towards the final degree grade outcome.

Conclusion

There are a number of potential implications from the findings of this study. Language, namely knowledge of technical vocabulary and receptive difficulty with oral communication, was found to be a major barrier to interaction between, and therefore integration with, cohorts during laboratory work. This suggests that the way in which TNE students are prepared for study in the UK should be reviewed. Despite the fact that the TNE students are taught in English in China, there may be an argument for more intensive, discipline-specific vocabulary input and development of listening skills.

In order to ensure interaction, and subsequent integration, between student cohorts, mixed nationality pairings should be considered when designing laboratory or similar workshop activities. However, this is a sensitive and complex part of the programme structure; thus changes should be carefully considered. One possible way to facilitate greater interaction and subsequent integration between the two cultural groups might be to explore whether the principles of 'compassionate group work' could be applied to the laboratory setting. This technique was developed and embedded within assessment at the University of Hertfordshire by Gilbert (2016a, 2017) to promote diversity and inclusion. In this work, students' individual, observable demonstrations of compassion were credit-bearing in some modules. The rationale was that when people feel socially safe in task-focused groups, their thinking processes are able to concentrate on the task rather than on the evolutionarily determined priority of (social) defence mechanisms. Students were trained in compassion-based micro skills for task-focused, face-to-face student group work in a short workshop at the beginning of the module and then gave a seminar in which their compassion skills were assessed. It was shown that credit for compassionate behaviours appeared to positively motivate students to attempt compassionate group management, regardless of their ethnic or national status (Gilbert 2016b; Gilbert et al. 2018). It may be possible to adapt the original model as used for seminar work to the oral environment of the laboratory.

Notes

1 Are there any barriers to communication with British students? Yes (76.9%), No (23.1%). n = 13.
2 How much interaction occurs between you and your [TNE] classmates during a typical laboratory session in the UK? A lot (1), some (2), not much (3), none (4); mean 1.00; n = 13; SD 0.000.
3 How much interaction occurs between you and your British classmates during a typical laboratory session in the UK? A lot (1), some (2), not much (3), none (4); mean 2.77; n = 13; SD 0.439.
4 When interacting with your [TNE] classmates in the laboratory in the UK, which language do you use? Mostly Chinese with some English (84.6%), Mostly English with some Chinese (0%), Chinese only (15.4%), English only (0%); n = 13.
5 When interacting with staff in the laboratory in the UK, which language do you use? Mostly Chinese with some English (7.7%), Mostly English with some Chinese (61.5%), Chinese only (0%), English only (30.8%); n = 13.
6 How much interaction occurs between you and staff during a typical laboratory session in the UK? A lot (1), some (2), not much (3), none (4); mean 2.00; n = 13; SD 0.816.
7 How useful do you feel interacting with the technician/demonstrator is for your learning? Very (1), fairly (2), quite (3), not very (4); mean 1.69; n =13; SD 0.751.
8 How useful do you feel interacting with the lecturer is for your learning? Very (1), fairly (2), quite (3), not very (4); mean 1.77; n = 13; SD 0.599.

9 How useful do you feel interacting with your [TNE] classmates is for your learning?
Very (1), fairly (2), quite (3), not very (4); mean 1.85; n = 13; SD 0.555.

10 How useful do you feel interacting with your British classmates is for your learning?
Very (1), fairly (2), quite (3), not very (4); mean 3.23; n = 13; SD 0.832.

Appendix

Interview guide questions

Areas to explore more:

Lab work in general:

- Were you told to do anything to prepare for labs in the UK?
- Benefits of working in pairs in the UK
- Would you prefer to be in [TNE] pair or UK and [TNE] pair? Explain
- Do you prefer asking Chinese/English staff for help?
- Lab follow-up in UK compared to [TNE]

Communication:

- If interaction is mainly with [TNE] students (in interviews) – why?
- Barriers to communication?
- What do you think the British students talk about in labs?

Lab work in UK?

- Benefits of UK labs?
- Challenges in UK lab sessions
- Is lab work different in the UK?
- How are your initial experiences?

Acknowledgements

We would like to acknowledge the University of Reading International Initiatives Fund for their financial support of this project.

Disclosure statement

No potential conflict of interest was reported by the authors

Ethics

Ethical approval was given for this study by the ethics committee in the International Study and Language Institute at the University of Reading.

References

Bergman, M. M. (Ed.) (2008), *Advances in Mixed Methods Research: Theories and Applications*. London: SAGE Publications. https://doi.org/10.4135/9780857024329.

Cho, J. Y. & Lee, E.-H. (2014). Reducing Confusion about Grounded Theory and Qualitative Content Analysis: Similarities and Differences. *The Qualitative Report*, 19 (32), 1–20. Retrieved 1 August 2020, from http://nsuworks.nova.edu/tqr/vol19/iss32/2.

Cranwell, P. B., Edwards, M. G., Haxton, K. J., Hyde, J., Page, E. M., Plana, D., Sedhi, G. & Wright, J. S. (2019). Chinese Students' Expectations Versus Reality When Studying on a UK-China Transnational Chemistry Degree Program. *New Directions in the Teaching of Physical Sciences*, 14 (1). https://doi.org/10.29311/ndtps.v0i14.3325.

Elo, S. & Kyngäs, H. (2008). The Qualitative Content Analysis Process. *Journal of Advanced Nursing*, 62 (1), 107–115. https://doi.org/10.1111/j.1365-2648.2007.04569.x.

Gilbert, T. (2016a). Embedding and Assessing Compassion in the University Curriculum. *The International Academic Forum: The European Conference on Education, 2016: Conference Proceedings* (pp. 77–87). The International Academic Forum.

Gilbert, T. (2016b). Assess Compassion in Higher Education? Why and How Would We Do That? *Link, University of Hertfordshire*. Retrieved 15 May 2020, from www.herts.ac.uk/link/volume-2,-issue-1/assess-compassion-in-higher-education-how-and-why-would-we-do-that.

Gilbert, T. (2017). When Looking is Allowed: What Compassionate Group Work Looks Like in a UK University. In P. Gibbs (Ed.), *The Pedagogy of Compassion at the Heart of Higher Education* (pp. 189–202). 1st ed. Switzerland: Springer. https://doi.org/10.1007/978-3-319-57783-8.

Gilbert, T., Doolan, M., Beka, S., Spencer, N., Crotta, M. & Davari, S. (2018). Compassion on University Degree Programmes at a UK University: The Neuroscience of Effective Group Work. *Journal of Research in Innovative Teaching & Learning*, 11 (1), 4–21. https://doi.org/10.1108/JRIT-09-2017-0020.

HE Global (June 2016). *The Scale and Scope of UK Higher Education Transnational Education*. Paragraph 1.7. Birmingham: Georgia Seora.

Hesse-Biber, S. N. (2010). *Mixed Methods Research: Merging Theory with Practice*. New York: The Guildford Press.

Hofstein, A. & Lunetta, V. N. (1982). The Role of the Laboratory in Science Teaching: Neglected Aspects of Research. *Review of Educational Research*, 52 (2), 201–217. https://doi.org/10.2307/1170311.

Hofstein, A. & Lunetta, V.N. (2004). The Laboratory in Science Education: Foundations for the Twenty-first Century. *Science Education*, 88 (1), 28–54. https://doi.org/10.1002/sce.10106.

Hou, J. & McDowell, L. (2014). Learning Together? Experiences on a China–U.K. Articulation Program in Engineering. *Journal of Studies in International Education*, 18 (3), 223–240. https://doi.org/10.1177/1028315313497591.

Johnson, R. B. & Onwuegbuzie, A. J. (2004). Mixed Methods Research: A Research Paradigm Whose Time Has Come. *Educational Researcher*, 33 (7), 14–26. https://doi.org/10.3102/0013189X033007014.

Lang, Q. C., Wong, A. F. L. & Fraser, B. F. (2005). Student Perceptions of Chemistry Laboratory Learning Environments, Student–Teacher Interactions and Attitudes in Secondary School Gifted Education Classes in Singapore. *Research in Science Education*, 35, 299–321. https://doi.org/10.1007/s11165-005-0093-9.

Lazarowitz, R. & Tamir, P. (1994). Research on Using Laboratory Instruction in Science. In D. L. Gabel (Ed.), *Handbook of Research on Science Teaching* (pp. 94–127). New York: Macmillan.

Lee, J. J. & Rice, C. (2007). Welcome to America? International Student Perceptions of Discrimination. *Higher Education*, 53, 381–409. https://doi.org/10.1007/s10734-005-4508-3.

Li, H. & Pitkänen, P. (2018). Understanding the Integration of Mainland Chinese Students: The Case of Finland. *Nordic Journal of Migration Research*, 8 (2), 107–115. https://doi.org/10.1515/njmr-2018-0008.

Lunetta, V. N., Hofstein, A., & Clough, M. (2007), Learning and Teaching in the School Science Laboratory: An Analysis of Research, Theory, and Practice. In N. Lederman, & S. Abel (Eds.), *Handbook of Research on Science Education* (pp. 393–441). Mahwah, NJ: Lawrence Erlbaum.

Moretti, F., van Vliet, L., Bensing, J., Deledda, G., Mazzi, M., Rimondini, M., Zimmermann, C. & Fletcher, I. (2011). A Standardized Approach to Qualitative Content Analysis of Focus Group Discussions from Different Countries. *Patient Education and Counseling*, 82 (3), 420–428. https://doi.org/10.1016/j.pec.2011.01.005.

Ramsay, G. A. & Howe, R. W. (1969a). An Analysis of Research on Instructional Procedures in Secondary School Science, Part I – Outcomes of Instruction. *The Science Teacher*, 36 (3), 62–70. Retrieved May 15, 2020, from www.jstor.org/stable/24151625.

Ramsay, G. A. & Howe, R. W. (1969b). An Analysis of Research on Instructional Procedures in Secondary School Science, Part II – Instructional Procedures. *The Science Teacher*, 36 (4), 72–81. Retrieved May 15, 2020, from www.jstor.org/stable/24152532.

Smith, K. (2014). Exploring Flying Faculty Teaching Experiences: Motivations, Challenges and Opportunities. *Studies in Higher Education*, 39 (1), 117–134. https://doi.org/10.1080/03075079.2011.646259.

Smith, R. A. & Khawaja, N. G. (2011). A Review of the Acculturation Experiences of International Students. *International Journal of Intercultural Relations*, 35 (6), 699–713. https://doi.org/10.1016/j.ijintrel.2011.08.004.

Tobin, K. (1990). Research on Science Laboratory Activities: In Pursuit of Better Questions and Answers to Improve Learning. *School Science and Mathematics*, 90 (5), 403–418. https://doi.org/10.1111/j.1949-8594.1990.tb17229.x.

Universities UK International. (January2018). *The Scale of UK Higher Education Transnational Education 2015–2016: Trend Analysis of HESA Data*. London: Leo Boe.

Ward, C., Masgoret, A.-M. & Gezentsvey, M. (2009). Investigating Attitudes Toward International Students: Program and Policy Implications for Social Integration and International Education. *Social Issues and Policy Review*, 3 (1), 79–102. https://doi.org/10.1111/j.1751-2409.2009.01011.x.

9 Spotlights on 'practiced' language policy in the internationalised university

Qi Chen and Florence Bonacina-Pugh

Introduction

With a view to responding to globalisation and transnational mobility, Higher Educational Institutions (HEI) are devising a set of internationalisation strategies. At the level of discourses, the internationalisation of HEIs often consists of "the integration of an international or intercultural dimension into the tripartite mission of teaching, research and service functions of Higher Education" (Maringe & Foskett, 2010, p. 1). In practice, however, it is often thought that HEIs pay lip service toward their strategic undertakings of internationalisation (De Vita & Case, 2003). Internationalisation is often reduced to a few changes such as the introduction of English as a medium of instruction, a high international student and staff ratio, exchange programmes and international partnerships, and new courses with 'global' or 'international' in their titles (De Wit, 2011; Warwick, 2014). Similarly, in the UK, large-scale surveys (e.g. Koutsantoni, 2006; Maringe, 2008) reveal that internationalisation strategies in HEIs predominantly focus on recruiting fee-paying international students, without engaging in the necessary changes to include the cultural and linguistic diversity brought about by international staff and students.

One key aspect of HEIs that needs to be considered in relation to internationalisation processes is language policy. Our study addresses this by looking at language policy at the level of practices (Spolsky, 2004, Bonacina-Pugh, 2012, 2020), that is, the language policies university staff and students orient to in their language practices. More specifically, we conducted the study in a chosen HEI in the under-represented context of Anglophone countries. In non-Anglophone countries, many international HEIs have changed their language policy to adopt English as a medium of instruction (e.g. Jenkins, 2014). In Anglophone countries such as the UK, the situation is different because a somewhat 'default' English monolingual environment is usually taken for granted in HEIs (Liddicoat, 2016). Given that HEIs in Anglophone countries rarely have 'declared' language policies (Shohamy, 2006), English continues therefore to be the assumed medium of instruction, perpetuating an English monolingual ethos (see also Preece & Martin, 2009). In this sense, internationalisation processes in HEIs in Anglophone countries rarely lead to apparent changes of language policy at the macro level of texts and discourses. However, little is known as to whether staff and students abide to the surrounding English monolingual discourses or whether they adopt a more inclusive 'practiced' language policy (Bonacina-Pugh, 2012, 2020), where languages other than English become visible and legitimate. In this chapter, we address this exact issue and put the spotlight on the 'practiced' language policy adopted in two post-graduate programmes, attended by a high number of international staff and students in a Russell Group university in the UK. We first briefly review research to date on the topic of language policy and multilingualism in HEIs in both non-Anglophone and Anglophone settings, and introduce the notion of 'practiced' language policy. The setting of our study and the methodological approach adopted, namely, Conversation Analysis, are then discussed. A Conversation Analysis of a corpus of interactions audio-recorded in two university workshops shows how the 'practiced' language policy adopted by staff and students in their daily teaching and learning activities reflects internationalisation processes.

Language policy, multilingualism and the internationalisation of higher education

Issues of language policy and multilingualism in relation to the internationalisation of HEIs *in non-Anglophone countries* have been the object of many previous studies (e.g. Soler & Gallego-Balsà, 2019). Some researchers have expressed, for instance, concerns over the danger of 'domain loss' of national languages due to the introduction of English as a medium of instruction in HEIs in European countries such as Norway and Sweden (Bolton & Kuteeva, 2012; Ljosland, 2007). Others have reported students' and staffs' conflicting views on the use of English as a medium of instruction in HEIs in East Asian countries such as Japan (Hashimoto, 2013; Higgins & Brady, 2016) and China (Galloway, Kriukow, & Numajiri, 2017).

Issues of language policy and multilingualism in HEIs *in Anglophone countries* have also been the focus of a few studies, but not often in relation to internationalisation processes. Liddicoat (2016) and Preece and Phan (2016), for instance, have highlighted the need for language policies in HEIs in Anglophone countries to value multilingualism as a resource. Preece (2010, 2019) has further shown how linguistic diversity in Anglophone HEIs stratifies students with an elite/non-elite binary according to social class. Others have illustrated how to protect and revitalise heritage languages such as Gaelic and Welsh in British HEIs (McPake, Tinsley & James, 2007), or how the marginalisation of languages other than English shapes students' and staff's transnational ethnic identities (Li & Zhu, 2013). The articulation of the three issues of multilingualism, the internationalisation of HEIs and language policy has, however, rarely been taken up in Anglophone contexts. This is probably because internationalisation is not seen as affecting language policies in Anglophone contexts in the same way as it is affecting language policies in non-Anglophone contexts where HEIs often adopt a new language policy, namely English as a medium of instruction. This chapter argues that even if there may be no salient changes at the level of language policy texts and discourses in HEIs in Anglophone countries, the 'practiced' language policy that staff and students orient to whilst engaging in an international teaching and learning environment is changing.

The notion of 'practiced' language policy was originally developed by Bonacina-Pugh (2012) and refers to the idea that language policy can be conceptualised 'as practice'. Practices are often studied in language policy research to see the extent to which language policies found at the levels of 'texts' and 'discourses' are implemented or resisted in practice (this is language policy *in* practice). Building on Spolsky's (2004) idea that there is a language policy at the level of practices, Bonacina-Pugh proposed to investigate practices to identify not so much whether a top-down language policy was implemented or not, but rather to see what actual language policy speakers have devised in practice. The notion of 'practiced' language policy posits that speakers refer to a set of interactional norms of language choice to interpret and produce their language choice acts, or in other words, to know when a particular language is appropriate or not. It is this set of norms of language choice that influences speakers' language choice acts, and which can therefore be considered as policy (this is language policy *as* practice). This set of interactional norms of language choice is dynamic and continuously negotiated by interactants.

Data set and methods

This study is part of a larger project (see also Bonacina-Pugh, Barakos & Chen, 2020) that aims to investigate whether internationalisation processes of HEIs in Anglophone countries have an impact on these HEIs' language policies. While it may appear at first sight that the language policies of HEIs in Anglophone countries have not changed because no new language policies have been put in place as a result of internationalisation (unlike in non-Anglophone countries where HEIs have explicitly changed their language policy to adopt English as a medium of instruction), we argue that the 'practiced' language policy adopted by staff and students is responsive to the changing linguistic and cultural landscape of HEIs generated by internationalisation. This larger project includes the study of language policy as 'texts', 'discourses' and 'practices' as conceptualised by Bonacina-Pugh (2012, building on Ball's 1993 notions of policy as text and discourse) in a UK HEI. It includes a corpus of language policy texts and discourses, as well as a corpus of audio recordings of classroom talk. The present chapter focuses on the latter corpus only and sheds light on the 'practiced' language policy that staff and students orient to in their teaching and learning activities.

This study was conducted in the academic year 2017–2018 in a Russell Group university in the UK portrayed as 'global' and 'one of the most international' universities on its website, with a quarter of its student population and three-tenths of its staff population being from overseas. We focused on two taught Master's programmes in the field of Language Education that recruited a total of 170 students, including 140 students from overseas. Data was collected during one course in Semester 2 that was attended by 40 students. Two groups of students were audio-recorded during their pre-workshop (without the tutor) and workshop activities (with the tutor) for a total of 12 hours over a period of eight weeks. Group 1 consisted of three Chinese students, one Taiwanese student and one Mexican student. Group 2 consisted of one Singaporean student, one Taiwanese student and four Chinese students. Together with the French and English bilingual tutor, these groups presented a linguistic repertoire that included English, Mandarin-Chinese, varieties of Chinese (such as Singaporean Hokkien and Taiwanese Hokkien), Spanish and French. In Group 1, students only had English as a shared language, whereas in Group 2, students shared English as well as Mandarin-Chinese.

As previously argued (Bonacina-Pugh, 2012), Conversation Analysis (CA) has proven to be a useful methodological tool and theoretical lens to identify 'practiced' language policies. To put it briefly, Spolsky and Shohamy (2000, p. 9) have shown how the language policy found at the level of practices consists of a set of "descriptive and explanatory rules" that can be deduced from the observation of a speech community's "habitual pattern of selecting among the varieties that make up its linguistic repertoire". To rephrase in Conversation Analytic terms, the language policy found at the level of practices consists of a set of interactional *norms* that can be deduced from the observation of a speech community's language choice *practices*. This set of language choice norms is what constitutes a 'practiced' language policy. These language choice norms are best identified by adopting an emic perspective to interaction, that is, by "studying behaviors as from inside the system" (Pike, 1967, p. 37). In our case, this means focusing on speakers' reactions to particular language choice acts. Any repair or translation sequences, for instance, would indicate that a particular language choice act is seen as deviant, which in turn points to what speakers would have considered as normative. In this sense, deviant cases analyses (e.g. ten Have, 2007) are helpful to uncover the implicit norms of language choice, that is, the 'practiced' language policy.

We use the term *medium of classroom interaction* to describe the "'linguistic code' that classroom participants actually orient-to while talking" (Bonacina & Gafaranga, 2011, pp. 330–331; see also Torras & Gafaranga, 2002), and the sub-categories of *monolingual medium* and *bilingual medium* (including *the mixed mode, the parallel mode* and *the half-way between mode*) to describe the language choice acts observed in our corpus. Investigating the 'practiced' language policy in the two workshops under study involves understanding the norms of language choice that participants orient to when choosing a medium of classroom of interaction.

Another CA concept that proved to be helpful in the analysis of the 'practiced' language policy in our corpus is that of 'participation framework'

(Goodwin, 2007a). We understand 'participation' here as being a 'communion of mutual engagement' (Goffman 1957), that is, when people engage in conversations, they also engage in the enterprises of maintaining shared attention and achieving mutual understanding with one another. Therefore, people in a multilingual speech community can draw upon multilingual resources in constructing such enterprises. Further, from a CA perspective, participation is a matter of participants' situated actions that are "temporally unfolding" on a moment-by-moment basis (Goodwin, 2007b, p. 12). During this process, participants "demonstrate to each other their ongoing understanding of the events they are engaged in by building actions that contribute to the further progression of these very same events" (Goodwin, 2007b, p. 12). A turn-by-turn CA analysis enables us to look into this temporally unfolding process by examining how participants (re)negotiate and reconfigure their engagement with on-going *participation frameworks*. As we shall see in the analysis of our data below, the notion of 'participation framework' is closely intertwined with the way in which the classroom participants under study manage the 'practiced' language policy at hand.

In brief, an ethnomethodological CA approach enables us to not only unravel a locally operated 'practiced' language policy, but also to unpack the nuances of how such a practiced language policy is negotiated, mutually understood and operated by conversational participants. Data was thus transcribed following the Jeffersonian conventions (Jefferson, 2004) in the ethnomethodological CA tradition (see full set of transcription conventions in the Appendix). To ensure intelligibility, we adopted a two-line transcription with the second-line-English translation vertically aligned to the first-line original Mandarin, and closely representing the original Mandarin word order with syntactic annotations (i.e. provided in brackets) (cf. Hepburn & Bolden, 2013).

The 'practiced' language policy in two university workshops

We now present four cases, two from each group,[1] to show the ways in which the internationalisation of this HEI has shaped the 'practiced' language policy oriented to by classroom participants in both teacher-led and peer-led participation frameworks. In particular, we aim to show how this 'practiced' language policy is mutually understood, jointly interpreted and collaboratively operated through an interplay between shifts of participation frameworks and switch of medium on a moment-by-moment basis.

The first case below in *Extract 1* shows an episode of interaction in a teacher-led participation framework during a workshop session (with the tutor). English is the shared language between the teacher and students, and French and Mandarin are in their linguistic repertoire. Prior to this extract, the teacher asked S2 to describe the online resource she found earlier, which is to be used as a language learning tool (with the use of cartoons, games and songs). In this extract, S2 presents her tool to the teacher.

Here, in lines 1–11, S2 is describing the design of this online resource to the teacher, who, at times, responds with 'continuers' (e.g. 'uhuh', 'mhm')

```
 1   S2: (.) and there is all those different kinds of
 2        (.) uhh (.) theme songs
 3        (.) and short video clips and games
 4        (.)
 5   T:  uhuh=
 6   S2: =from the (.) famous (.) [ cartoon ] characters
 7   T:                           [characters ]
 8   T:  [uhm ]
 9   S2: [like] peppa pig (.) like dora and whatever=
10   T:  =mhm=
11   S2: =and then you can click on each of the games and songs
12        (.)
13   T:  u[hm ]
-->14 S2: [and] someti- and there is- (.) uh- uh- the-the-the
15        (.) there is a (.) sing along (.) uh- function?
16        (.)
17   T:  [ mhm ]
18   S2: [for the] theme song (.) so they can read
-->19      (.) the- (.) uh the words?
-->20      (.) it's like a karaoke (.)
-->21 T:  ahhhhh okay so (.)
22        that's to develop what of the four skills I asked=
```

Figure 9.1 Extract 1 – Group 1 – "It's like a karaoke"
● S2: Mandarin and English bilingual student

(Gardner, 2001). In line 14, S2 starts a 'searching for a word' act (Hayashi, Raymond & Sidnell, 2013). She first displays uncertainties and hesitations with restarts ('and someti- and there is-', 'there is a') and repetitions ('uh- uh-', 'the-the-the') in formulating the sentence 'there is a (.) sing along (.) uh- function?', which ends with a rising intonation that further shows uncertainty of her word-choice here. She then extends her turn in line 18–19 with a further word search on 'the words?', for which she possibly means 'lyrics of the songs'. She finally reaches the searched-for item in line 20, 'it's like a karaoke', therefore establishing mutual understanding with the teacher responding 'ahhhhh okay'. In this word search, it is interesting to see that S2 sticks to the use of English as a monolingual "medium of classroom interaction" (Bonacina & Gafaranga, 2011, p. 319). Despite her difficulties finding the missing word, she does not draw on her Mandarin repertoire nor solicits assistance from her Mandarin-speaking peers. This case therefore indicates S2's orientation to a 'practiced' language policy according to which the shared language (e.g. English) is to be adopted as *medium of classroom interaction* in a teacher-led participation framework.

We now look at a case of a peer-led participation framework during a pre-workshop session (without the tutor), with a view to see whether the norm(s) of language choice that students orient to in that framework are the same as in the teacher-led one described above. *Extract 2* shows interactions among Group 2, a linguistically homogeneous group where all students share English and Mandarin. Here, the two students are talking about the children's books they brought to class with them for one of the workshop activities.

As can be seen, S1 consistently uses Mandarin (lines 1, 3, 5, 7, 9) while S2 consistently uses English (lines 2, 4, 6, 8). We can see that their talk-in-interaction is conducted smoothly without any signs of repair or need for translation; neither the use of Mandarin nor the use of English is oriented to as being problematic or deviant by students. Therefore, it can be said that a *parallel mode of the bilingual medium of classroom interaction* is adopted here

```
1    S1:  (  )小孩子的书就      (   )一大堆        (.) 哈哈哈哈
               children books   lots of them     hahahaha
2    S2:  hahahaha
3    S1:  我拿几个不同类型的=
          I took various types
-->4   S2:  =so- (.) so this i[s your own book?
5    S1:                      [拿过来借一下
                              (1) borrowed them
6         (.)
-->7   S1:  [呃 (.) 有些是借
           uh   some of them are borrowed
8    S2:  [or how do you-
9    S1:  (.) 有些是          (.) 自己的
             some of them are      my own
```

Figure 9.2 Extract 2 – Group 2 – "So this is your own book?"
• S1, S2: English and Mandarin bilingual students

(Bonacina & Gafaranga, 2011), where each speaker uses their preferred language. Thus, both S1 and S2 seem to orient to a local norm of language choice according to which the shared preferred language(s) can be used in peer-led participation frameworks.

So far, we have seen how the 'practiced' language policy in the two workshops under study consists of the following norm of language choice: when there is a shared language(s) among participants, that language(s) is adopted as the medium of classroom interaction. In the next two cases, we show the importance of participation frameworks in agreeing on a shared preferred language(s). *Extract 3* is also a case from Group 2, but in a teacher-led participation framework during the workshop session (with the tutor). All students in Group 2 share English and Mandarin in their repertoire. In this extract, the teacher is explaining to students that the game 'Scrabble' could be a useful language learning tool.

In lines 13–15, the teacher conducts a 'translation quest' (Bonacina-Pugh, 2013) and asks students whether there is a Mandarin equivalent to the English 'Scrabble'. In doing so, the teacher legitimises the use of Mandarin in a teacher-led participation framework despite the fact that Mandarin is not in her linguistic repertoire (see also Bonacina-Pugh, 2020 for more detail on how 'practiced' language policies legitimise multilingual classroom talk).

```
1    T:   scrabble (.) yeah (.) it's a good game
          ((a few lines omitted))
-->13  T:   does it have a Chinese equivalent?
14        (.)
15   T:   a name
-->16  S3:  °yeah°
17        (.)
18   S3:  °so-° (.) °um°
19        (.)
-->20  S5:  [°拼字游戏吗°?
           (is it) word puzzle game
21   S3:  [°我每天都玩这个游戏°=
            I everyday play this game
22   S4:  =°怪不得°
           no wonder
```

Figure 9.3 Extract 3 – Group 2 – "Does it have a Chinese equivalent?"
• S3, S4, S5: English and Mandarin bilingual students

Interestingly, however, this invitation to use a language other than English is not taken up by the Mandarin-speaking students in the class, who prefer to switch to a peer-led participation framework to use Mandarin. This is evidenced by the fact that S3's response in line 16 is in English and shows hesitation markers such as pauses, self-interruptions and a soft voice (yeah (.) so- (.) um). In line 20, S5 switches to Mandarin and offers a candidate answer for a translation of 'Scrabble' in Mandarin (拼字游戏吗 *(is it) word puzzle game*). In the meantime, S3 also switches to Mandarin, commenting on his experience of playing this game, and is responded to by S4 in Mandarin (lines 21–22). Here, S5, S3 and S4's turns-at-talk show that in responding to the teacher's translation quest, they progressively move away from the teacher-led participation framework to talk among themselves, at which point Mandarin is used. This extract therefore confirms that students seem to orient to a norm of language choice according to which 'only the shared language can be adopted as the *medium of classroom interaction*'. Since Mandarin is not shared by the teacher, they feel it cannot be used in a teacher-led participation framework. For that reason, they respond to the teacher's invitation to use Mandarin by switching to a peer-led participation framework. It further shows that despite the teacher's invitation to use a language other than the shared language (i.e. English) in a teacher-led framework, it is not taken up by students. In this extract, students uphold the teacher-led participation framework as a monolingual space and prefer switching to a peer-led participation framework to use Mandarin.

Similarly, *Extract 4* shows how a request for explanation conducted by a student initiates a (re)negotiation of the medium through a shift of participation framework. As can be seen, talk is conducted within a linguistically heterogeneous group in a peer-led participation framework in a pre-workshop session (without the tutor), in which S1, S2, S4 and S5 are Mandarin-speaking students, and S3 is a Spanish-speaking student, which means English is the only shared language.

- S1, 2, 4, 5: Mandarin and English bilingual students
- S3: Spanish and English bilingual student

The talk starts when students are discussing the notion of 'tracing', and the *medium of classroom interaction* adopted here is English starting in line 1. S3 asks S2 a question in line 1, checking her understanding of 'tracing'. S2 and S1 are verbally engaging in the discussion whereas S4 and S5 take on a more receptive role (lines 2–10). In line 11, S5 asks a question in Mandarin, "'tracing'该怎么描述呢 *(how (do you) describe it)*", which is clearly a request for explanation on the meaning of 'tracing' directed to her Mandarin-speaking peers, as well as a switch of medium from English to Mandarin. Similar to *Extract 2*, this switch of medium to Mandarin by S5 initiates a *schisming* away from the on-going participation framework. This *schisming* is evidenced by S2 and S4 soon responding to S5 in Mandarin (lines 13–14). Meanwhile, S3 builds

```
 1    S3: so (0.2) do you know what 'tracing' is right=
 2    S2: =yeah=
 3    S3: =yeah so (0.2) it gives you different worksheets
 4        (0.2) with di[fferent themes]
 5    S2:              [   ohhh     ]
 6    S2: ohh=
 7    S1: =ah[ hh]
 8    S3:    [for] 'tracing'
 9    S3: (0.2) but I cannot open them
10        (0.3)
-->11 S5: 'tracing' 该怎么描述呢?
              how (do you) describe it
12        (0.3)
13    S2: 嗯=
          umm
14    S4: =嗯?
          um
15    S5: (.) 是- (0.3) 描
          is- (0.3) trace
16        (0.2)
17    S3: maybe I can send [it to ] your [email]=
18    S2:                  [  嗯  ]
                              um
19    S4:                                [ 描  ]
                                          trace
20    S5: =描
          trace
21    S4: [嗯]
          um
22    S2: [嗯]
          um
23        (0.5)
24    S3: a[nd you can see] it
25    S4:  [ 怎么    了? ]
            what's the matter
26        (0.2)
-->27 S2: like
28        (1.7)
29    S2: learning to write with [proper gui]dance
30    S3:                        [  yes  ]
```

Figure 9.4 Extract 4 – Group 1 – "How do you describe it?"

upon her previous turn in line 9 and continues her talk in lines 17 and 24; here her talk is directed to S1, who previously responded to her talk in line 7. The *schisming* is then continued in lines 18–22, when the candidate answer explanation for 'tracing', that is, '描(*trace*)', is accepted by all participants. The two parallel turn-taking systems therefore continue until lines 27 and 29 when S2 switches back to English, and gives a statement of her understanding of 'tracing' (learning to write with proper guidance). This is responded to by S3 with 'yes' in overlap, signalling the re-establishment of shared attention and mutual understanding among all participants. In sum, this extract further shows the reflexive interplay between a switch of medium and a shift of participation framework. In other words, to switch medium of classroom interaction, participants often have to switch participation framework.

Conclusion

Overall, we have shown that the teacher and students adopt a 'practiced' language policy that consists of the following norm: only shared language(s) can be adopted as the medium of classroom interaction. When English is the only shared language among participants, whether in a teacher-led or a peer-led participation framework, a *monolingual English medium* is adopted (e.g. *Extracts 1, 3* and *4*). When there is more than one shared language, these languages can be adopted in a bilingual medium of classroom interaction. For instance, in *Extract 2*, participants used a *parallel mode of the bilingual medium* in a peer-led participation framework where each participant used their preferred language. We have also shown that the classroom participants played with that norm of language choice to suit their interactional needs. They would often initiate *schismings* from one participation framework to another, where a preferred language would become the shared (and therefore legitimate) language among participants. Moving back and forth between different participation frameworks enabled students in particular to check understanding and seek clarification in the language of their choice. These shifts of participation frameworks meant that different languages were shared at different times in classroom talk. This, in turn, legitimised multilingual practices as they were in line with the local 'practiced' language policy according to which any language(s) can be used in classroom interaction as long as it is a shared language. We argue that the notion of 'participation framework' is useful to understand the 'practiced' language policy in our context. Further research is needed to see its relevance to the study of 'practiced' language policy in other contexts.

To conclude, this study provides valuable insights into the intersection of language policy, higher education internationalisation and multilingualism. Our findings are in line with the call for the need to value multilingualism as a resource in language policies in HEIs in Anglophone countries (Liddicoat, 2016; Preece & Phan, 2016). As discussed earlier, the taken-for-granted 'default' English monolingual environment is seen as a common phenomenon in HEIs in Anglophone countries such as the UK. What we have shown through our empirical data is, however, that the internationalisation of higher education is, to a certain extent, influencing language policy as practice, insofar as classroom learning is becoming increasingly more multilingual. Languages other than English were used and seen as legitimate by the teacher and students at the local level of the practiced language policy. This was specifically the case of Mandarin, where its use supported students' learning. Languages other than English and Mandarin, however, remained largely invisible. We therefore argue that further work is needed for the multilingual repertoire of staff and students to be included and visible in internationalisation-at-home strategies in UK higher education, in order to create more space and opportunities for teaching and learning.

Note

1 Not all students in the groups are talking in every extract.

Appendix

```
(.)              pause less than 0.2 second
[   ]            overlapping talk
=                latching utterance
(   )            unidentifiable talk
°talk°           softer than surrounding talk
-                cut-off talk
:                extended syllable
?                rising intonation
'talk'           quoted talk

哈哈             original talk in Mandarin-Chinese
haha             English translation
```

Figure 9.5 CA transcription conventions

References

Ball, S. J. (1993). What is policy? Texts, trajectories and toolboxes. *Discourse: Studies in the Cultural Politics of Education*, 13(2), 10–17. https://doi.org/10.1080/0159630930130203.

Bolton, K., & Kuteeva, M. (2012). English as an academic language at a Swedish university: Parallel language use and the "threat" of English. *Journal of Multilingual and Multicultural Development*, 33(5), 429–447. https://doi.org/10.1080/01434632.2012.670241.

Bonacina-Pugh, F. (2012). Researching "practiced language policies": Insights from conversation analysis. *Language Policy*, 11(3), 213–234. https://doi.org/10.1007/s10993-012-9243-x.

Bonacina-Pugh, F. (2013). Multilingual label quests: A practice for the "asymmetrical" multilingual classroom. *Linguistics and Education*, 24(2), 142–164. https://doi.org/10.1016/j.linged.2012.12.006.

Bonacina-Pugh, F. (2020). Legitimizing multilingual practices in the classroom: the role of the 'practiced language policy'. *International Journal of Bilingual Education and Bilingualism*, 23(4), 434–448. https://doi.org/10.1080/13670050.2017.1372359.

Bonacina-Pugh, F., Barakos, E. and Chen, Q. (2020). Language policy in the internationalisation of Higher Education in Anglophone countries: The interplay between language policy as 'text', 'discourse' and 'practice'. *Applied Linguistics Review* (published online ahead of print 2020), 000010151520190148. https://doi.org/10.1515/applirev-2019-0148.

Bonacina, F., & Gafaranga, J. (2011). "Medium of instruction" vs. "Medium of classroom interaction": Language choice in a French complementary school classroom in Scotland. *International Journal of Bilingual Education and Bilingualism*, 14(3), 319–334. https://doi.org/10.1080/13670050.2010.502222.

De Vita, G., & Case, P. (2003). Rethinking the internationalisation agenda in UK higher education. *Journal of Further and Higher Education*, 27(4), 383–398. https://doi.org/10.1080/0309877032000128082.

De Wit, H. (2011). *Trends, Issues and Challenges in Internationalisation of Higher Education*. Amsterdam: Centre for Applied Research on Economics & Management, School of Economics and Management of the Hogeschool van Amsterdam.

Galloway, N., Kriukow, J., & Numajiri, T. (2017). Internationalisation, higher education and the growing demand for English: An investigation into the English medium of instruction (EMI) movement in China and Japan. *British Council ELT Research Papers* (Vol. 17). British Council.

Gardner, R. (2001). *When Listeners Talk: Response Tokens and Listener Stance.* Amsterdam: John Benjamins Publishing Company.

Goffman, E. (1957). Alienation from interaction. *Human Relations,* 10(1), 47–60. http s://doi.org/10.1177/001872675701000103.

Goodwin, C. (2007a). Participation, stance and affect in the organization of activities. *Discourse & Society,* 18(1), 53–73. https://doi.org/10.1177/0957926507069457.

Goodwin, C. (2007b). Interactive Footing. In E. Holt & R. Clift (Eds.), *Reporting Talk: Reported Speech in Interaction* (pp. 16–46). Cambridge: Cambridge University Press.

Hashimoto, K. (2013). "English-only", but not a medium-of-instruction policy: The Japanese way of internationalising education for both domestic and overseas students. *Current Issues in Language Planning,* 14(1), 16–33. https://doi.org/10.1080/14664208.2013.789956.

Hayashi, M., Raymond, G., & Sidnell, J. (2013). *Conversational Repair and Human Understanding.* Cambridge: Cambridge University Press.

Hepburn, A., & Bolden, G. B. (2013). The conversation analytic approach to transcription. In J. Sidnell & T. Stivers (Eds.), *The Handbook of Conversation Analysis* (pp. 57–76). Oxford; Boston, MA: Blackwell Publishing Ltd.

Higgins, R. M., & Brady, A. (2016). Language policy, planning, and enactment: The necessity and empowering potential at the local level. *Current Issues in Language Planning,* 17(3–4), 242–259. https://doi.org/10.1080/14664208.2016.1212650.

Jefferson, G. (2004). Glossary of transcript symbols with an introduction. In G. H. Lerner (Ed.), *Conversation Analysis: Studies from the First Generation* (pp. 13–31). Amsterdam: John Benjamins Publishing Company.

Jenkins, J. (2014). *English as a Lingua Franca in the International University: The Politics of Academic English Language Policy.* Abingdon, Oxon: Routledge.

Koutsantoni, D. (2006). *Internationalisation in the UK.* Paper presented at the Leadership Challenges of Globalisation and Internationalisation Leadership Summit, London. www.lfhe.ac.uk/publications/reports.html.

Li, W., & Zhu, H. (2013). Translanguaging identities and ideologies: Creating transnational space through flexible multilingual practices amongst Chinese university students in the UK. *Applied Linguistics,* 34(5), 516–535. https://doi.org/10.1093/applin/amt022.

Liddicoat, A. J. (2016). Language planning in universities: Teaching, research and administration. *Current Issues in Language Planning,* 17(3–4), 231–241. https://doi.org/10.1080/14664208.2016.1216351.

Ljosland, R. (2007). English in Norwegian academia: A step towards diglossia? *World Englishes,* 26(4), 395–410. https://doi.org/10.1111/j.1467-971X.2007.00519.x.

Maringe, F. (2008). *Globalisation and internationalisation in HE.* Paper presented at the ICHEM conference, University of Minho, Portugal, 1–3 April.

Maringe, F., & Foskett, N. (Eds.) (2010). *Globalization and Internationalization in Higher Education: Theoretical, Strategic and Management Perspectives.* London & New York: Continuum International Publishing.

McPake, J., Tinsley, T., & James, C. (2007). Making provision for community languages: Issues for teacher education in the UK. *Language Learning Journal,* 35(1), 99–112. https://doi.org/10.1080/09571730701317705.

Pike, K. L. (1967). *Language in Relation to a Unified Theory of the Structure of Human Behavior*. The Hague: Mouton.

Preece, S. (2010). Multilingual identities in higher education: Negotiating the "mother tongue", "posh" and "slang." *Language and Education*, 24(1), 21–39. https://doi.org/10.1080/09500780903194036.

Preece, S. (2019). Elite bilingual identities in higher education in the Anglophone world: The stratification of linguistic diversity and reproduction of socio-economic inequalities in the multilingual student population. *Journal of Multilingual and Multicultural Development*, 40(5), 404–420. https://doi.org/10.1080/01434632.2018.1543692.

Preece, S., & Martin, P. (2009). Imagining higher education as a multilingual space. *Language and Education*, 24(1), 3–8. https://doi.org/10.1080/09500780903343070.

Preece, S., & Phan, L.-H. (2016). BAAL/CUP Seminar 2014: The Multilingual University: Linguistic diversity in higher education in English-dominant settings and English-medium instructional contexts. *Language Teaching*, 49(1), 141–145. https://doi.org/10.1017/S0261444815000361.

Shohamy, E. (2006). *Language Policy: Hidden Agendas and New Approaches*. New York: Routledge.

Soler, J., & Gallego-Balsà, L. (2019). *The Sociolinguistics of Higher Education: Language Policy and Internationalisation in Catalonia*. Gewerbestrasse, Switzerland: Springer International Publishing.

Spolsky, B. (2004). *Language Policy*. Cambridge: Cambridge University Press.

Spolsky, B., & Shohamy, E. (2000). Language Practice, Language Ideology, and Language Policy. In R. D. Lambert & E. Shohamy (Eds.), *Language Policy and Pedagogy: Essays in Honor of A. Ronald Walton* (pp. 1–41). Amsterdam: John Benjamins Publishing Company.

ten Have, P. (2007). *Doing Conversation Analysis*. London: SAGE Publications.

Torras, M. C., & Gafaranga, J. (2002). Social identities and language alternation in non-formal institutional bilingual talk: Trilingual service encounters in Barcelona. *Language in Society*, 31(4), 527–548.

Warwick, P. (2014). The international business of higher education: A managerial perspective on the internationalisation of UK universities. *International Journal of Management Education*, 12(2), 91–103. https://doi.org/10.1016/j.ijme.2014.02.003.

10 We (don't) need to talk

Communication among international students in group projects

Jill Doubleday

Introduction

In this chapter, I report findings concerning group work communication, drawing on data from a larger project investigating UK international students' perceptions of their English. Further details of this larger project are given below. Group work communication can be considered as a form of classroom interaction because it is part of the teaching and learning activities that students engage in. The relevance of students' perceptions of their English in this context is that this affected how they communicate. In the research project discussed here, group projects were a common form of assessment, with most groups formed of only non-native English speakers (NNESs). My interview data offer an insight into how communication was (mis)managed by group members, and the impact of this on individuals. I also consider the wider context in which the group projects took place, looking at the role of lecturers and policymakers, and consider the impact on practice and student learning. The chapter begins with an outline of the wider research context, followed by a discussion of previous studies in the field and the theories that informed the research.

Literature review

In UK higher education, international students constitute a significant proportion of the student cohort. This is especially marked at postgraduate taught level, with a third of all students in 2017–18 originating from outside the UK (Higher Education Statistics Agency, 2019). In academia, the term 'international student' is typically used to mean 'non-native English speaker', with 'native English speakers' being referred to as 'home students'. These labels are not without problems, however. In linguistics, there has been considerable debate around the term 'native' (e.g. Davies, 2003; Widdowson, 1994), and recent work has been critical of the treatment of 'international students' as one homogenous group (e.g. Baird and Baird, 2018; Blaj-Ward, 2017; Jones, 2017). However, in the absence of other widely known terms, in this chapter I use 'non-native English speaker' (NNES) synonymously with 'international student' to refer to those students whose native language is not English as defined by the prevailing language policy used for admissions purposes, and who therefore need to provide proof of their English proficiency to gain entry to university.[1] I use 'home student' to mean those students considered to be native English speakers (NESs) in the same context.

Two bodies of research informed the group work study discussed here. The first focuses on international student experiences in UK higher education, specifically those investigating interactions between NNESs and NESs. A common finding has been that international students prefer working with other international students (e.g. Beaven and Spencer-Oatey, 2016), and that interacting with home students is challenging (e.g. Bond, 2019; Harvey, 2016). At the same time, home students have been found to view international students' English negatively, especially if they feel it might lower grades for group assignments (e.g. Elliott and Reynolds, 2014; Spencer-Oatey and Dauber, 2017).

The second area of research that is relevant here, and my main guiding framework of interaction, is English as a Lingua Franca (henceforth ELF), by which I mean "any use of English among speakers of different first languages for whom English is the communicative medium of choice and often the only option" (Seidlhofer 2011, p. 7). In relation to perceptions and interaction, ELF scholarship was key in shaping my approach to data collection and interpretation. Research into the use of accommodation strategies is of particular interest, since this shows how interactants achieve communicative effectiveness through, for example, repetition, clarification and paraphrasing (e.g. Kaur, 2011; Mauranen, 2006). While these strategies are not unique to ELF, nor even to intercultural communication, some researchers have argued that ELF interlocutors may be more willing to make efforts to accommodate, being more aware of the possibilities for communication breakdowns (e.g. Kaur, 2009, Mauranen, 2012). Indeed, studies conducted in the UK and elsewhere have found that NNESs are more willing and able to accommodate than NESs (e.g. Carey, 2010; Jenkins, 2014). At the same time, however, researchers have found that some NESs have a positive attitude towards accommodation (e.g. Kalocsai, 2013; Margić, 2017; Dippold et al., 2019). Similarly, it should not be assumed that communication among only NNESs is harmonious. In addition to the uncooperative behaviour reported by Jenks (2012), several studies have found that NNESs negatively evaluate other NNESs' English, particularly in high-stakes activities such as assessment (e.g. Kuteeva, 2014; Spencer-Oatey and Dauber, 2017). Assessed group projects, the focus of the research discussed here, are clear examples of high-stakes activities.

Methodology

Having discussed the wider context, I now move on to the specific setting of the study. The research took place at the University of Southampton, which was in 2016–17 the 19th highest recruiter of international students in the UK, enrolling 7110. Almost 40% of these students (2834) were from China (University of Southampton, 2020a).[2] As noted above, around a third of ISs at postgraduate taught (PGT) level were from outside the UK in 2017–18, with business and administrative studies attracting a significant proportion of these (UKCISA, 2019). Southampton reflects these UK figures, so although it attracts students from over 135 countries (University of Southampton, 2020b), diversity is limited in some disciplines. At the time of this study, for example, Chinese students were in the majority at PGT level in the Business School.

As already stated, the data discussed here form part of a larger study, in which documents were analysed to establish the university's English language policy. These findings informed interviews, during which participants were asked about topics related to the policy.[3] The two aspects relevant to this chapter concern intercultural communication (i.e. communication between individuals from different linguacultural backgrounds). First, no written policy was found regarding lecturer facilitation of group work, in terms of managing intercultural communication. Second, of several possible entry routes available to international students, most required demonstration of proficiency measured by approximation to native-like English. Full findings are available in Doubleday (2018), and I return to both issues in the discussion below.

Two rounds of semi-structured interviews were conducted with 18 PGT international students. Ethical approval was given on the basis that, although the university itself was identifiable due to the analysis of website documents, participants would remain anonymous. Pseudonyms were used, and nationalities were not revealed except in the case of Chinese participants. This was because the high proportion of Chinese PGT students not only made identification of individuals unlikely, but was also sometimes commented on by participants, meaning that revealing their nationality was necessary to discuss the implications of my findings. Participant details are given below in Table 10.1.

Each participant was interviewed twice, towards the start of their degree programme, and again in the second semester, in order to investigate how their perceptions changed over time. Participants were asked how confident they felt about their English, and about their experiences of studying in

Table 10.1 Participant nationalities and disciplines (N = 18)

Nationality	8	CHI (Chinese)
	7	EUSA (European, Eurasian, South American or Asian, excluding Chinese)
	3	MID (Middle Eastern)
Faculty	13	Business, Law and Arts
	2	Humanities
	2	Social, Human and Mathematical Sciences
	1	Physical Sciences and Engineering

English. Topics included carrying out assignments, listening to lecturers, seminar discussions, and group work (see Doubleday, 2018 for interview schedules). In interviews, I initially defined 'group work' broadly to include any instances of communication for academic purposes, including brief in-class discussions. However, as 15 participants had taken part in assessed group project work, they tended to focus on this during interviews. Interviews were recorded and transcribed. Data were analysed using a combination of content and discourse analysis (Fairclough, 2003; Schreier, 2012).

Findings

Although my research focus was on language policy and practices, participants made relevant a range of other factors when discussing group work. These included age, personality, previous experience of group work, disciplinary background, work experience and what some referred to as 'cultural' differences, as will be seen below. In this chapter, I discuss findings under the two most prevalent themes in my data on group work, Chinese students and native(-like) English speakers. It will be seen, however, that there is some overlap between the two.

Chinese students

Pax (EUSA) was one of several participants who discussed communication difficulties related to Chinese students, saying that a lack of feedback made him uncertain whether he was understood:

> the problem is that the Chinese people I have in my master even if they don't understand they won't say anything so you can ask 'are you ok' and they say 'yeah yeah yeah' and you ask again 'do you know what you have to do' 'uh-um' {shakes head}

Pax found a way round this, by supplementing spoken interaction with written:

> you know I solved that problem using Facebook, every time I have a team coursework I open a chat and now I know if they can't listen or understand if I write like 'how are we going to do that' and it's easier for them if they read that

Another participant, Sandi (EUSA), was the only non-Chinese student in a group of six. She commented that it was 'very difficult to communicate with them', going on to differentiate between group members:

> sometimes they had to translate it because there are two girls who have lots of difficulties with English so they listen to you and then translate it to them in Chinese and then these girls say something and he translates back and that's weird (laughs) because if he doesn't get me as well

Here the solution was for one group member to act as an interpreter. Sandi's concern with this is the risk of mistranslation, which is similar to Pax's worry that ideas may not be understood.

At the same time, several Chinese participants provided insights into their perceptions of communication in group work. Three worked in all-Chinese groups. When asked how they felt about this, given it rendered English redundant, none responded negatively. Cindy and Barbet felt socialising to be a more appropriate way to gain experience in speaking English, while Patti explicitly stated that group work did not involve talking, saying

> yeah but I think it's just for to finish the work we will focus on the work not focus on speaking

None of the three, then, saw oral communication in English as important in group work.

In contrast to the findings so far discussed, another participant, Eveline (EUSA), described Chinese group members who were effective communicators. She had no difficulties understanding them, saying that they made an extra effort to make their pronunciation clear. When they asked her to speak more slowly, however, she chose instead to use the whiteboard. Like Pax, she switched to written communication.

Native(-like) English speakers

The second theme of this chapter is native, or native-like, English speakers. I discuss two participants who emphasised the importance of group members' English skills.

In her second interview, Eveline (EUSA) talked about a critical group assignment worth 60% of the overall grade, saying "we were lucky because I worked with English people so they checked the grammar". Eveline elaborated on the group members as follows:

> there was err one guy even if he comes from Africa in his country they err they speak English maybe it was Ghana but I'm not so sure... and then there was another girl that even if she wasn't English she spoke English perfectly without any I don't know any problems so err our group it was I think it was I don't know full of good people so I was happy about that because of course when you work with English people you can take advantage about that because they can help you

Eveline felt that the "English people" in her group were happy to help, since she was contributing by preparing a specific aspect. She also felt her previous experience of group work was valuable:

> I know how to manage a group work and on the other hand for their case
> they didn't know how to approach and how to work so it was a situation
> in which I had to I don't know organise the group manage the relation-
> ship inside the group even if I wasn't English even if I don't know but I
> knew how to collaborate with them

Here Eveline emphasises the importance of group dynamics, referring to
managing relationships between group members. Previous experience was also
key in another group assignment in which Eveline worked with two female
NNES students, "much older than me", who she described as both experienced in group work and proficient in English.

When Evelyn experienced difficulties, she tended to ascribe this to 'cultural'
differences. Although she reported no problems with the two older women
referred to above, her view of Chinese people was different:

> I think it depends about the culture because for Chinese people they don't
> know how to approach you since they come from a different part of the
> world and everything is different so I can understand they may not they
> cannot have a normal relation with you they have some gap they have
> like a wall err in front of them

It is noteworthy that, in her first interview, Eveline had not talked about
group work with Chinese students negatively at all. In fact, she had said she
had no problem understanding them because they accommodated. By the
second interview she saw it differently, perhaps because the project had been
given a low mark or perhaps because she was able to compare it to two other
experiences, both positive. The result is that she sees a "wall" between herself
and Chinese people, which she attributes to their coming from "a different
part of the world".

For Eveline, the effectiveness of group work depends on several factors –
age, previous experience of group work, English proficiency and 'cultural'
background. The extent to which each influences the other is not always clear,
but some participants tended to generalise a negative experience with one or
two individuals to all of their compatriots, and to blame the problems on
'culture' rather than age or experience. This seems to be the case with the final
participant I discuss, Tabora.

Tabora (MID) first talked about a group project in which she worked with
three other students, two Chinese and one British, explaining that they split into
pairs to carry out tasks before coming back together. She chose the British student because "with Chinese I can't understand them and they can't understand
me". However, she also empathised with one of the Chinese students, who could
not make himself understood, saying, "he has a problem with pronunciation, we
all have this problem but maybe he's more than us".

Then, like Eveline, she talked about culture to explain her preference for
the British student:

yeah so we can discuss thing and I think we have the same culture cultural thing which is we love to speak and give background about everything before we start work on it and the Chinese they love to work without even describe they don't know how to describe thing

She is critical of Chinese students and conflates their approach ("they love to work without even describe") with their English ability ("they don't know how to describe thing"). Tabora's generalisations appeared to stem from a negative experience she had described in her first interview. Before her PGT programme, she had taken a year-long pre-sessional course on which almost all her course mates were Chinese. In her view, their lack of fluency had a detrimental impact on her own, and this seems to have resulted in Tabora's reluctance to work with Chinese students. She also felt she shared a cultural approach with British people, "we love to speak". However, this view has changed by her second interview, when she described a second group work experience, working with five other people, three of whom were British:

I think... English people they talk too much and they work less than the others so in the meeting we talked like 45 minutes we just talking and we didn't do anything actually so I don't like that I'm like ok I'm pragmatic person so let's just start work this is just a lot of talking it is nothing important and so they discuss if this is a door or not a door

Here, Tabora feels "English people" are too talkative, and she is frustrated with the lack of progress. But she further explained that this was a multi-disciplinary project, saying the tension may have been caused by different disciplinary approaches in terms of the level of detail needed. It is worth noting here that Tabora's frustration may relate to the fact that she ran her own business at home, so was used to simply getting on with the task at hand. She had routinely used English to communicate with her employees. Later in the interview, she returned to the topic, saying that she had declined an invitation to speak at a conference. This was due to a lack of confidence in her English, though not in herself. She went on to explain what being confident in English would mean to her:

like if I'm very confident I would just tell others to just stop talking please and let us work because ideas just like that {knocks on desk} one two three four and you don't want to you don't need to just speak about is that a door or not so in that sense

It seemed difficult for this experienced, confident businesswoman to accept that English had held her back, given her extensive experience of using it, but she eventually conceded that this was the case. This led her to change her view on her relationship with English, which until then she had seen as simply a communication tool. This negative experience affected her profoundly, to the extent that I apologised for having caused her to talk about it, but Tabora reflected that our interview had been beneficial, somewhat like therapy. Tabora's experience demonstrates the significant impact that group work communication can have on an individual. Her experience also highlights the diversity within the label 'home students'. With her first group project, she felt a shared cultural approach in terms of talking about the work, but with a different group of British people, there was too much talking and Tabora felt unable to object to this.

Discussion

To sum up, the linguistic challenges in intercultural group work discussed here include unfamiliar accents, mismatches in proficiency and confidence, and different priorities, in terms of both how important it is to use native-like English, and how much to talk. Here, 'language proficiency' is not meant in a restricted sense of fluency or accuracy, but encompasses the ability to employ communicative strategies, discussed above in relation to ELF. These challenges, along with others noted above that influence the effectiveness of group work, such as personality and previous experience, can be attributed to three main causes: a lack of linguistic diversity in group work, an absence of lecturer intervention and limited intercultural communication skills.

To elaborate on the first point, in groups where all members share another common language, it is unreasonable to expect English to be used. This may not be a problem for that particular group assignment, but it does deny those students an opportunity to use English, which may impact upon them more widely. Patti, the Chinese student discussed above, was the only participant whose confidence levels in her oral skills dropped during the study. Lack of diversity may also be an issue when all but one member of a group shares a common language besides English. Sandi, for example, was concerned that her ideas may not have been translated accurately.

The second point concerns lecturers. None of the participants were given guidance in managing group work, including how to ensure that communication was effective. This links to the third cause, that of limited intercultural communication skills. As we have seen, participants reported inventive strategies to deal with communication problems, such as switching to written communication or translation, as a temporary fix for that particular group project. Only Eveline reported an example of accommodation, when her Chinese groupmates adjusted their pronunciation to speak more clearly.

The source of these problems seems to lie with recruitment and language policies. Lecturers are limited in their ability to promote intercultural communication if the institution's recruitment policy results in students from one linguacultural background dominating. They cannot create linguistically diverse groups if a majority of students share a language. In terms of language policy, the main policy mechanism is English language entry requirements for NNESs. All the participants in this study had at least the minimum level of English required, but this proficiency level is measured in limited terms, as approximation to native speaker norms. As Harding and McNamara (2018, p. 579) argue, a test is needed that assesses "ELF-related strategic behaviour" such as accommodation skills.

Intercultural communication skills are needed by all students, however, not just NNESs. The issue of NESs developing such skills is partially addressed in the Quality Assurance Agency's (2015, p. 9) guidance, which suggests that universities

> will find it helpful to consider having in place training provision to support home students in developing intercultural knowledge and skills, particularly on programmes with significant numbers of international students

While this is a welcome development, it is advised only for certain home students, with international students and staff not mentioned. Spencer-Oatey and Dauber take a more inclusive stance, pointing out that there is a need to make both staff and students aware of "effective strategies for handling communication challenges" (2017, p. 231). However, given the range of factors that interacted with linguistic ones to affect group work, I would argue that there is a need to take a broader approach. Baker (2015) has pointed out that critical approaches to intercultural communication acknowledge the fluidity and heterogeneity inherent in cultures, such as differences in identifications such as class, gender and profession. This does not mean that national cultures are ignored, but that it is important to see them as one form of culture or grouping (Baker, 2018). Similarly, Zhu (2015, p. 66) notes that, while intercultural communication studies often take difference as their starting point, it is essential to recognise that communication problems may be unrelated to culture. She therefore advises researchers to consider how interaction is affected by any differences the speakers perceive to be relevant. I return to this point in the 'impact' section below.

Challenges

One challenge of investigating classroom discourse in this context was how to take account of the other factors that impact upon the effectiveness of group work. As noted above, participants perceived personality, age, experience and background as relevant. It was therefore not always possible to separate 'language' from these other factors.

Another challenge was that I did not observe the group interactions each participant talked about, nor did I talk to the other group members. Accounts therefore need to be acknowledged as one-sided, from the participants' perspective only.

Impact on practice and student learning

This study highlights that a broader approach to intercultural communication would be beneficial. As we have seen, participants commented on a range of factors unrelated to national culture, such as different disciplinary approaches and experiences of group work. We have also seen that some participants who had negative experiences with students from a particular national culture went on to make assumptions about others from that culture.

Training for both staff and students developed from the critical view of culture outlined above could focus on three As: *awareness* that not all differences stem from language or from essentialist views of culture; *attitude* in terms of developing respect for difference and a willingness to accommodate; and *ability* to accommodate to interlocutors. Such training could, I believe, also lead to wider acknowledgement of the diversity within the groups labelled as 'home' and 'international' students.

Conclusion

To conclude, I return to the title of this chapter. Initially, I had opted for "We need to talk", to signal that there was a need for more effective oral communication among students. However, after further thought, I added "(don't)" in brackets to reflect the fact that some participants felt that communication could be effective without talking in English. I have discussed examples of written communication from Pax using Facebook and Eveline using the whiteboard, and of three students who felt that group work did not require discussion.

The issue of not talking remains an empirical question needing further investigation, to understand its impact not only on group assignments, but also on individuals.

Notes

1 There is range of entry routes, including a specified minimum score in an approved test such as IELTS (International English Language Testing System), successful completion of a pre-sessional course or holding a UK university degree. For full details, see Doubleday (2018).
2 2016–17 is the period for which the most recent figures are available for numbers of Chinese students at Southampton, so I have cited comparable data here. In 2017–18, Southampton enrolled 7190 international students in total.
3 For full details of the project, see Doubleday (2018).

References

Baird, M. & Baird, R. (2018). English as a lingua franca: changing 'attitudes'. In J. Jenkins, W. Baker & M. Dewey. (Eds.). *The Routledge handbook of English as a lingua franca* (pp. 531–543). London: Routledge.

Baker, W. (2015). *Culture and identity through English as a lingua franca: Rethinking concepts and goals in intercultural communication.* Boston, MA; Berlin: De Gruyter Mouton.

Baker, W. (2018). English as a lingua franca and intercultural communication. In J. Jenkins, W. Baker & M. Dewey. (Eds.). *The Routledge handbook of English as a lingua franca* (pp. 25–36). London: Routledge.

Beaven, A. & Spencer-Oatey, H. (2016). Cultural adaptation in different facets of life and the impact of language: a case study of personal adjustment patterns during study abroad. *Language and Intercultural Communication*, 16 (3), 349–367. doi:10.1080/14708477.2016.1168048.

Blaj-Ward, L. (2017). *Language learning and use in English-medium higher education.* Cham: Springer.

Bond, B. (2019). International students: language, culture and the 'performance of identity', *Teaching in Higher Education*, 24 (5), 649–665. doi:10.1080/13562517.2019.1593129.

Carey, R. (2010). Hard to ignore: English native speakers in ELF research. *Helsinki English Studies*, 6, 88–101.

Davies, A. (2003). *The native speaker: Myth and reality.* Bristol: Multilingual Matters.

Dippold, D., Bridges, S., Eccles, S. & Mullen, E. (2019). Taking ELF off the shelf: developing HE students' speaking skills through a focus on English as a lingua franca. *Linguistics and Education*, 54. doi:10.1016/j.linged.2019.100761.

Doubleday, J. (2018). *International postgraduate students' perceptions of their English in a UK university context.* PhD thesis. University of Southampton. https://eprints.soton.ac.uk/428631/ (Accessed 2 June 2020)

Elliott, C. J. & Reynolds, M. (2014). Participative pedagogies, group work and the international classroom: an account of students' and tutors' experiences. *Studies in Higher Education*, 39 (2), 307–320. doi:10.1080/03075079.2012.709492.

Fairclough, N. (2003). *Analysing discourse: Textual analysis for social research.* London: Routledge.

Harding, L. & McNamara, T. (2018). Language assessment: the challenge of ELF. In J. Jenkins, W. Baker & M. Dewey (Eds.). *The Routledge handbook of English as a lingua franca* (pp. 570–582). London: Routledge.

Harvey, L. (2016). 'I am Italian in the world': a mobile student's story of language learning and ideological becoming. *Language and Intercultural Communication*, 16 (3), 368–383. doi:10.1080/14708477.2016.1168049.

Higher Education Statistics Agency (HESA). (2019). *Where do students come from?* Available at: www.hesa.ac.uk/data-and-analysis/students/where-from (Accessed 2 June 2020)

Jenkins, J. (2014). *English as a lingua franca in the international university: The politics of academic English language policy.* London: Routledge.

Jenks, C. (2012). Doing being reprehensive: some interactional features of English as a lingua franca in a chat room. *Applied Linguistics*, 33 (4), 386–405. doi:10.1093/applin.ams014.

Jones, E. (2017). Problematising and reimagining the notion of 'international student experience'. *Studies in Higher Education*, 42 (5), 933–943. doi:10.1080/03075079.2017.1293880.

Kalocsai, K. (2013). *Communities of practice and English as a lingua franca: A study of Erasmus students in a central-European context.* Berlin: De Gruyter Mouton.

Kaur, J. (2009). Pre-empting problems of understanding in English as lingua franca. In A. Mauranen & E. Ranta (Eds.). *English as a lingua franca: Studies and findings* (pp. 107–123). Newcastle: Cambridge Scholars Publishing.

Kaur, J. (2011). Raising explicitness through self-repair in English as a lingua franca. *Journal of Pragmatics*, 43 (11), 2704–2715. doi:10.1016/j.pragma.2011.04.12.

Kuteeva, M. (2014). The parallel language use of Swedish and English: the question of 'nativeness' in university policies and practices. *Journal of Multilingual and Multicultural Development*, 35 (4), 332–344. doi:10.1080/01434632.2013.874332.

Margić, B. (2017). Communication courtesy or condescension? Linguistic accommodation of native to non-native speakers of English. *Journal of English as a Lingua Franca*, 6 (1), 29–55. doi:10.1515/jelf-2017-0006.

Mauranen, A. (2006). Signalling and preventing misunderstanding in English as a lingua franca communication. *International Journal of the Sociology of Language*, 177, 123–150. doi:10.1515/IJSL.2006.008.

Mauranen, A. (2012). *Exploring ELF: Academic English shaped by non-native speakers*. Cambridge: Cambridge University Press.

Quality Assurance Agency for Higher Education (QAA). (2015). *Supporting and enhancing the experience of international students in the UK: A guide for UK higher education providers.* Available at: www.qaa.ac.uk/docs/qaa/international/international-students-guide-15.pdf?sfvrsn=7375f781_4 (Accessed 2 June 2020)

Schreier, M. (2012). *Qualitative content analysis in practice*. London: Sage.

Seidlhofer, B. (2011). *Understanding English as a lingua franca*. Oxford: Oxford University Press.

Spencer-Oatey, H. & Dauber, D. (2017). The gains and pains of mixed national group work at university. *Journal of Multilingual and Multicultural Development*, 38 (3), 219–236. doi:10.1080/01434632.2015.1134549.

UK Council for International Student Affairs (UKCISA). (2019) *International student statistics: UK higher education.* Available at: https://ukcisa.org.uk/Research–Policy/Statistics/International-student-statistics-UK-higher-education (Accessed 2 June 2020)

University of Southampton (2020a). *Information for students from China.* Available at: www.southampton.ac.uk/uni-life/international/your-country/asia/china.page (Accessed 2 June 2020)

University of Southampton (2020b). *Our international student community.* Available at: www.southampton.ac.uk/uni-life/international.page (Accessed 2 June 2020)

Widdowson, H. G. (1994). The ownership of English. *TESOL Quarterly*, 28, 378–389. doi:10.2307/3587438.

Zhu, H. (2015.) Negotiation as the way of engagement in intercultural and lingua franca communication: frames of reference and interculturality. *Journal of English as a Lingua Franca*, 4 (1), 63–90.

Part III

Classroom interaction: Interventions and reflections

11 Developing practice through intervention

Marion Heron and Doris Dippold

Introduction

In Chapter 1 we provided a topographical account of research into classroom interaction across the educational sector. A search of the literature on pedagogic interventions in higher education (HE) revealed few studies, so perhaps it is not surprising that we once again look to the compulsory school sector and the second language learning literature to document and analyse classroom interventions and to find applications to the HE context, with the aim of highlighting lessons learned. Changes in practice are at the heart of the research described with the ultimate aim of supporting students' learning. This chapter considers some key intervention studies which have been carried out in either the compulsory school sector or the second language classroom to shed light on key features and ways forward for the disciplinary context. We therefore focus on the following questions:

- What are the features of key intervention studies?
- What was the impact on students' learning?
- What can we gain from these studies and apply to the HE context?
- What is the way forward?

An overview of the intervention studies points to a range of underpinning dimensions which are summarised in Table 11.1. Articulating these dimensions or features may help us to develop ideas for further work in HE. Whilst not all studies fall neatly into one or the other columns, there is a tendency to do so.

These studies will be explored to consider to what extent they can inform our understanding of classroom interaction in the HE disciplinary context, and how there might be convergence and or divergence of practice. Most importantly, the chapter will consider how student learning in HE might be optimised through a development of tutors' awareness of their own classroom discourse. What is common to all the pedagogic interventions reported on below is the teacher development perspective. It is through the awareness of teachers of their classroom talk and interaction that interventions may take place to make changes in practice.

Table 11.1 Dimensions of intervention studies

Student facing	Teacher facing
Development of student talk	Development of teacher talk
Large scale	Small scale
School context	HE context
Development of conceptual understanding	Development of linguistic proficiency
Attainment measured in terms of subject knowledge	Attainment measured in terms of critical thinking skills

Examples of pedagogic interventions

The Oracy Project

Perhaps one of the most widely known pedagogic interventions is the Cambridge Oracy Project. This was developed by Neil Mercer and colleagues with the aim of developing the quality of student talk in class, namely by encouraging the use of exploratory talk (see Chapter 1, this volume). Exploratory talk describes classroom discourse in which children work together to reason, share knowledge and co-construct knowledge. The school project was entitled 'Thinking together' and has been reported on in a number of papers (Mercer & Dawes, 2014). In essence, the intervention involved training the children to use established guidelines and participation frameworks which would support the use of exploratory talk. Underpinning this was the development of a classroom culture in which children could share ideas and challenge each other in a supportive environment. The established guidelines, referred to as Talk Rules, included rules such as 'challenge your peers' and 'ask for reasons'. The researchers report that these interventions have resulted in a number of benefits, such as developed reasoning skills, as measured by standardised tests in maths and science, and the quality of the children's talk. Arguably the concept of Talk Rules could be equally applied to a HE context since research has noted that students, in particular international students, struggle to understand how small-group interactive events are interactionally organised (Engin, 2017; Fejes, Johansson & Dahlgren, 2005). It makes sense therefore to make these implicit rules of participation explicit through agreed Talk Rules.

Dialogic teaching project

The dialogic teaching project is a recent intervention carried out across a number of schools and reported on in Alexander and Hardman (2017), Alexander (2018) and Jay et al (2017). The aim was to "improve the quality of classroom talk and thereby increase students' engagement, learning, and attainment" (Alexander et al, 2017, p. 1). The study comprised control groups and intervention groups. Teachers were trained in the use of dialogic teaching pedagogy (Alexander, 2001) through a professional development programme over two phases. Key strands of the training were video analysis for self-evaluation. Findings indicated that both teachers and students extended their talk repertories. Interaction also became more inclusive, and teachers were more aware of their classroom talk. In particular, in phase 2 of the intervention, teachers used more open questions than the control group. There were also more extended student contributions in the intervention group. In terms of construction of conceptual knowledge, through the measurement of standardised tests, it was found that in the intervention groups pupils were two months ahead of those in the control groups in English and science.

In terms of application to HE, there are a number of learning points. One is the professional development of teachers to incorporate elements of dialogic teaching into their practice. Whilst this might not be appropriate in large-group teaching (e.g. lectures with large cohorts), there is no reason why dialogic teaching features such as cumulative talk and reciprocity cannot be part of HE practice. In seminars in particular, we would hope that students listen to each other and build on each other's ideas. Jacques and Salmon (2007, p. 108) write about seminars in the following way:

> When seminars go well, they can be a most exhilarating experience. An effective seminar discussion demands patience from the tutor, preparation by the students, and a suitable mix of personal qualities. The exceptional tutor may succeed in elevating a seminar to a memorable level of intellectual ferment.

In HE, if we want to promote 'intellectual ferment', then the classroom talk and the educational goals must align (Walsh, 2006).

Teacher scheme for educational dialogue analysis (T-SEDA)

T-SEDA is a further project which has developed out of the University of Cambridge, this time focusing on teacher development schemes (Howe et al, 2019; Vrikki et al, 2019). The project was based on previous research by the authors which established that when children use elaborated responses and querying through extensive participation, their curriculum mastery is improved, as measured by standardised tests (Howe et al, 2019). The aim is to develop teachers' analysis of their own classroom interaction and discourse as a starting point for individual action research projects. The researchers report that classroom dialogue is productive student and teacher talk which stimulates critical thinking and helps develop conceptual understanding. A coding analysis was first developed, which was then prepared as a teacher training toolkit. A key feature of the toolkit is teachers' recording and analysis of the classroom dialogue using the coding to better understand to what extent students are given the opportunity for reasoning, challenging and elaborating on ideas.

The project has now finished, with their website (Teacher Scheme for Educational Dialogue Analysis, 2018) reporting that teachers have developed a more nuanced understanding of classroom talk and equitable participation.

There are a number of applications of the T-SEDA scheme to the wider HE context. Firstly, the basic premise of the coding scheme, that these talk moves are crucial to constructing conceptual understanding, as has been argued in Chapter 1 and elsewhere in this book, are also key HE aims. We want our students to challenge, reason and elaborate. The coding scheme which reflects these talk moves can be used in a similar way to the intervention in the project. HE teachers can carry out small action research projects in which they first evaluate their classroom talk and then develop activities to encourage more educational dialogue talk moves. Encouraging a data-led approach to reflection on teaching as advocated by Walsh and Mann (2015) can be supported through the use of these codes. HE teachers can analyse excerpts of classroom transcripts (either their own, or example transcripts) to be sensitised to the centrality of classroom talk and interaction in learning.

Video-based teacher development

Lefstein and Snell's (2013) book *Better than best practice* is a resource book for teachers and school leaders to use to raise awareness of and reflect on classroom talk and interaction. One of the book's main premises is that all classroom talk takes place in specific sociocultural conditions and therefore there is no such thing as 'best' practice in terms of dialogic pedagogy. The aim of the book and programme is to sensitise teachers to the "problems and possibilities of dialogic pedagogy" (p. 9). Although no claims are made about students' development of understanding, the aim to raise teacher awareness of classroom talk is apparent in the conversations around the video clips of school classrooms. Despite the extensive use of video for teacher development in school settings (Tripp & Rich, 2012), the use of video clips for professional development in an HE context is rare. HE teacher education would benefit from the use of video extracts and group collaborative feedback sessions to highlight and reflect on the classroom interaction. With reference to Leftstein and Snell's recognition of the importance of sociocultural and educational context to classroom interaction and dialogue, conversations around video clips would surface disciplinary differences in classroom interaction (see Chapter 6).

Higher education

An example of a small-scale teaching intervention in HE is described in Engin (2017). The study followed an action research approach. Drawing on the work of Mercer and Dawes (2014), a group of international Master's students were introduced to the principles of exploratory talk and classroom talk rules. The first week's session was dedicated to orientation to the approach, and each following week the students engaged in a discussion activity in small-group and large-group settings. The discussions were audio recorded for thematic coding of dialogic and non-dialogic interactions. These extracts were used in stimulated recall interviews with the students. Findings revealed the very complex nature of dialogic interaction in HE seminar contexts and why students were reluctant to verbally participate on occasion due to linguistic challenges, topic challenges and a lack of understanding of the process and procedures of seminar participation. However, despite these challenges, interviews with teachers and recordings of classroom talk revealed that the teachers' approach of encouraging classroom talk through an application of Talk Rules (Mercer, 2000) supported students' confidence in participating in classroom talk.

Conclusion

As stated earlier, HE has a lot to gain from incorporating ideas, techniques and interventions from school contexts. Teacher education interventions in particular stand out as affording opportunities for systematic reflection on classroom interaction and the development of action plans. Interventions may be at an individual level, or can be part of an already established professional development route, such as the Postgraduate Certificate in Teaching and Learning, a programme which many institutions require their new lecturers to take. Similarly, reflection on practice using an evidence-informed approach (Walsh & Mann, 2015) can be organised more informally through communities of practice, or continuing professional development (CPD) sessions.

This chapter has reviewed the current terrain of pedagogic interventions in developing classroom interaction and classroom discourse. What is clear is that there are few accounts of pedagogic interventions in the HE disciplinary classroom. It is therefore timely to focus on small-scale practices and interventions which have addressed this neglected area. The following chapters describe interventions in specific contexts and promise innovative ideas and practices for HE practitioners and policy makers.

References

Alexander, R. (2018) Developing dialogic teaching: genesis, process, trial, *Research Papers in Education*, 33(5), 561–598,

Alexander, R. A., & Hardman, F. C. (2017). *Changing talk, changing thinking: Interim report from the in-house evaluation of the CPRT/UoY Dialogic Teaching project.* Research report. University of York and Cambridge Primary Review Trust. Available at http://eprints.whiterose.ac.uk/151061/1/Alexander_Hardman_hardman_2017_.pdf.

Alexander, R. J. (2001). *Culture and pedagogy: International comparisons in primary education.* Blackwell Publishing.

Alexander, R. (2018). Developing dialogic teaching: Genesis, process, trial. *Research Papers in Education*, 33(5), 561–598.

Engin, M. (2017). Contributions and silence in academic talk: exploring learner experiences of dialogic interaction. *Learning, Culture and Social Interaction*, 12, 78–86.

Fejes, A., Johansson, K., & Dahlgren, M. A. (2005). Learning to play the seminar game: Students' initial encounters with a basic working form in higher education. *Teaching in Higher Education*, 10(1), 29–41.

Howe, C., Hennessy, S., Mercer, N., Vrikki, M., & Wheatley, L. (2019). Teacher–student dialogue during classroom teaching: Does it really impact on student outcomes? *Journal of the Learning Sciences*, 28(4–5), 462–512.

Jacques, D., & Salmon, G. (2007). Enabling group interaction: the role of tutor and emoderator. In: Jacques, D. & Salmon, G. (eds) *Learning in groups: A handbook for face-to-face and on-line environment*, 159–194. Abingdon: Routledge.

Jay, T., Willis, B., Thomas, P., Taylor, R., Moore, N., Burnett, C., Merchant, G., & Stevens, A. (2017). *Dialogic teaching: Evaluation report and executive summary*. Project report. Education Endowment Foundation. Available from http://shura.shu. ac.uk/17014/1/Dialogic_Teaching_Evaluation_Report.pdf.

Lefstein, A., & Snell, J. (2013). *Better than best practice: Developing teaching and learning through dialogue*. Routledge.

Mercer, N. (2000). *Words and minds: How we use language to think together*. Routledge.

Mercer, N. (2010). The analysis of classroom talk: Methods and methodologies. *British Journal of Educational Psychology*, 80(1), 1–14.

Mercer, N., & Dawes, L. (2014). The study of talk between teachers and students, from the 1970s until the 2010s. *Oxford Review of Education*, 40(4), 430–445.

Teacher Scheme for Educational Dialogue Analysis (2018). Available from www.educ. cam.ac.uk/research/projects/tseda/.

Tripp, T., & Rich, P. (2012). Using video to analyze one's own teaching. *British Journal of Educational Technology*, 43(4), 678–704.

Vrikki, M., Kershner, R., Calcagni, E., Hennessy, S., Lee, L., Hernández, F., ... & Ahmed, F. (2019). The teacher scheme for educational dialogue analysis (T-SEDA): Developing a research-based observation tool for supporting teacher inquiry into pupils' participation in classroom dialogue. *International Journal of Research & Method in Education*, 42(2), 185–203.

Walsh, S. (2006). *Investigating classroom discourse*. Abingdon: Routledge.

Walsh, S., & Mann, S. (2015). Doing reflective practice: A data-led way forward. *ELT Journal*, 69(4), 351–362.

12 Dialogic interaction in the higher education classroom

A Philosophy for Children (P4C) approach

Fufy Demissie

Introduction

The significance of talk for learning is "as old as language itself" (Murphy et al., 2017, p. 435). Informed and influenced by Socratic and Aristotelian traditions, and more recently, by Dewey, Freire, Wells and Bakhtin, talk remains central to pedagogy across a wide range of educational contexts (Skidmore & Murakami, 2016). There is strong evidence to show that high-quality talk is powerful because it enables learners to arrive at "new understandings through collaborative constructions" (Murphy et al., 2017, p. 433), improves cognitive skills (Alexander, 2004; Jay et al., 2017), nurtures positive attitudes for learning (such as self-confidence and self-expression) (Gorard et al., 2017), and promotes civic engagement and empowerment (Nagda & Gurin, 2007). Students' ability to think critically and reflectively is therefore a priority for most academic disciplines (Brookfield & Preskhill, 2005; Darling-Hammond, 2006). Yet, for many students it is a learning process that presents cognitive (unfamiliarity with articulating arguments) and affective (fear of expressing own ideas) challenges (Gunn, 2007).

This chapter outlines how, in an attempt to address some of the barriers to productive classroom talk, the Philosophy for Children (P4C) pedagogy was integrated into an initial teacher education course. P4C is a relational inquiry-based dialogic approach designed to develop critical, creative, collaborative and caring thinking (Lipman, 2003). After highlighting some of the common issues in classroom talk in higher education (HE), the chapter outlines the key features of P4C pedagogy and its underpinning principles (including an illustrative example of a P4C enquiry). The three cases exemplify its impact on the students' readiness to engage in classroom discussion and their tutors' pedagogical practices. The final section evaluates P4C's role in addressing some of the barriers to productive classroom interaction. In conclusion, the chapter argues that, despite popular assumptions about students' lack of willingness and/or ability to learn dialogically, holistic pedagogies such as P4C can create a valuable opportunity for high-quality classroom interactions. The term 'tutors' is used to refer to the HE context and 'teachers' to the school context.

Issues in approaches to facilitate educational talk

Learning dialogically may be more transformative than traditional teacher-centric approaches (Gibb, 2010), but it is challenging nonetheless (Gunn, 2007). One reason is that students are generally more accustomed to traditional tea-cher-centric pedagogies, rather than learning that involves collaborative reflection and meaning making (Van der Meer, 2012). Even in HE contexts, Initiation, Response, Feedback (IRF) exchanges dominate; based on tutors' questions (Initiation), student' response (R) and tutors' feedback on students' response (F) (Hardman, 2016). Students are also likely to lack confidence in their own ideas and/or articulate their thinking to peers and tutors (Engin, 2017). Additionally, many students are hesitant about challenging others' views, and insecure about being challenged by their peers (Gunn, 2007). These uncertainties create a threat to individuals' sense of self and identity and therefore are likely to discourage participation and engagement in classroom discussions (Rogers & Freiberg, 1994).

A related issue is the influence of students' assumptions and beliefs about knowledge. Research suggests that dualist assumptions about knowledge, that is, views about knowledge as absolute (i.e. right or wrong) can affect attitudes towards dialogic classrooms (Perry, 1968). In other words, when students expect that authority figures (i.e. tutors) have the right answer, they are unli-kely to engage in enquiry, reasoning and knowledge co-construction with their peers (Van der Meer, 2012). Instead, a more contextual mind-set, where views and judgements are seen as conditional and open to challenge, makes dialogic interactions easier to embrace (Magolda, 2004). However, for many students, such a mind-set is problematic because dualist beliefs about knowl-edge are deeply ingrained (Kember, 2001). It is possible, nonetheless, that structured pedagogical approaches can cultivate students' appreciation of contextual knowledge, and embrace open-mindedness, and a readiness to test and evaluate ideas (Moon, 2008).

Finally, popular teaching strategies rarely address the complexities of dialogic classroom interactions. Jacques's influential work on classroom pedagogy, for example, focuses on strategies to manage the social and emotional barriers to the HE classroom (such as grouping strategies), but neglects the cognitive dimensions (Jacques, 2000; Jacques & Salmon, 2007). Others, such as problem-based learning, do the opposite; they emphasise the cognitive dimensions (such as problem-solving, evaluation) but miss out the affective aspects. Added to this, professional development for HE tutors make few references to the specific skills needed for high-quality classroom discussions. Thus, to better address the barriers to effective classroom discussions, classroom pedagogy needs a more holistic underpinning. In other words, tutors need the skills to provide safe and enabling conditions for dialogue, and the confidence to model and nurture process skills such as critical thinking and evaluation (Murphy et al., 2017).

The evidence from school-based research suggests that dialogic approaches such as P4C are effective in addressing the cognitive and affective barriers to classroom talk (Alexander, 2004; Gorard et al., 2016; Jay et al., 2017). Whilst these findings are school rather than HE based, the insights are highly relevant as the ideas that underpin the role of talk in learning (such as Dewey, Vygotsky) are universal rather than context specific. The following sections outline the key features of P4C (using an illustrative example of a P4C inquiry), and the findings from three case studies about P4C in an initial teacher education department.

Philosophy for Children (P4C)

Philosophy for Children is an inquiry-based dialogic pedagogy that originated in the US in the 1960s. Similar to most talk-based pedagogies, it draws on pragmatism (Dewey, 1933), socio-cultural theory (Vygotsky, 1978), inter-subjectivity for meaning making (Bakhtin, 1981) and the power of co-constructing knowledge (Freire, 1970). The catalyst for P4C was a genuine concern about an education system that prioritised knowledge transmission at the expense of "fostering of thinking" (Lipman, 2003, p. 4). In philosophy, Lipman saw a discipline that was "key to the improvement of thinking" because it involves "learning to think about the thinking in the disciplines, whilst at the same time learning to think self-correctively about one's own thinking" (1988, p. 40). In other words, philosophy offers a way of a way of thinking about ideas and concepts through reasoning, justifying questioning assumptions, questioning and wondering. Significantly, Lipman and Sharp also saw P4C as a means to encourage pupils' active participation in a democratic praxis and a space to learn how to "exercise citizenship when they become adults" (1988, p. 60). Sharp, Lipman's close collaborator, also argued that P4C was more than a pedagogy, but "a way of life involving the instilling and perfecting of cognitive, emotional and behavioural habits" (Sharp, 2004, p. 256).

P4C is a holistic pedagogy. It creates a safe and structured environment (ground rules) and is: learner-centred (students co-construct new knowledge), enquiry-based (based on questions), collaborative, and designed to develop the cognitive (meta-cognition and thinking skills) and affective (caring and collaborative thinking) skills and dispositions (Society for the Advancement of Philosophical Enquiry and Reflection in Education, SAPERE, 2010). Its structure is uniquely designed to operationalise these principles. In the ground rules, participants are invited to suggest behaviours that are most likely to facilitate openness and discussion, such as taking turns, agreeing with the point and not the person, and so on, whilst the ice-breaker games help to build relationships. Similarly, once the stimulus (provocation) is presented, participants are invited to generate discussible questions before voting on the one that they would most like to discuss. In the dialogue stage, participants are encouraged to express viewpoints, and to build on each other's ideas, as well as to justify and reflect on their views and position, whilst at the same time taking account of what has been said in the group (Lipman, 2003, see Box 12.2).

The facilitator's role is an important part of the structure and embodies key elements of P4C's principles (Splitter & Sharp, 1995). It is a complex role because it requires the facilitator to constantly monitor the cognitive and social and emotional environment of the classroom, and keep track of the dialogue so as to enable the participants to build on each other's contributions and to make progress (SAPERE, 2010). Practically it involves choosing relevant and sufficiently provocative stimuli and arranging the room in a circle to build trust and relationships. Pedagogically, the facilitator is encouraged to avoid indoctrination, respect students' opinions, maintain relevance, model genuine curiosity, and listen and build trust and confidence (Lipman, 1988). In addition to this, facilitators are also encouraged to sensitively model and encourage the 4Cs (critical, caring and collaborative and creative thinking). For example, if someone makes a sweeping statement, he/she might intervene with, '*So does everyone agree with that?*' '*Who thinks differently?*' Or '*Can you give us an example?*' Lipman also argued that teachers' attitudes to enquiry are crucial because unlike traditional didactic approaches, the focus in P4C is on the

> process of discussion, and not aimed at achieving one specific conclusion, teachers do not need to present themselves to their students as possessing great store of information. It is better to appear to the class as a questioner who is interested in stimulating and facilitating discussion
>
> (Lipman, 1988, p. 103)

Box 12.1 The P4C methodology (SAPERE, 2010)

1   Ground rules
2   Ice breakers
3   Presentation of stimulus
4   Generating questions
5   Airing questions
6   Voting for a question: to extend the democratic ideals
7   First thoughts
8   Building dialogue
9   Last thoughts

Box 12.2 An example of a P4C enquiry in a university context (time frame: 1–1:30 hours)

Chairs are arranged in a circle and the facilitator invites the students to consider. Common suggestions include 'some person speaks at one time', 'disagree with the point not the person', 'don't laugh', 'listen', and confidentiality. **(Ground rules – step 1)**

The facilitator then presents an 'ice breaker' such as name games. The aim is to build connection and solidary between the members, i.e., a community. **(Ice breaker – step 2)**

The stimulus: A relevant object, image, text or dilemma. As the students were going on an international placement, the stimulus was a series of images from the countries they would be visiting **(Presentation of the stimulus – step 3).**

They were then invited to get into small groups and to generate 'discussible questions' **(Generating questions – step 4):**

- Why is safeguarding so strict in the UK but not in other countries?
- Do uniforms hide society's inequalities?
- What diversity do other countries have in terms of SEND (Special Educational Needs and Disability)?
- Does poverty affect the quality of teaching?
- How much do resources impact on learning?

After reflecting on the questions (**Airing questions – step 5**) they voted for the following (**Voting – step 6**):

Why is safeguarding so strict in the UK but not in other countries?

First they shared their initial thoughts about the question **(First thoughts – step 7).** The discussions **(Building dialogue – step 8)** raised issues about context and how differences in society may lead to different policies and actions. At the end they were invited to reflect on whether their thinking has shifted, and what question the discussion had raised for them in relation to their own context **(Last thoughts – step 9)**

The students began to explore how their own assumptions and values influence their views and developed awareness of alternative perspectives on the issue. Throughout the facilitator used Socratic questioning, such as *"what counts as safety?" "what assumptions are we making about risks in different contexts?"* and *"how many people think that safeguarding is always a positive action?"*

Case studies of P4C in an Initial Teacher Education (ITE) department

Context

The following case studies took place in a large teacher education department located in a region where many of the schools have adopted the P4C approach. Additionally, P4C is also a key part of the ITE curriculum. In the first year, P4C is used in the Professional Learning module that includes topics such as 'professionalism', 'inclusive practice' and 'behaviour management'. In the second year of their studies, students complete a four-hour introductory course on P4C accredited by SAPERE (see Box 12.3). All teaching staff have also completed the same four-hour introductory course. In the final year, approximately 20% of the students choose to complete a further six-hour course to achieve the Level 1 certificate and/or choose to make P4C the focus of their dissertation.

The case studies were designed to gain insights into P4C's impact on students' perspectives, classroom interactions and tutors' pedagogies. They include a practitioner development activity on the use of P4C in a first-year module, a student survey about their perceptions of P4C, and finally, an in-depth reflective account by four final-year students on the impact of P4C on their professional and personal lives.

Box 12.3 Introductory course for Philosophy for Children (P4C)

The SAPERE introductory course for Philosophy for Children (P4C)

In this SAPERE (Society for the Advancement of Philosophical Enquiry and Reflection in Education) accredited four-hour course, participants are initially introduced to the aims and purpose of Philosophy for Children before being presented with the underlying ideas and principles.

Community of enquiry: "A group of people used to thinking together with a view to increasing their understanding and appreciation of the world around them and of each other" (SAPERE, 2010, p. 10)

Concepts: To draw participants' attention to discussible and contested concepts for the enquiry/discussion, e.g. beauty, justice, fairness.

The four dimensions of thinking (4Cs): An introduction to the skills and dispositions involved in creative, critical and collaborative thinking. These thinking modes are introduced as fundamental to addressing the community's question.

The role for the facilitator: This is introduced as crucial to sustaining and nurturing the community of enquiry through the facilitator modelling and enacting the 4Cs in the inquiry/discussion.

Additionally, participants take part in two philosophical enquiries to experience the key ideas (e.g. a community of enquiry and the 4Cs in practice; see Box 12.1).

Case study 1

The Professional Learning module addresses key aspects of the teachers' professional role such as planning, inclusive practice, professionalism, behaviour management and curriculum. The usual format for these seminars involves tutor exposition of key concepts and small-group discussion based around prompt questions such as "*can you describe what you understand by the term 'curriculum'?*" In this case, however, tutors presented stimuli such as images of classrooms around the world, which led students to generate questions such as "*Why are art and physical education classed as a luxury, rather than a necessity?*" and "*How important are uniforms in school?*"

Two key themes emerged following a series of professional dialogues about our experiences. The first related to the volume and quality of students' participation that exceeded tutors' expectations. Tutors' comments ranged from surprise at students' "*willingness to engage sharing and challenging opinions*", noting how "*they did give examples to justify their opinions*", the "*impressive levels of level of discussion and engagement of all involved*" and how a P4C-led discussion '*worked very effectively as means of developing critical thinking*". As the account shows, some tutors also noted how students applied P4C principles in other contexts:

> So I split them into two halves and they had all read these journal articles and they used evidence from the articles to prepare an argument for the debate. So I let everyone speak for each side and then opened it up, and what I found was, minutes after I opened it up, it started turning it into P4C and they were checking on each other "*hang on, you can't say that*", "*you were supposed to take this position*" … and they were naturally taking it into more P4C. And it needed that, because when we looked at the grid, the debate was good for lots of aspects of building up their logical argument and giving evidence and things like that… but it didn't have the different perspectives bit, the critical thinking to push them all up to. And once they started getting into the P4C, that's when the real multiple perspectives started to come in which it almost sat naturally… I was really impressed with the second years.

The second theme related to the role of the tutor/facilitator and the inherent challenges of managing and leading fruitful discussions. These included the issue of silent classrooms, facilitating an inclusive environment in classroom discussion, creating a safe and enabling environment, and developing the art of questioning. One of the tutors, for instance, reflected on the dilemmas of garnering student involvement:

> Different kinds of dynamics going on, so I said to them… let's get into circles or as a whole… so they voted as a whole group… so it started off an interesting discussion, listening to each other and some people were saying "*building on…*", "*I disagree*" then in the end, quite a lot of people, quiet ones who didn't say anything… I tried not to get involved, but I did say, let's hear from the people we didn't hear from. And not really anybody did and in the end, it got to two people discussing it and I said… I am aware now that there are a lot of people not involved in this discussion let's move on… quite a few pauses I left drift, which is quite hard, I did actually wait… So then I said, let's see if we do it a different way for the second question.

The second example refers to another tutor's account of her uncertainties about her facilitation style:

> It's weird I think because I am putting pressure and worrying about my contribution, I will sit and try and facilitate an enquiry and think didn't like this, didn't like this and I will come out afterwards and I will be reflecting, how did that go and as I am talking I go oh yeah, there was this and there was this... that was really valuable... and it's only in reflecting afterwards that I realise that there were great things that came out of it.

Case study 2

The purpose of this survey was to gain some insights into second-year students' perceptions of P4C at university. In addition to being taught through P4C in their first year, they had also completed a four-hour introductory course in P4C (see Box 12.2). They responded to the following questions:

- Which part of the P4C methodology do you find most engaging?
- What has taking part in P4C improved?
- What is your current understanding of P4C?
- What would you like more of?

Of the ones who responded (25% of the cohort), over 80% chose the chance to discuss as the best thing about P4C, followed by the use of different stimuli for discussion (60%). In response to the question on how P4C has impacted on their learning, over 70% cited the opportunity to explore ideas, and 62% cited their understanding of critical thinking. Just under half of the participants (46%) wanted to see P4C-type approaches in their other seminars. These findings were also supported by comments, including "*it has helped me with critical thinking which was useful for my assignment*", "*I welcome discussion as I think it opens up perspectives that we may not have previously considered*" and "*I think it is good for conflict resolution*". Though it was a small sample, the findings highlight there is an appetite for spaces for discussion and recognition of its value.

Case study 3

Four final-year students who undertook an extended P4C qualification (an additional six-hour training) elected to take part in a peer learning project. The brief was to lead P4C enquiries with first-year students. In consultation with the seminar tutor, they chose a suitable stimuli (related to the seminar focus) and in pairs facilitated the seminar discussion. Data about their experiences was collected using the 'Listening Room' (Heron, 2019), where pairs of students undertake a guided recorded conversation without the presence of the researcher. The conversation lasted for 60 minutes and was based on six cue cards (Belonging, Becoming, Journey, Happiness, Confidence and Success) in relation to their experience of P4C at university.

A collaborative group analysis (involving six colleagues) was then undertaken on the data. The findings indicate that P4C improved confidence in how to lead P4C enquiries, and promoted personal growth, transformation and the development of critical thinking in their professional and personal lives.

A: I don't think I would have felt like the right person to tell someone about it but I feel like after having done (P4C) with adults you feel like, well, I can talk about that, I can talk about doing it at school, I can talk about doing it at uni and I can talk about facilitating it in uni.

B: I think doing the P4C sessions it's your confidence in almost backing your own opinion. But then having the confidence to justify it as well and have the confidence to support it if you change it, you know. There was also evidence of person growth and transformation

B: I feel like it gave us more of an ability to think about our questioning and the language that we use as facilitators... which I hadn't really done much of before when doing it with children. But after doing it with first years I feel like I do it more with children now because I've had to do it properly with older people. In relation to critical thinking:

A: Like the skills are so transferable as well, you know, everyone has got an opinion on everything, but just being able to have that critical thinking, the way you can process information, different viewpoints and express opinions effectively without it being negative, I think it's a really good skill to have. Yeah, and we're like *what did you mean by that?* And, oh, *could you elaborate on that?* Or *I like what you said when you said this.* We have all those languages that we use but I feel like in first year we just said our opinion and then we'd disagree and that was that.

A: It's that stubbornness of not opening yourself up to other opinions because that can really stunt discussion. Yeah. I'm a lot better at hearing other people's opinions.

Reflections

Taken together, these findings suggest that overall, integrating the P4C pedagogy in the ITE curriculum had a beneficial impact on students and tutors. Both students and tutors were highly engaged, and the quality of the classroom discussion during P4C was superior to traditional seminars. The students' learning experience had been enriched because the discussions were beginning to transform their understanding and implications of important teaching-related concepts. Some of the conclusions they came to, for example, about classroom discipline, challenged accepted wisdoms about best practice. For some, the experience led to personal growth and transformation in areas such as critical thinking that is a challenge for many (Mezirow & Taylor, 2009).

From the tutors' perspective, P4C provided an opportunity to deeply reflect on their seminar practices, and to be introduced to ways of deepening questioning and creating a more conducive learning environment for dialogue and interactions.

The apparent benefits of this learning approach raise important questions about common assumptions about students and tutors (Van Der Meer, 2012). For example, the idea that students are reluctant, or unable, to engage in discussion and dialogue is a common one. Often this is attributed to the highly test-driven education culture in English high schools that encourages teacher-centric learning approaches that is at odds with the co-construction models of learning in HE (Moon, 2008). However, the findings here show that this deficit view is problematic, as even first-year students (in the first few weeks of their study at university) were willing and able to articulate their viewpoints and to question each other and consider multiple perspectives. The tutors' experience and reflections also raise questions about whether professional development sufficiently addresses the skills and dispositions needed to facilitate high-quality classroom discussions (Ellis & Hogard, 2018).

There are many aspects of the P4C pedagogy that contributed to the benefits outlined above. P4C embodies many elements of transformative pedagogies such as: authentic relationships (Rogers & Freiberg, 1994; Noddings, 2012), dialogue (Freire, 1970; Bakhtin, 1981), individual experience and learner autonomy (Mezirow & Taylor, 2009), meta-cognition (Brookfield & Preskill, 2005), student autonomy (Chin & Osborne, 2008) and the collaborative dimension (Dewey, 1933). Much of the value of P4C is due to the structured methodology that encapsulates and reinforces the key principles (see Boxes 12.1 and 12.2). Moreover, its user-friendly nature makes it accessible to students and tutors and creates a shared understanding of its aims and principles. Significantly, P4C also equips tutors with specific tools to manage the learning environment (e.g. manage the dominant voices by giving limited number of talk tokens or explicitly inviting the quieter members to speak) and to model and incorporate critical, caring, collaborative and creative thinking (4Cs) during the dialogue.

The findings in these studies highlight the potential benefits of a holistic pedagogy such as P4C, which are lacking in many popular teaching approaches. However, in addition to the small-scale nature of these case studies, there are other limitations. P4C is a complex and multifaceted pedagogy, so it is not clear which specific aspect of the pedagogy makes the key difference to students' willingness to participate. Critics may also question the wider relevance of the findings given the highly contextual nature (teacher education) and the prevalence of reflections on personal experiences (of tutors and students), rather than observational or comparative studies with non-P4C approaches. Observational data could have also corroborated or contradicted tutors' impressions of improved student engagement and participation. At the same time, however, the multi-layered nature of P4C makes it difficult to isolate a specific skill or disposition as a focus for enquiry. Despite these limitations, P4C offers a principled and well-structured approach that makes it a worthy candidate for professional development activities, especially since there are few other pedagogical approaches that take into account the challenges of dialogic interaction in HE classrooms.

Conclusion

Dialogic interaction should be an integral part of the HE learning experience because it develops and embeds the skills and dispositions for intellectual growth and transformation. The interventions described in this chapter challenge popular assumptions about student disinterest in dialogic classroom interactions, their capacity for independent thought and tutors' confidence in facilitating fruitful classroom discussions. Given the right context, it seems that even first-year students can articulate reasoned arguments and are open to consider alternative perspectives. This suggests that for high-quality discussion to flourish, students need learning contexts that not only create a safe learning environment, but also knowledge of the relevant skills and dispositions. With its structured methodology and careful attention to the affective and cognitive elements of dialogic learning, the Philosophy for Children pedagogy offers one way of unlocking students' potential and building tutors' confidence in supporting their learning.

References

Alexander, R. (2004). *Towards dialogic teaching: Rethinking classroom talk.* York: Dialogos.

Bakhtin, M. (1981). *The dialogic imagination: Four essays*, ed. Michael Holquist, trans. Caryl Emerson and Michael Holquist. Austin, TX: University of Texas.

Brookfield, S., & Preskill, S. (2005). *Discussion as a way of teaching: Tools and techniques for democratic classrooms.* San Francisco, CA: Jossey-Bass.

Chin, C., & Osborne, J. (2008). Students' questions: a potential resource for teaching and learning science. *Studies in Science Education*, 44 (1), 1–39.

Darling-Hammond, H. (2006). Constructing 21st-century teacher education. *Journal of Teacher Education*, 57 (3), 300–314.

Dewey, J. (1933). *How we think: A restatement of the relation of reflective thinking to the educative process.* Boston, MA; New York [etc.]: D.C. Heath and company.

Ellis, R., & Hogard, E. (2018). *Handbook of quality assurance for university teaching.* London: Routledge.

Engin, M. (2017). Contributions and silence in academic talk: exploring learner experiences of dialogic interaction. *Learning, Culture and Social Interaction*, 12, 78–86.

Freire, P. (1970). *Pedagogy of the oppressed.* New York: Continuum Books.

Gibb, M. (2010). *Dimensions of quality.* The Higher Education Academy. www.advance-he.ac.uk/knowledge-hub/dimensions-quality (Accessed 1 August 2020).

Gorard, S., Siddiqui, N., & See, B. H. (2016). An evaluation of Fresh Start as a catch-up intervention: a trial conducted by teachers. *Educational Studies*, 42(1), 98–113.

Gorard, S., Siddiqui, N. & See, B. H. (2017). Can philosophy for children improve primary school attainment? *Journal of Philosophy of Education*, 51 (1), 5–22.

Gunn, V. (2007). *Approaches to small group learning and teaching*. Glasgow: University of Glasgow, Learning and Teaching Centre. www.gla.ac.uk/media/media_12157_en.pdf (Accessed 20 May 2014).

Hardman, J. (2016). Tutor-student interaction in seminar teaching. *Active Learning in Higher Education*, 17 (1), 63–76.

Heron, E. (2019). Friendship as method: reflections on a new approach to understanding student experiences in higher education, *Journal of Further and Higher Education*, 44 (3), 393–407.

Jacques, D. (2000). *Learning in groups: A handbook for improving group work*. London: Kogan Page.

Jacques, D., & Salmon, G. (2007). *Learning in groups: A handbook for face to face and online environments*. Abingdon: Routledge.

Jay, T., Willis, B., Thomas, P., Taylor, R., Moore, N., Burnett, C., Merchant, G. & Stevens, A. (2017). *Dialogic teaching: Evaluation report and executive summary*. Project report. London: Education Endowment Foundation.

Kember, D. (2001). Beliefs about knowledge and the process of teaching and learning as a factor in adjusting to study in higher education. *Studies in Higher Education*, 26(2), 205–221.

Lipman, M. (1988). *Philosophy goes to school*. Philadelphia, PA: Temple University Press.

Lipman, M. (2003). *Thinking in Education* (2nd ed). Cambridge, UK; New York: Cambridge University Press.

Magolda, B. (2004). Evolution of a constructivist conceptualization of epistemological reflection. *Educational Psychologist*, 39 (1), 31–42.

Mezirow, J., & Taylor, E. (2009). *Transformative learning in practice: Insights from community, workplace and higher education*. San Francisco, CA: Jossey-Bass.

Moon, J. (2008). *Critical thinking: An exploration of theory and practice*. London: Routledge.

Murphy, K., Wilkinson, I., Soter, A. & Firetto, C. (2017). Instruction based on discussion. In Mayer, R. & Alexander, P. (Ed.), *Handbook of research on learning and instruction* (pp. 432–459). London: Routledge.

Nagda, B., & Gurin, P. (2007). Intergroup dialogue: A critical-dialogic approach to learning about difference, inequality and social justice. *New Directions for Teaching and Learning*, 111, 35–45.

Noddings, N. (2012). The caring relation in teaching, *Oxford Review of Education*, 38 (6), 771–781.

Perry, E. (1968). *Patterns and development in thought and values of students in Liberal Arts College: A validation of a scheme*. US Department of Health, Education and Welfare. https://eric.ed.gov/?id=ED024315 (Accessed 6 December 2019).

Rogers, C., & Freiberg, H. (1994). *Freedom to learn*, 3rd revised edition. Upper Saddle River, NJ: Prentice Hall.

SAPERE (2010). *Handbook to accompany the Level 1 course*, 3rd edition. Abingdon, Oxon.

Sharp, A. M. (2004). The other dimension of caring thinking. *Critical & Creative Thinking: The Australasian Journal of Philosophy in Education*, 12 (1), 9–14.

Skidmore, D., & Murakami, K. (2016). *Dialogic pedagogy: The importance of dialogue in teaching and learning*. Bristol: Multilingual Matters.

Splitter, L., & Sharp, A.M. (1995). *Teaching for better thinking: The classroom community of inquiry.* Melbourne, Victoria: ACER (Australian Council for Educational Research Ltd.).

Van Der Meer, J. (2012). 'I don't really see where they are going with it': Communicating purpose and rationale to first year students. *Journal of Further and Higher Education,* 36 (1), 81–94.

Vygotsky, L. (1978). *Mind in society: The development of higher psychological processes.* Cambridge, MA: Harvard University Press.

13 Implementing a dialogic pedagogy in university seminar-based teaching

Benjamin Poore

Introduction

In June 2017, I attended a Learning and Teaching Forum workshop delivered by Dr Jan Hardman, titled 'Transforming teaching and learning through a dialogic pedagogy'. Hardman (2016) has written of dialogic teaching in which "teachers break out of the limitations of the recitation script through higher order questioning and feedback strategies which promote a range of alternative discourse strategies" (p. 64). I was intrigued by this idea, and by Hardman's highlighting of the "lack of research on tutor–student interaction and discourse" conducted in higher education settings (2016, p. 65). As a drama academic teaching on a BA in Theatre, I imagined that much of my practice was already dialogic; students and staff work together on practical and production projects and interact regularly and informally. Dialogic approaches can also be seen in traditions of teaching drama in schools (Fleming, 2011) and drama teaching is often characterised as collaborative and student centred (Lehtonen, 2016). However, after the workshop I began to wonder whether staff–student interaction in drama seminars was as dialogic as I had assumed. Since the withdrawal of a (non-credit-bearing) study skills module two years earlier, we no longer set time aside to explain to new students what a seminar is, what staff expectations are for students' conduct and participation, and how seminars are intended to enhance learning, whereas the study skills module had covered these basics of university study. Given such a lack of guidance, it was perhaps unsurprising that the proportion of students engaging in talk activities in seminars was low. Other factors may well be at play in seminars, however. In the introductory module discussed in this chapter, students were facing a new learning environment with peers and lecturers whom they were only just getting to know and trust, for example. Students may also have had variable prior experiences of classroom participation depending on the type of school or college and educational norms in their country of origin. As seminar teaching was one of the main forms of staff–student contact on the Theatre degree programme, I posited that opportunities were being missed to support cognitive development through dialogic talk that reflects reasoning and justification of ideas.

My central research questions related to the value and utility of talk in university teaching: does the application of dialogic approaches to talk in seminars lead to better-argued written work in the assessment, and do dialogic methods enhance students' sense of the value of seminars as contact events? These questions were particularly pertinent to the context in which the research was initially carried out, an introductory core module called 'Introduction to Play Analysis'. The assessment was based entirely on a single essay, and in this sense the module was not unusual for an arts and humanities degree programme. If interaction could be made more meaningful in the two-hour weekly seminars – the contact event in which students on this module spent the greatest amount of time – then it might improve the quality of thought, argumentation and expression in essays.

Theories and frameworks

This section outlines the classroom interventions to enhance spoken interaction that were undertaken in the action-research project and explains their methodology as well as the theory guiding them. Dialogic pedagogy was chosen as a framework for interaction because it offered a chance to model learning and teaching at university level along different lines from what students may have been used to in schools. In doing so, I hoped to improve student engagement and attendance, retention, and investment in learning, and to build student confidence and autonomy in responding to and organising talk in the seminar. There were 60 students in the cohort, of whom ten per cent were from other EU countries and eight per cent were from other overseas countries. Of those educated in the UK, the majority studied in schools and sixth-form colleges and took A Level and/or BTEC qualifications, sometimes in Drama and Theatre Studies (though not always, as this was not an entrance requirement for the course). Hence, prior experience of learning in the subject might range from exclusively desk-bound discussions that were focused on identifying themes, imagery and literary features, to workshop sessions focused on devising performance rather than analysing text.

Theoretical principles

I drew on Alexander's (2006, p. 29) notion of a repertoire of approaches for facilitating dialogic talk, including whole-class discussion, paired talk, small-group talk and teacher-directed discussion. I developed these as the term progressed, drawing also on Resnick and colleagues' distinction between *talk formats* and *talk moves*: a talk format might be a lecture, a recitation, or a whole-group discussion, while a talk move is a specific question or suggestion to support the development of 'accountable talk' Michaels, O'Connor & Resnick, 2008. Accountable talk has three dimensions: "accountability to the community, accountability to knowledge, and accountability to accepted standards of reasoning" (Michaels, O'Connor & Resnick 2008, p. 286).

Hence, while the first week's seminar featured mostly teacher-led discussion, and introduced basic talk moves, seminars in the middle of term gave students greater agency in deciding the duration and nature of a task, and in running and monitoring whole-group discussions, including drawing conclusions and deciding when a task was satisfactorily completed. This can be interpreted as a development from talk which is accountable to the learning community ("talk that attends seriously to and builds on the ideas of others") to talk which is accountable to standards of reasoning (involving explanation and self-correction) and talk which is accountable to knowledge ("based explicitly on facts" and "written texts") (Michaels, O'Connor, & Resnick, 2008, p. 286; 287; 289). Students were introduced to this theory of accountable talk explicitly, both at the beginning of the term and as a means of exploring what new talk moves could achieve as they were introduced.

In these mid-term seminars I also introduced more complex small-group activities such as 'jigsaw teaching', where students alternate between talk in specialised and mixed groups working on a range of concepts (Kember & McNaught, 2007, p. 85). By the end of term, students were practising peer teaching (Kember & McNaught, 2007, p. 93), where a part of the group that had seen a stage production explained and analysed it with the part that had not seen it, with their talk structured by a series of production images shared with them in advance. Throughout the term, time was set aside for students to reflect on the quality of the talk activity itself. This meta-level talk is a feature of, among others, Neil Mercer's approach to dialogic learning (Mercer, Dawes, & Staarman, 2009). In terms of my own role in the seminar room, I saw the adoption of a *dialogic stance*, reflecting and responding to students' contributions, as key. For Boyd and Markarian (2015), a dialogic stance is defined not so much by interactional form – open versus closed questions, for example – as by responsiveness to the interactive functions of talk within the learning environment (p. 294). The features of effective seminar teaching identified by Richmond, Boysen and Gurung (2016, p. 56) were useful in identifying what this stance might look like: caring and supportive, possessing a good rapport with students, having strong communication skills, exhibiting ethical and principled behaviours, and creating opportunities to engage students. I also found the concept of *immediacy* a useful one for dialogic learning: the seminar leader is present, attentive and responsive throughout (Richmond, Boysen, & Gurung, 2016, p. 61). I sought means of decentring myself as the sole source of authority and analytical judgement in the room, by, for example, setting up a group discussion activity and asking the students to nominate someone other than myself to lead or co-lead the discussion. This interpretation of a dialogic stance responds to the thinking of Paolo Freire and the idea of re-learning the subject material with the students (Skidmore & Murakami, 2016, p. 3).

Methodology

The structure of the project was based on an action-research methodology. In the first term of teaching the new first-year cohort, I would implement a dialogic approach to seminar planning and teaching. Seminars were video and audio-recorded so that evidence could be analysed. In the first seminar, students were asked to identify their own learning goals in response to the official module learning aims and outcomes. They were also asked to construct and agree their own 'ground rules for talk' (Mercer & Littleton, 2007, pp. 61–62) to try to ensure that everyone had a stake in the success of the seminars and that there was common agreement of standards of behaviour and discussion (Exley & Dennick, 2004, p. 21). In the second and third terms of the academic year, a Teaching Fellow became the seminar leader and I observed the sessions. Both the Teaching Fellow and I kept a reflective journal for each session we taught to record our impressions of how effectively dialogic practice was being embedded in seminar work. As each seminar was taught three times over one to two days with up to 20 students per group, there were opportunities to reflect on the seminar structure and to adjust our techniques from week to week and even between seminars taught in the same week.

To measure the students' qualitative experience of seminar teaching, at the start of the investigation I surveyed second and third-year students on their experiences of seminars at university in an attempt to establish a 'baseline' of student responses without the dialogic intervention. I then surveyed first-year students at the end of the academic year on their experiences of seminar learning. This data was gathered in an anonymous online survey using a seven-point Likert scale, as well as through the anonymous standard module evaluation survey. The quality of written work was to be assessed through the summative essays for the first-year modules in 'Introduction to Play Analysis' and 'Dramaturgy'. I ensured that two experienced colleagues were allocated to moderation for these tasks to try to ensure objectivity and avoid confirmation bias. A successful intervention would, I expected, be indicated – though not conclusively proven – by improved marks across the cohort compared to previous years for these modules, before the dialogic principles were implemented.

The challenges of investigating and developing classroom discourse

In this section I discuss some challenges encountered during the research process, all of which had a significant impact on the outcomes. Perhaps the deepest challenge to the investigation was the actual application of a dialogic pedagogy to an introductory university seminar series. This can be seen, firstly, at the level of programme and module design. As noted above, the module 'Introduction to Play Analysis' incorporated various elements of an earlier study skills module, and a considerable number of skills necessary for the study of Theatre at degree level are also introduced at this stage. Students are expected to get used to reading plays independently and in greater numbers than at school or sixth-form college; they must become familiar with the conventions of citation; they develop skills of close reading and drama-turgical analysis of primary texts and learn to use and evaluate secondary sources. Students learn to frame arguments in essays where the content is much less predetermined than it was under school examination systems, and analytical essay writing of this kind continues to be a key means of assess-ment for the rest of the degree programme. Students may be encountering historical play texts for the first time and learning the basics of verse drama. The historical range of plays studied on this module is also intended to act as a form of 'survey course' for performance history and the history of playwriting. There are many new skills to practise and much new subject knowledge to assimilate. In such a context, students might wish for an author-itative seminar leader rather than one who cedes power to the students, as is the case with dialogic approaches (Teo, 2019, p. 176).

This preference for a single source of authority might be especially under-standable for students after a school experience that, in the UK at least, is likely to have focused in its latter years on the syllabus and the requirements of the examination boards, and the teacher's ability to interpret these for students. As the evidence below indicates, this appears to have been the case. Students in their first terms at university can find it difficult to adjust to an environment that foregrounds personal and intellectual development, and where much of the taught material is not immediately 'useful' or examinable but represents the foundational principles of a higher level of subject inquiry. In the design of the investigation, I had tried to anticipate students' concerns on this issue by having lectures and seminars serve two distinct purposes: the lectures would present a range of possible approaches to the analysis of plays, with worked-through examples, while the seminars would be a more open, reflective and dialogic space for students to build their own responses to the material. Nevertheless, module evaluation feedback indicated that students felt there was too much material in a one-hour lecture and that they were unable to capture it all. Comments included:

> "The module in lectures seemed rushed and hard to keep up... I feel like the lecture could be 2 hours long instead of 1"
> "If it could be slowed down just a little so I have time to comprehend the first thing before moving onto the next then I feel I would benefit more from it."
> "The lectures however need to be longer so the lecturer can develop his points and not run out of time."
> "I enjoyed the content of the module but I feel as if it was almost packed with too much information."

Somewhat surprisingly, therefore, the introduction of a dialogic pedagogy in seminars seemed to increase student reliance on lectures as the most significant source of information, increasing the prominence of 'transmission-model' teaching. In seminar reflection, students also expressed frustration that the readings set for each week had not been given sufficient prominence in seminars, and also asked whether seminars themselves could be video-recorded and shared (the department already has a default policy of lecture capture, so all lectures on this module are recorded with audio and screen capture for student review and revision). Moreover, while students in seminar feedback acknowledged the value for their learning of reflecting on the quality of the talk activity itself, this too may have contributed to a concern that information on plays and play analysis was being displaced by meta-level talk.

These student responses indicate the difficulty in implementing a dialogic pedagogy with students after years of schooling which has emphasised 'teaching to the test' ("Teaching to the test", 2015). Rather than thinking of the seminars, in particular, as experiential learning, it seems that some students saw effective teaching as explicit 'coverage' in seminars of their independent reading, while some wanted to collect all possible module content for future viewing, storage and reflection. In addition to students requesting permission to make personal recordings of seminars or to have them automatically recorded, this desire also manifested itself in some students favouring note-taking over active involvement in seminar talk. This in turn may reflect not only an increased focus on assessment in the UK education system but also the framing of education as a 'consumer good', particularly since the tripling of tuition fees, first legislated for in 2010 (Cini & Guzmán-Concha, 2017, p. 623). The collection of study materials and recordings of teaching events – rather than the full participation in those events – might therefore become a way of demonstrating a tangible return for course fees. As Teo (2019) suggests, the valuing of dialogic pedagogy cannot take place in isolation from other elements of the education system, or from society at large (p. 176). Alternatively, student enthusiasm for information conveyed as lectures may reflect personal preferences for less interactive forms of learning and discomfort with the perceived "exposed" nature of dialogue in the peer-facing seminar configurations (Parsons, 2018, p. 27).

The impact of the study on student learning

Measured purely in terms of student attainment, the dialogic approach does appear to have had benefits for first-year marks in 'Introduction to Play Analysis' and, less markedly, 'Dramaturgy'. The mean for 'Introduction to Play Analysis' increased by 7.1 marks compared to the previous year, by 8.07 marks compared to 2015/16, and by 4.52 marks compared to 2014/15. The increase in median marks was 7, 9 and 6 marks compared to previous years. For 'Dramaturgy', the mean mark increased by 1.85 in comparison with 2016/17, by 2.22 in comparison with 2015/16, and by 6.25 marks compared with 2014/15. Median marks increased by 3, 3.5 and 8 marks in comparison with previous years.

In terms of grade distribution, improvement was again most noticeable in 'Introduction to Play Analysis', where the number of Firsts awarded was 17, an increase of 10 on the previous highest number of Firsts awarded for this module (awarded in 2016/17). The number of 2:1 marks awarded was the highest in the module's history (26) and the number of 2:2s (13) considerably lower than in 2016/17 (21) or 2015/16 (18). In 'Dramaturgy', nine students were awarded first-class marks, the joint-highest in the module's three-year history, but the number of 2:1s matched that of 'Introduction to Play Analysis' (26), with 17 students achieving a 2:2. Returning to the first research question posed at the beginning of this chapter, then, it can be said that there was a correlation between the application of dialogic approaches to talk in seminars and higher-quality written work in the summative assessment. While the dialogic pedagogy intervention may not have been the relevant factor in these results, it is notable that in every other module that year (students took six modules overall), the cohort had a lower mean score than the previous year's intake, suggesting that the higher mark distribution in 'Introduction to Play Analysis' and 'Dramaturgy' was not necessarily the result of a more able intake. In two of those modules – including 'Introduction to Performance', which students study alongside 'Introduction to Play Analysis' – the mean for the cohort was lower than for the previous two years. However, other modules, such as 'Acting' and 'Directing', are taught very differently and are assessed on practical work and reflective (rather than analytical) writing, and so the comparison with attainment in other models can only be indicative rather than conclusive.

Certainly, the Hawthorne effect cannot be discounted when students are being filmed and are aware that they are participating in pedagogical research. The Hawthorne effect is defined as "the tendency, particularly in social experiments, for people to modify their behaviour because they know they are being studied, and so to distort (usually unwittingly) the research findings" (Payne & Payne, 2004, pp. 107–111). This might apply both at the level of students feeling special

Table 13.1 'Introduction to Play Analysis'

Year	First	2:1	2:2
2017/18	17	26	13
2016/17	7	20	21
2015/16	4	15	18

Table 13.2 'Dramaturgy'

Year	First	2:1	2:2
2017/18	9	26	17
2016/17	7	24	23
2015/16	9	17	17

because they were being studied (Payne & Payne, 2004, p. 109), and at the level of students perceiving a 'tangible benefit' to co-operating with the researcher in terms of attention and resources (Payne & Payne, 2004, p. 110). However, the improvement in essay grades suggests that the positive effects of dialogic inter-action continued beyond the students' classroom performance.

Student perception data was collected using the online survey I had constructed, based on 11 key features of successful seminar and small-group teaching. First-year students were invited to complete the survey after the year's teaching had been completed. The survey questions used the word 'discussion' where the term 'dialogue' may have been more precise (see Alexander, 2006, pp. 22, 27); however, I was attempting to make the questions accessible for both the cohort that were the subjects of the research and the other cohorts that had no experience of dia-logic methods. Hence, I identified specific dialogic practices in several questions rather than making a strict distinction between 'discussion' and 'dialogue' (see Appendix). The survey results (see Figures 13.1 and 13.2) suggest that first-year students, experiencing dialogic approaches to seminar learning, were much more likely that second and third-year students to agree with Statement Three ("In seminars, students are encouraged to participate in discussions"), Statement Four ("Students are encouraged and enabled to teach each other in seminars"), State-ment Seven ("A wide range of opinions is listened to and valued"), Statement Eight ("In group and whole-class discussions, points are listened to and responded to by people other than the seminar leader"), Statement Ten ("After discussions and group work in seminars, we often talk as a class about the quality of the dis-cussion itself") and Statement 11 ("The tutor often probes student responses for more elaboration, justification and evidence, and to invite other students to comment on the contribution").

Returning to the second research question stated at the opening of the chapter, the application of dialogic methods did enhance first-year students' sense of the value of seminars as contact events, for this group of respondents at least. There are some significant issues with the validity of these results, however, given the low number of first-year respondents to the seminar-specific survey (eight first-year students and 22 second and third-year students). This was also a self-selecting sample, meaning that students may have chosen to participate because of their strong feelings about their seminar experiences, whether positive or negative; their different experiences of seminar teaching, and being surveyed at a different point in their programme of study, also make direct comparisons problematic.

Additionally, as noted previously, the introduction of a dialogic pedagogy created greater student concern than in other cohorts over the coverage of module content, despite the improvement in results. Second and third-year students were more likely to 'Agree' or 'Strongly Agree' with Statement Five, "We always cover the key concepts thoroughly in seminars". The most popular answer for second- and third-year respondents was 'Agree' while for first-year students it was 'Somewhat Agree'. Combined with the student module evaluation comments quoted earlier, the results do suggest an area of concern.

■ Year 1   ▪ Years 2&3

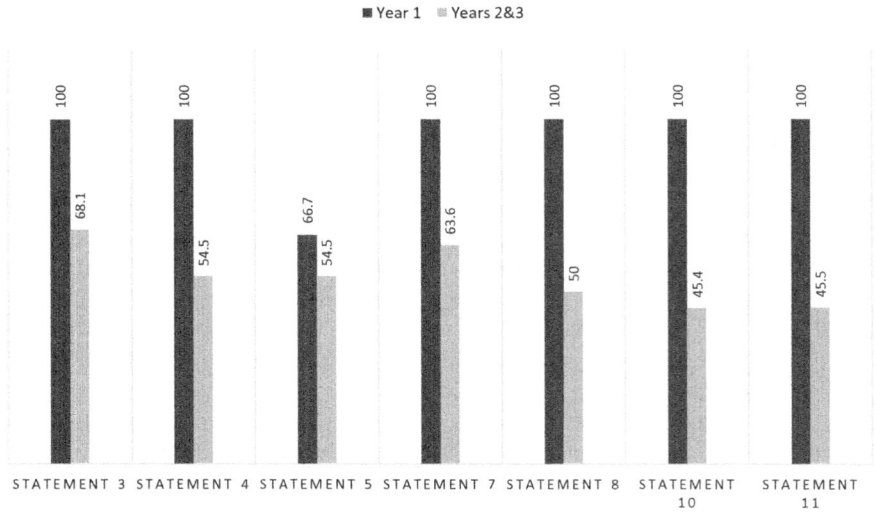

Figure 13.1 Student survey: 'Agree' scores

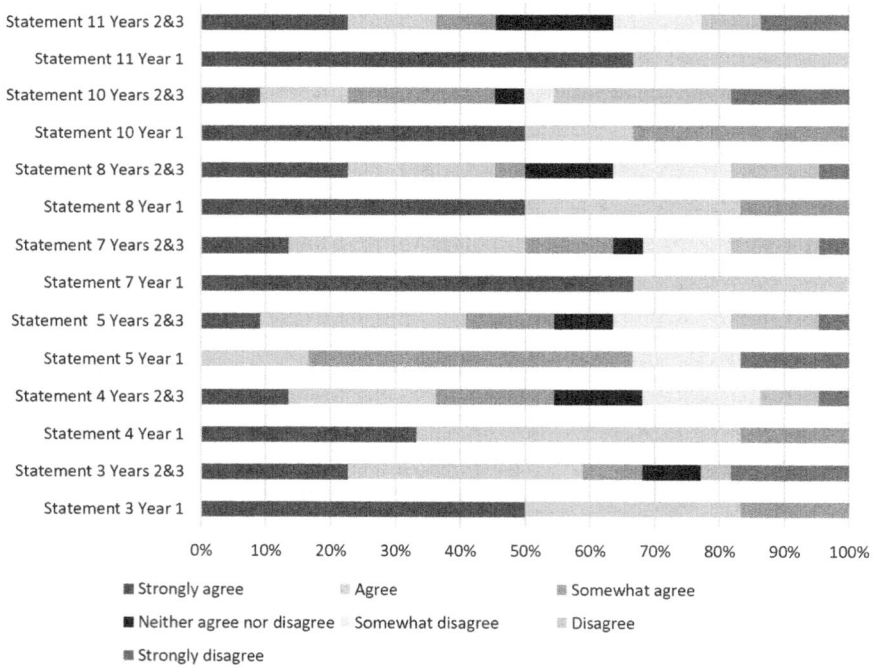

Figure 13.2 Student survey: all scores

The impact of the study on theory and practice

Given the positive impact on assessment results, I have continued to use a dialogic pedagogy approach in the first-year 'Introduction to Play Analysis' and 'Dramaturgy' modules. However, the limitations of this methodology in the context of assessments based on writing or solo work have led to a reconsideration of the design of these modules and how they are assessed. As Teo (2019) suggests, "[e]xisting models and modes of assessment tend to still treat student knowledge as fixed, discrete and assessable through individualized and standardized pen and paper tests" (p. 176). For future academic years, the programme team is considering assessment by both written work and a peer-evaluated discussion for 'Introduction to Play Analysis'. The 'Dramaturgy' module was redesigned in 2018/19 to emphasise the development of dramaturgical skills rather than the content of particular plays and the number of plays set for study was reduced from eight to six. This was intended to address student concerns – expressed in module evaluations – that not all plays were being given equal coverage, while at the same time de-emphasising the idea of 'coverage' of a preordained curriculum of texts. 'Dramaturgy' continues to be assessed by both essay and solo presentation, but again proposals have been put forward to adjust this presentation to facilitate dialogic exchanges.

In response to student feedback about the pace of lectures, I initiated a follow-on, action-research project in 2019/20 to redesign lectures along more interactive and inclusive lines. The project led to more robust connections between the experience of lectures and dialogue and discussion in the seminars that follow. The follow-on project also builds on the dialogic pedagogy approach by being team-taught with another lecturer in both lectures and seminars. As Game and Metcalfe (2009, p. 46) suggest,

> By having more than one teacher present in front of the class, the position of the knowing teacher is diffused. If students can see teachers engaged in dialogue, working out difficult questions between them, they come to trust teachers, seeing them not as people with a complete knowledge, but as people devoted to learning and thinking.

By focusing on the 'live' experience of lectures and foregrounding staff and student co-presence, the intervention was able to improve lecture attendance and course engagement, to improve student satisfaction with the module, and to make students more verbally and physically active participants in lectures as well as seminars. Particularly in its team-teaching elements, the project represented a powerful iteration of a dialogic stance. However, it remains a further challenge to replicate such experiences online in a teaching landscape profoundly altered by COVID-19.

Conclusion

As noted above, the limitations of the project's methodology are that student perceptions captured in the online survey only represented a small proportion of both the year group that was participating in the dialogic teaching seminars, and the two year groups that were not, since the survey was voluntary and in addition to required student module evaluations. Although further qualitative data was collected in group interviews with first-year students, who were asked the questions featured in the survey, these responses could not be included in case participants had also completed the anonymous online survey. Group-interview participants were also self-selecting and may have been more likely to attend if positively disposed towards the module or seminar participation.

However, the success of the dialogic pedagogy initiative in seminars, in terms of student attainment, has a number of implications for future practice. Students certainly need to be supported in the transition from school and college to university study, and alongside a dialogic pedagogy that fosters the co-construction of knowledge, this support might involve additional contact hours on the module that focus on instruction for independent study skills. The disposition towards learning that this dialogic intervention sought to inculcate in students is not necessarily one which yields immediate assessment results, but rather it is intended to benefit the student across their undergraduate career. To be able to carry out such investigations requires a degree of privilege in a higher education sector that is marked by increasing casualisation and precarity (Cini & Guzmán-Concha, 2017, p. 624). Less securely employed lecturers are likely to find it harder to risk the potential initial student anxieties that have been shown here to accompany a dialogic approach when student module evaluations can be taken into account for their own hiring or promotion decisions. As Teo (2019) notes, "There is a deep-seated sense of insecurity that comes with relinquishing control and ceding 'authority' to students, who may begin to question their teacher's competence" (p. 176). Therefore, in insecure times, dialogic pedagogy requires longstanding support from senior staff if it is to deliver on its potential for transforming student learning.

Appendix: Seminar survey

Statement 1

Seminars contain a variety of types of activity, which keep me engaged.

Statement 2

Seminars provide a caring and supportive learning environment.

Statement 3

In seminars, students are encouraged to participate in discussions.

Statement 4

Students are encouraged and enabled to teach each other in seminars.

Statement 5

We always cover the key concepts thoroughly in seminars.

Statement 6

The seminar leader always provides a clear structure for the seminar.

Statement 7

A wide range of opinions is listened to and valued.

Statement 8

In group and whole-class discussions, points are listened to and responded to by people other than the seminar leader.

Statement 9

It is always clear what the discussion in seminars is building towards.

Statement 10

After discussions and group work in seminars, we often talk as a class about the quality of the discussion itself.

Statement 11

The tutor often probes student responses to ask for more elaboration, justification and evidence, and to invite other students to comment on the contribution.

References

Alexander, R. (2006). *Towards dialogic teaching: rethinking classroom talk* (4th ed.). Dialogos.

Boyd, M. P., & Markarian, W. C. (2015). Dialogic teaching and dialogic stance: moving beyond interactional form. *Research in the Teaching of English*, 49, 272–296. Accessed 28 December 2019. www.jstor.org/stable/24398703?seq=1#metadata_info_tab_contents.

Cini, L., & Guzmán-Concha, C. (2017). Student movements in the age of austerity: the cases of Chile and England. *Social Movement Studies*, 16, 623–628. Accessed 29 December 2019. https://doi.org/10.1080/14742837.2017.1331122.

Exley, K., & Dennick, R. (2004). *Small group teaching: tutorials, seminars and beyond.* Routledge.

Fleming, M. (2011). *Starting drama teaching.* Routledge.

Game, A., & Metcalfe, A. (2009). Dialogue and team teaching. *Higher Education Research and Development,* 28, 45–57. Accessed 29 December 2019. https://doi.org/ 10.1080/07294360802444354.

Hardman, J. (2016). Tutor–student interaction in seminar teaching: implications for professional development. *Active Learning in Higher Education,* 17, 63–76. Accessed 26 December 2019. https://doi-org.libproxy.york.ac.uk/10.1177/1469787415616728

Kember, D., & McNaught, C. (2007). *Enhancing university teaching: lessons from research into award-winning teachers.* Routledge.

Kim, M.-Y., & Wilkinson, I. A. (2019). What is dialogic teaching? Constructing, deconstructing, and reconstructing a pedagogy of classroom talk. *Learning, Culture and Social Interaction,* 21, 70–86. Accessed 29 December 2019. https://doi.org/10. 1016/j.lcsi.2019.02.003.

Lehtonen, A. M.-V. (2016). Promoting creativity in teaching drama. *Procedia – Social and Behavioral Sciences,* 217, 558–566.

Mercer, N., & Littleton, K. (2007). *Dialogue and the development of children's thinking.* Routledge.

Mercer, N., Dawes, L., & Staarman, J. K. (2009). Dialogic teaching in the primary science classroom. *Language and Education,* 23, 353–369. Accessed 29 December 2019. https://doi.org/10.1080/09500780902954273.

Michaels, S., O'Connor, C., & Resnick, L. B. (2008). Deliberative discourse idealized and realized: accountable talk in the classroom and in civic life. *Studies in the Philosophy of Education,* 27, 283–297. Accessed 29 December 2019. https://doi-org.libp roxy.york.ac.uk/10.1007/s11217-007-9071-1.

Parsons, C. S. (2018). Learning the ropes: the influence of the roundtable classroom design on socialization. *Journal of Learning Spaces,* 7, 23–34. Accessed 27 December 2019.

Payne, G., & Payne, J. (2004). *Key concepts in social research.* Sage. Accessed 28 December 2019. https://dx-doi-org.libproxy.york.ac.uk/10.4135/9781849209397.n22.

Richmond, A., Boysen, G., & Gurung, R. A. (2016). *An evidence-based guide to college and university teaching: developing the model teacher.* Routledge.

Skidmore, D., & Murakami, K. (2016). Dialogic pedagogy: an introduction. In D. Skidmore & K. Murakami, *Dialogic pedagogy* (pp. 1–16). Multilingual Matters.

"Teaching to the test". (2015). In S. Wallace, *A dictionary of education.* Oxford University Press. Accessed 28 December 2019. www.oxfordreference.com/view/10.1093/acref/ 9780199679393.001.0001/acref-9780199679393-e-1014.

Teo, P. (2019). Teaching for the 21st century: a case for dialogic pedagogy. *Learning, Culture and Social Interaction,* 21, 170–178. Accessed 18 December 2019. https:// doi.org/10.1016/j.lcsi.2019.03.009.

14 Reflecting on the cultural assumptions we bring to teaching

One strategy for improving classroom interaction

Jane G. Bell and Jane Richardson

Introduction

Universities are ostensibly meritocratic and have a duty to reduce barriers to participation in order to meet the requirements of the Equality Act (2010); however, not all students have the same opportunities to succeed. In this chapter it is argued that facilitating development of an inclusive, negotiated culture in the classroom may reduce the likelihood of discrimination or bullying and lead to more effective classroom interaction in which differences are respected and valued. However, for this to take place cultural awareness and reflexivity is required on the part of the facilitator. A broad definition of culture is adopted, which includes organisational cultures and groups linked by common interests and experiences, neurological difference or physical or mental impairments. Classroom interaction is considered meaningful if it supports students to access the discourses and practices of the academic community on their own terms (Kettle, 2017). In other words, the interaction between student and teacher is viewed as an exchange and students as assets to the internationalised university, not problems to be solved (Ryan, 2011).

The research presented here was originally prompted by a serious mobbing or sustained group bullying incident on an in-sessional course, which resulted in the student victim becoming suicidal. Research also suggests that over a fifth of UK university students have current mental health issues, while almost a third have experienced a serious mental health issue which required professional help (Pereira et al., 2019). This psychological distress has been attributed to a number of causes including leaving home for the first time, the transition from school to HE and financial pressures (Pereira et al., 2019). Another possible factor may be increasing student diversity. In 1970, only 8.4% of the population were awarded a degree (Bolton, 2012, p. 14). By 2017, this figure had risen to 42% (ONS, 2017). In Scotland, the number of disadvantaged students entering university rose by 90% between 2006 and 2016 (Blackburn, Kadar-Satat, Riddell & Weedon, 2016). Aspects of student diversity include first language, age, economic background due to increased numbers of 'first generation' students, neurodiversity, health, sexual orientation, gender identity and other cultural influences.

The wellbeing of faculty staff and students are inextricably linked; hence, there is a clear need to facilitate greater diversity awareness among teaching staff as well as among students. The strategy employed to improve classroom interaction, a diversity awareness induction session for pre-sessional English teachers, was trialled in 2019. The research consisted of a thematic analysis of teachers' reflections after the induction session. The theory underpinning the research is outlined below, followed by an analysis of 25 reflections, written by participants after the induction session. A high percentage of the teachers on the Herriot-Watt University pre-sessional programme have extensive research experience or are based in universities year-round, while our own practice comprises both seminar teaching and lectures; hence, 'teacher' is used throughout to refer to both teachers and lecturers.

Theoretical framework

Social practice model of teaching

Teaching and learning are social practices and therefore classroom interaction is affected by how the participants view each other in terms of group membership. A 'group' could be identified by features such as gender, ethnicity, disability, vocation or age and each has their own distinctive 'culture' which is constantly evolving. One individual can belong to many groups and institutions also have distinctive cultures. Interaction in a classroom is therefore of an intercultural nature on many levels and can lead to the creation of a 'community of practice' (Wenger, 1998, p. 2) involving shared goals and identity.

A key factor in effective intercultural communicative competence is self-awareness and knowledge of one's own culture (Deardorff, 2006). Therefore, facilitating cultural awareness in students requires culturally aware staff who avoid the 'othering' of students (Dippold et al., 2019) when they are labelled as

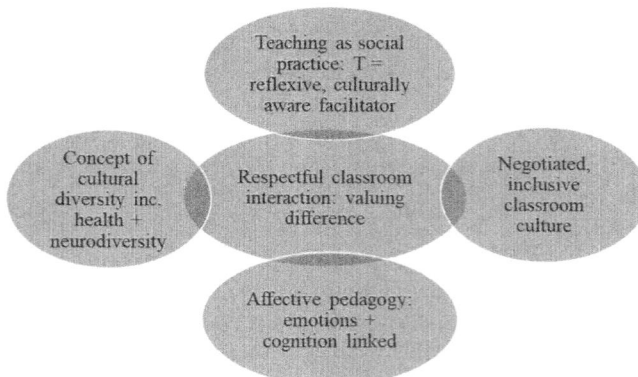

Figure 14.1 Theoretical framework

'international', and instead view them as individuals able to draw on a range of cultural resources. In order to avoid stereotyping or applying the deficit model of students with regard to culture or neurological type, interaction between students and teachers should be viewed as reciprocal, rather than unidirectional. Communication between teacher and student or between students then occurs where meaning is negotiated to reach common understanding, rather than either side relying on preconceived notions of 'them' and 'us' (Holliday, Hyde, & Kullman, 2010). On our in-sessional courses, one aspect of this reciprocal approach entails involving students in decision-making about class or homework activities whenever possible.

Concept of cultural diversity

Culture can be broadly defined as shared understandings and values which shape personal and group identities. It is understood not as fixed features of nationality or ethnicity, but as contextual, dynamic, mutable, and different for every individual. The aspects of cultural identity that a person chooses to reveal may vary depending on context, and an individual may have membership of many different cultures, which may change over time. Following Jameson (2007), cultural identity is defined for the purposes of this analysis as encompassing and shaped by a person's vocation, social class, environment, philosophy, language(s), culture-related elements of biology or health such as age, neurodiversity, physical and/or sensory impairments (for example, Deaf Culture), and other aspects of a person's life which are significant to them.

Impact of culture on classroom interaction

Factors such as previous academic culture and conflicting cultural values can significantly influence the ability of students or staff to work effectively together. Adapting to a new academic culture can challenge students' expectations of classroom participation, assessment and teacher and student roles (Dippold, 2015; Scudamore, 2013). Cultural values relate to a person's ideas of right and wrong and are often emotive and deeply felt; hence, conflicting values may lead to misunderstandings or conflict. The importance of student emotions will be further discussed in the section titled 'The role of emotion in classroom interaction'. Power and privilege are also considered integral to cultural identity (Jameson, 2007) and hence influence classroom interaction, in areas such as the perception of "permission to speak".

Negotiated inclusive classroom culture

Intercultural communication in a Higher Education (HE) context is understood here as interaction between people who are members of a range of cultural groups (e.g. social, political, linguistic, organisational, national or transnational), whose world views and values may also be shaped by neurological differences or aspects of health. Development of a new culture rooted in a specific context can enable students to negotiate new understandings and avoid national stereotypes and essentialist cultural categories. This principle mirrors that of a community of practice, in which members are united by common goals and interests (Dippold, 2015).

The role of emotion in classroom interaction

As part of an overall aim to adopt a more holistic view of students and teachers as complex individuals, it is important to acknowledge the centrality of emotions in intercultural communication and classroom interaction. Emotions can affect university students' learning, teaching quality, and teacher and student wellbeing (Mendzheritskaya & Hansen, 2019). Affective pedagogy is an approach in which the emotional states of students are acknowledged to be key factors in learning:

> [The] affective and cognitive dimensions of education are interrelated. Students' feelings about themselves as learners and about their academic subjects can be at least as influential as their actual ability.
>
> (Lang, 1998, p. 5)

The causal relationship of the correlations between teachers' emotions and teaching approaches, and between students' emotions and learning approaches, is still unclear. However, it seems likely that in both cases, it is bidirectional. Trigwell (2009) found a correlation between positive teacher emotion and learner-centred teaching, and, conversely, a link between negative teacher emotions and a transmissive, teacher-centred teaching approach (cited in Postareff & Lindblom-Ylänne, 2011, p. 800). Students are also aware of and influenced by teachers' emotions, and links have been made between student emotions and the depth of their learning approaches (Trigwell et al., 2012).

Rationale for diversity awareness teacher induction session

Teachers have a responsibility to model inclusive behaviour and to create safe, respectful learning spaces for their students. If teachers are to be reflexive, empathetic role models for their students, it is important to provide a forum in which they can reflect on professional challenges. Reflective practice is an evidence-based, transformational process which can enable self-development and inform future practice; importantly, it can also reveal differences between professed teacher beliefs and actual teaching practice (Farrell & Ives, 2015).

In order to avoid unthinkingly imposing Western values or practices on students, it is important to accept that education is never culturally neutral. Teaching can be viewed as 'a cultural artefact, deeply embedded in cultural values about knowledge, teacher-student relations, classroom interaction and the role of talk in learning' (Kettle, 2017, p. 119). The pedagogic principles and practices of every academic field are shaped by the cultural perspectives of its practitioners. For example, teachers trained in the UK are likely to have adopted the principles of Socratic dialogue, communicative and/or constructivist teaching practices and a relatively low power difference between students and staff. They may favour persuasive discourse over authoritative discourse (Bakhtin, 1981), in other words, the role of facilitator over the transmissive approach. For teachers to be aware of their students' academic assumptions and expectations, they also need to be aware of their own.

Academic culture in the UK is evolving. At Heriot-Watt, 45% of students self-identify as having learning difficulties (HWU, 2019), making the concept of a 'normal' student increasingly difficult to define. Approximately 10% of the UK population is neurodivergent, in other words cognitively different from the neurotypical majority (Singer, 1998). Examples of neurodivergence include those on the autism spectrum and individuals with dyslexia, ADHD and dyscalculia. It is thought that a significant number of neurodivergent students are diagnosed for the first time at a UK university, perhaps due to low awareness or risk of stigma in the student's previous culture. Moreover, some neurodivergent students may choose not to disclose their status in UK HE due to bullying experiences at school and fear of further discrimination (Van Roekel et al., 2010). Understanding this aspect of student diversity is key to creating a respectful classroom culture.

Aims of diversity induction session

The primary aim of this research was to focus on teachers and their role in creating a more inclusive learning environment, reducing the potential for student distress or conflict by enhancing classroom interaction. Hence, the aims of the diversity induction session were to:

- raise awareness of staff and student diversity in HE
- develop a community of practice among teachers
- enable teachers to share their extensive, varied intercultural experience and knowledge
- elicit ideas for accommodating diversity in the classroom, and
- expand the typical EAP definition of 'diversity' beyond first language and previous academic culture, given the growing importance in HE of reducing barriers to participation for students with mental health issues or neurodivergence

Findings: Analysis of pre-sessional teacher reflections

A thematic analysis (Bryman, 2008) was conducted of the teachers' 500-word reflections and several key themes emerged which were significant in terms of our theoretical framework. Direct quotations from teachers are indicated by T#. The main themes were as follows:

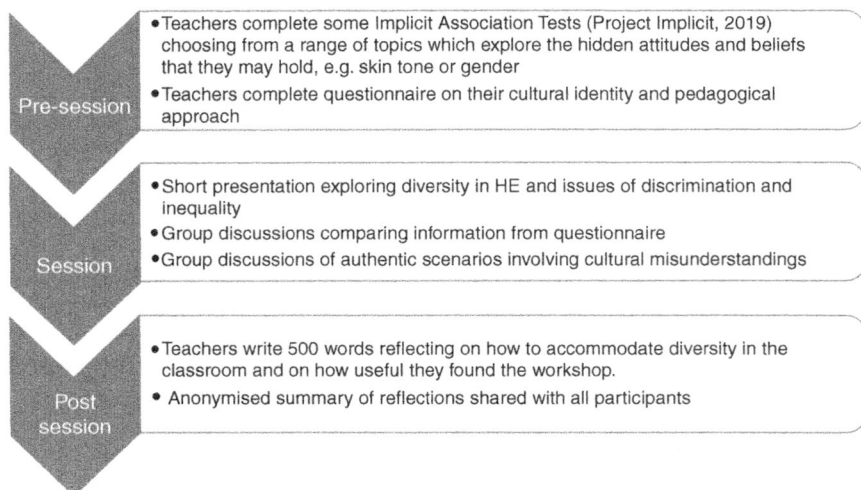

Figure 14.2 Induction session outline

1   Evaluation of the diversity induction session
2   Student diversity
3   Teacher identities
4   Pedagogical implications of student diversity

Evaluation of teacher induction session

The reflections suggest that the aims of the session were met to a large degree. Many teachers commented that there was a sense of "singing from the same hymn sheet" [T12], which suggests a community of practice was developing. Only one teacher [T25] disagreed, asserting that such awareness-raising was common in the public domain and therefore unnecessary. Teachers seemed committed to continuing the induction CPD process, requesting input in future sessions from the Student Wellbeing Services on mental health and neurodivergence, and more time for discussion of lesson planning to maximise the benefits of student diversity and support students. The rich intercultural experience and knowledge shared in these reflections shows the teachers' engagement with the issues and an acknowledgement of the social nature of teaching, and discussion continued in CPD sessions throughout the rest of the programme.

Student diversity

During the workshop, a broader definition of student diversity emerged. Participants discussed the effects of aspects of student diversity such as age, previous academic culture, neurodiversity and mental health. Discussion of the multiple cultural assumptions embedded in their practice [T12] led teachers to question prevalent stereotypes about, for example, mature students being more motivated and autistic students choosing Maths subjects; and they observed that students may have different understandings of concepts such as autonomy and hence may not always value a 'student-centred classroom' [T1].

Besides appreciating the cultural impacts on their teaching practice and being aware that academic cultures are changing, teachers also showed considerable empathy for their students and their different learning preferences and personalities. Regarding the growing recognition of student mental health issues in HE, one commented:

> [In] some cultures this would not be discussed openly or even recognised as different from homesickness, cultural problems etc.... HW has set up a unit to address these issues, and a member of staff at the unit commented that he had not come across any L2 speaker presenting with depression, and commented that the majority of students presenting with this condition were Arts students.
>
> [T4]

Other participants also voiced concerns that depressed students might be unable to access medical support due to difficulty in "articulating this very complex condition". This relates to comments by others about cultural variation in recognition or understanding of neurodiversity, discussed in the section titled 'Pedagogical implications of student diversity'.

Several teachers wanted to learn more about how to accommodate neurodivergent students, and some teachers felt apprehensive about teaching these students. One commented:

> In the past I have taught a very small number of students who were neurologically different. Despite having been advised about their situation, I sometimes felt intimidated and unsure about my approach to the student in question.
>
> [T10]

Participants displayed considerable sensitivity to the dangers of cultural stereotyping, and expressed a desire to understand the students as individuals. For example, T3 commented:

> ...individuals constitute a layering of beliefs, values and attitudes developed through personal, social, national and international histories. A range of filters is in operation in terms of arriving at shared definitions. The filters might be ascribed to a group context but need to be ultimately considered for the individual.

The influence of previous academic culture on student expectations was noted by several teachers. Regarding teacher and student roles, T1 noted:

> Ss can sometimes expect a more authoritarian, sage-on-the-stage, role for the teacher and are sometimes resistant to classroom interactions which are less teacher-centric and more student ⊠ student. Some students... resist roles and interactions and assessments in which more emphasis is put on student autonomy.

For this reason, we regularly enable new students in groups to compare their expectations about UK HE culture with previous experiences, using a questionnaire. This task typically reveals a range of expectations about, for example, student and teacher roles, participation, autonomy and assessment in UK universities. This induction session enables students to begin negotiating a new class culture.

Some teachers criticised institutional methods of 'othering' students, in other words a deficit model:

> Too often, when institutions talk about 'diversity' they are really talking about 'divergence' from some standardized state of being as if something is lacking, so they contextualize women as 'not men', BAME as 'not white', or gay as 'not straight'. In some colleges, international students from India are streamed into ESOL classes for speaking 'not standard English'. But we are all divergent. We can all be defined as who we are not. If we are all lacking something, then together we complete the group.
>
> [T7]

Pedagogical implications of student diversity

> To me, diversity in the classroom is about giving people space to develop their potential with individuality and dignity.
>
> [T7]

How to plan lessons to accommodate student diversity was the most challenging question posed in the induction session, and participants would have preferred more discussion time. Tellingly, few written reflections addressed this topic but most participants agreed this should be the key focus of a future induction session.

Several teachers expressed a desire for more information about how to recognise and accommodate mental health issues in the classroom:

> An L2 student recently told me she suffered from social anxiety. I had no idea how to deal with this, or in reality what this meant for her in a classroom situation.
>
> [T4]

T4 also reflected on how best to accommodate student neurodiversity, given that a student's condition may be undiagnosed or unstated due to cultural reasons:

> I think a formal diagnosis is not necessary or even practicable; in some of the students' home countries this is not easily available, if at all.

Many teachers expressed a pragmatic desire to accommodate student diversity as best they could, given that not all students are able or willing to divulge information about their mental health condition or neurodivergence. Suggestions regarding ways of ensuring inclusivity included supporting students to work in groups and devising tasks and assessments to take into account learning differences:

> Allowing flexibility regarding task-type (e.g. autistic students allowed to opt out of working in groups), encouraging students to identify their own strengths and weaknesses and divide up group work accordingly, creating groups of mixed gender, experience and culture, if possible.
>
> [T1]

'Identifying strengths' is key, since neurodivergent individuals often possess abilities or skills that neurotypical individuals lack (Singer, 1998).

Another teacher reflected on the nature of student autonomy, considering the affective factors involved in learning:

> I started to wonder more about the relationship between confidence and autonomy at HE undergraduate and postgraduate levels, and how a pre-sessional tutor can navigate that relationship in a diverse class of undergraduates and postgraduates, whether it's a multi-cultural or uni-cultural cohort.
>
> [T6]

Regarding the effects of previous academic cultures, some teachers acknowledged the effects of cultural variation in rhetorical conventions, for example:

> I once coached an Arab student whose IELTS exam writing usually began with a lengthy paragraph praising his school and teachers… He'd apparently never had the Anglophone cultural value placed on concision explained to him… but adapted very quickly and his IELTS writing score jumped two whole bands when he next sat the exam.
>
> [T1]

T5 advocated cultural humility:

> We might not be able to change the world, but we [can influence] what happens in our classrooms. However, it's imperative we do this in a way

that does not 'other' our students or indeed promotes Western European modes of thinking (and educating) as superior.

These reflections show that teachers were open to extending the definition of diversity and to considering ways to accommodate this diversity through adopting a more learner-centred and affective pedagogy, by facilitating more inclusive group work for example.

Teacher identities

Regarding diversity in HE, many teachers reflected on their own identities, referring to cognitive differences, use of 'low-prestige' varieties of English, recognised biases, teaching approaches (TEFL[1] vs EAP) and the fact that their identity changed depending on their teaching context: "I am not the same 'I' across groups, institutions, syllabuses, lessons" [T6]. They also reflected on what they felt they had in common: as "like-minded liberals" we "share a common perspective on diversity" [T5]. This was echoed by T8:

> [As] someone who works within a university and educational settings, I suspect I occupy a world with other individuals who, while very different, share certain commonalities such as a value of questioning, the importance we place on lifelong learning, criticality and more often than not a liberal leaning disposition.

Some interpretations of the values embodied in the role of an EAP professional also revealed awareness of a political responsibility: we are "front line 'promoters' of a hegemonic language" [T14].

Some teachers expressed empathy with neurodivergent students, due to the lack of understanding they had experienced themselves. One reflected on:

> the very real distress this caused me as it went undiagnosed… I was very good at Maths… but in teenage years [exam performance] became erratic… No one realised that I could not correctly sequence and record numbers of more than 4–6 digits, so although I knew the answer I could not record it accurately, particularly under exam pressure… I was advised to give up Maths and labelled 'lazy' or erratic. I felt very frustrated and confused.
>
> [T4]

A number of participants commented on the importance of teacher self-awareness. For example, T8 acknowledged that

> it is sometimes more difficult to be objective about our own personal issues than those we observe externally… it is clearly not enough to simply be aware of the possible issues our students may face.

Several commented on the usefulness of the unconscious bias tests they had completed before the session. For example:

> We had an interesting discussion about... whether those biases can be overcome. I think they can. I think acknowledging the unconscious takes away its power.
>
> [T7]

> the unconscious bias test we had to do for this workshop was very revealing. For me it revealed I have a strong preference for younger people over older people.
>
> [T2]

Impact

The teacher induction had a number of effects. Evidence of the continuing impact of the session could be seen in discussions in staff meetings about possible reasons for poor student participation, for example. Whereas such discussions often focus on factors such as language proficiency or motivation, on this course the possibility of neurodivergence or mental health issues was often noted. It was impossible to measure the extent to which the induction session increased participants' sense of membership of a community of practice, although teachers provided one another with ample peer support. Future research could further investigate this.

Regarding the impact on our future practice, the following changes will be implemented as a consequence of teacher feedback.

1. Future teacher diversity awareness induction sessions

Based on teacher feedback, these will include:

a   input from the Wellbeing Services, including information on neurodiversity and mental health support for students
b   exploration of practical methods of applying an affective, inclusive pedagogy to classroom interaction which reduces barriers to participation and contributes to a negotiated culture based on mutual respect
c   reflection by teachers on relations of power in the classroom, including the relative prestige accorded to varieties of English

In relation to point c, more discussion of the different Englishes spoken in the classroom could be facilitated by students choosing a variety of English to research, for example Malaysian English (Galloway & Rose, 2018). An acceptance by teachers that their students may speak a different English to themselves is an example of embracing diversity in the classroom and giving students some agency. Raising students' awareness of how English has spread and adapted to local conditions will build confidence in their identity as English users and their proficiency in using it for global communication, not as a 'native speaker' (Galloway & Rose, 2018).

2. Student diversity awareness sessions

These will entail small-group discussions of a questionnaire which enable students to:

- question assumptions about peers and UK academic culture
- discuss research on the benefits of diverse teams, including the unique strengths of neurodivergent individuals
- analyse authentic examples of cultural misunderstanding related to cross-cultural variation in turn-taking or politeness strategies
- understand procedures students should follow if incivility, micro-aggressions or bullying occur
- learn about some effects on of neurodiversity and mental health issues on classroom interaction
- develop critical thinking skills through discussion of counter-stereotypes (Goclowska, Crisp & Labuschagne, 2012)

3. Adding to and developing the learning outcomes of group work assessments

Group work is a common component of university assessment and therefore one way of highlighting the importance of diversity is to include learning outcomes for effective intercultural communication and collaboration in group assessment. The following learning outcomes are based on the Common European Framework of Reference for Languages (CEFR) B2 level competences (Council of Europe, 2018) and have been added to group assessment criteria on our courses:

- identify and appreciate ideas and perspectives of other people which may be different to yours
- collaborate in a team by developing your own and other people's ideas in order to construct new meaning and find solutions to problems

Conclusion

This research was motivated by the apparent increase in student emotional distress in UK universities and the possible links between emotional wellbeing and academic performance. This prompted the researchers to consider how affective pedagogy could facilitate development of a negotiated, inclusive classroom culture. Classroom interaction is central to students' experience of HE and it is argued that when it is managed effectively by self-aware teachers who appreciate and value diversity, it can help to safeguard students in ways which extend beyond the classroom. Potential benefits include enhanced intercultural communication skills as a result of deeper understanding of the benefits of diversity and development of supportive social relationships.

The diversity induction session involved many teachers who return to teach on the pre-sessional programme year after year, and served as the beginning of an extended dialogue, in the form of CPD sessions and discussion of materials design. While much of the impact of the session is difficult or impossible to measure, two key effects were our subsequent inclusion of new assessment criteria to all group assessments, and further development of the student induction session. The anonymised summary of the teachers' rich reflections shared with participants was described as 'fascinating', 'thought-provoking' and prompted further discussions. Teacher reflection is arguably an essential component of any continuing professional development, and as academic culture evolves, so must we.

Study limitations

The study is small-scale and therefore not generalisable. Participants were invited to reflect on any aspect of the workshop that interested them, resulting in data which lacked a specific focus. However, teachers' topic choices were revealing in themselves and a wide range of insights were presented. As the reflections were anonymous, there was no opportunity to elicit expansion of teachers' views. Future research could include focus groups in order to explore some themes in greater depth.

Note

1 TEFL – Teaching English as a Foreign Language.

References

Bakhtin, M. M. (1981) Discourse in the novel (C. Emerson & M. Holquist, Trans.). In M. Holquist (ed.), *The Dialogic Imagination* (pp. 342–354). Austin, TX: University of Texas Press.

Blackburn, L. H., Kadar-Satat, G., Riddell, S. & Weedon, E. (2016) *Access in Scotland: Access to Higher Education for People from Less Advantaged Backgrounds in Scotland.* The Sutton Trust. Retrieved 10 June 2020 from: www.suttontrust.com/wp-content/up loads/2020/01/Access-in-Scotland_May2016.pdf.

Bolton, P. (2012) *Education: Historical Statistics.* House of Commons Library. Retrieved 5 April 2020 from: https://researchbriefings.parliament.uk/ResearchBrief ing/Summary/SN04252#fullreport.

Bryman, A. (2008) *Social Research Methods.* Oxford: Oxford University Press.

Council of Europe (2018) *Common European Framework of Reference for Languages: Learning, Teaching, Assessment: Companion Volume with new descriptors.* Retrieved 3 December 2019 from www.coe.int/lang-cefr.

Deardorff, D. K (2006) Identification and assessment of intercultural competence as a student outcome of internationalization'. *Journal of Studies in International Education*, 10(3), 241–266.

Dippold, D. (2015) *Classroom Interaction: The Internationalised Anglophone University.* Basingstoke: Palgrave Macmillan.

Dippold, D., Bridges, S., Eccles, S. & Mullen, E. (2019) Developing the global graduate: How first year university students narrate their experiences of culture. *Language and Intercultural Communication*, 19(4), 313–327.

Farrell, T. S. C. & Ives, J. (2015) Exploring teacher beliefs and classroom practices through reflective practice: A case study. *Language Teaching Research*, 19(5), 594–610.

Galloway, N. & Rose, H. (2018) Incorporating Global Englishes into the ELT classroom. *ELT Journal*, 72(1), 3–14.

Goclowska, M., Crisp, R. & Labuschagne, K. (2012) Can counter-stereotypes boost flexible thinking? *Group Processes & Intergroup Relations*, 16(2), 217–231.

Harvard University (2018) *Project Implicit: Harvard Unconscious Bias Test.* Retrieved 16 March 2018 from https://implicit.harvard.edu/implicit/takeatest.html.

Holliday, A., Hyde, M. & Kullman, J. (2010) *Intercultural Communication: An Advanced Resource for Students* (2nd Ed.). Routledge Applied Linguistics. Abingdon, Oxon: Routledge.

HWU (2019) *Heriot-Watt University Student Data Summary: April 2019.* Retrieved 1 October 2019 from www.hw.ac.uk/services/docs/StudentData19.pdf.

Jameson, D. A. (2007) Reconceptualizing cultural identity and its role in intercultural business communication. *Journal of Business Communication*, 44(3), 199–235.

Kettle, M. (2017) *International Student Engagement in Higher Education: Transforming Practices, Pedagogies and Participation.* Blue Ridge Summit, PA: Multilingual Matters.

Lang, P. (1998) Towards an understanding of effective education in a European context. In P. Lang, Y. Katz & I. Menezes (eds.), *Affective Education: A Comparative View* (pp. 3–18). London: Cassell.

Mendzheritskaya, J. & Hansen, M. (2019) The role of emotions in higher education teaching and learning processes. *Studies in Higher Education*, 44(10), 1709–1711.

Office for National Statistics (2017) *Steady increase in the number of graduates in the UK over the past decade.* Retrieved 7 February 2020 from: www.ons.gov.uk/emp loymentandlabourmarket/peopleinwork/employmentandemployeetypes/articles/gra duatesintheuklabourmarket/2017#steady-increase-in-the-number-of-graduates-in-the-uk-over-the-past-decade.

Postareff, L. & Lindblom-Ylänne, S. (2011) Emotions and confidence within teaching in higher education. *Studies in Higher Education*, 36(7), 799–813.

Pereira, S., Reay, K., Bottell, J., Walker, L., Dzikiti, C., Platt, C. & Goodrham, C. (2019) University Mental Health Survey 2018: A large scale study into the prevalence of student mental illness within UK universities. *The Insight Network.* Retrieved 16 January 2020 from: https://uploads-ssl.webflow.com/561110743bc7e45e78292140/ 5c7d4b5d314d163fecdc3706_Mental%20Health%20Report%202018.pdf.

Ryan, J. (2011) Teaching and learning for international students: Towards a transcultural approach. *Teachers and Teaching*, 17(6), 631–648,

Scudamore, R. (2013) *Engaging Home and International Students: A Guide for New Lecturers.* Higher Education Academy. Retrieved 3 January 2021 from: www.heaca demy.ac.uk/system/files/RachelScudamoreReportFeb2013.pdf.

Singer, J. (1998) Why can't you be normal for once in your life? From a 'problem' with no name to the emergence of a new category of difference. In M. Corker & S. French (eds.), *Disability Discourse*. Buckingham: Open University Press.

Trigwell, K. (2009) *Relations between teachers' emotions in teaching and their approaches to teaching in higher education: A pilot study*. Paper presented at the Biannual International Meeting for the European Association for Learning and Instruction (EARLI), August 25–29, Amsterdam, the Netherlands.

Trigwell, T., Ellis, R. A. & Han, F. (2012) Relations between students' approaches to learning, experienced emotions and outcomes of learning. *Studies in Higher Education*, 37(7), 811–824.

Van Roekel, E., Scholte, R. H. & Didden, R. (2010) Bullying among adolescents with autism spectrum disorders: Prevalence and perception. *Journal of Autism and Developmental Disorders*, 40(1), 63–73.

Wenger, E. (1998) Communities of practice: Learning as a social system. *Systems Thinker*, June.

15 An experiment in how to teach strategies for effective classroom interaction

Are we getting it right?

Elizabeth Long

Introduction

In this chapter, I will analyse an on-going intervention for the explicit teaching of oracy skills to groups of first-year undergraduates, the aim of which is to develop skills and strategies for effective classroom interaction to enhance learning, and provide the groundwork for a wide range of oral communications which will take place during a university career. I will discuss how this is delivered and assessed in the classroom through a non-disciplinary module, the challenges faced and the benefits perceived by the students and tutors. Are we taking the right approach and how can we know? The term 'oracy' may not be familiar to all in higher education (HE), but here it is used to describe the skills of talking with an audience in mind (Barnes, 2008), combined with active listening and understanding (Gaunt & Stott, 2019). Explicit teaching of oracy skills in HE is still in its relative infancy, so this chapter aims to add to the practical research in the area of classroom interaction, rather than provide any definitive answers to these questions.

Context

As part of their Liberal Arts degree, in which interdisciplinary teaching and learning is key to the curriculum, first-year undergraduates at Richmond, the American International University in London (RAIUL), take a number of modules designed to develop their academic literacy, numeracy, scientific reasoning and creative expression. In line with the university's mission and values ("Our Vision, Mission & Values – Richmond University", 2020), tutors aim to work collaboratively with students and thus have moved towards a far more interactive style of teaching in these modules; they wish to foster a spirit of independent learning amongst the students, especially through group discussion to promote the sharing of ideas. Australian researchers investigating the oracy demands of two first-year modules have described many university classrooms as a "talkative environment" (Doherty et al, 2011, p. 22). However, tutors at Richmond regularly report informally a lack of classroom engagement in this style of pedagogy: "they don't discuss";

"they don't join in the group activities"; "why are most of them silent?". Is it that many students do not have the necessary oracy skills to engage in such classroom interactions, nor the expectation of classroom contribution? Responding to this, an experimental module called Fundamentals of Academic Language and Oracy is delivered to small groups of students (maximum 16), whose competence in academic English is judged as being at a lower level than their peers, according to an entry diagnostic test; its main aim is to empower students through learning the fundamentals of formal and semi-formal spoken communication as required in academic life both in a physical and an online classroom – in other words, classroom interaction in a range of situations.

Theoretical considerations

Because interest in the value of speaking for learning appears to have been growing during the 21st century (Skyrme, 2010), it seems that it is an area that warrants further research. Relevant research is taking place in English schools, underpinned by the work of Neil Mercer and others at Hughes Hall in Cambridge ("About us", 2020), some of which is discussed here.

When people use mainly spoken language to create ideas, a process called 'interthinking' is taking place, meaning how "people are able to think creatively and productively together" (Littleton & Mercer, 2013, p. 1). These authors argue that the oracy skills required for interthinking should be integrated into classroom education. It is not enough simply to provide opportunities for students to talk, but it is through helping them to learn to talk effectively that problems are solved and learning takes place.

Littleton and Mercer's research has taken place mostly in primary schools (Mercer & Littleton, 2007). They have explained how children's involvement in what can be called 'exploratory talk' during group work promotes the development of reasoning. Examples of exploratory talk include challenging, clarifying, explaining and justifying. Building on this research from 2007, they suggest that people of any age can learn to use interthinking across a range of situations (Littleton & Mercer, 2013).

Teachers in London's School 21, for pupils aged from 5 to 18, have used this research to justify giving the same status in the curriculum to oracy as to literacy and numeracy, with the aim of providing a level playing field for pupils of all backgrounds. They argue that oracy skills should be both a classroom pedagogy and a set of teachable skills: "learning to talk and through talk", recognising that the different contexts in which someone is speaking require different sets of oracy skills (Gaunt & Stott, 2019, p. 8). In order to understand these differences, and how they overlap, they base their work on the Oracy Skills Framework, which has been developed with the University of Cambridge's Faculty of Education, breaking down the skills into four strands: physical, linguistic, cognitive, and social and emotional ("Oracy – Voice 21", 2020). The application of these strands in the module under discussion is explained below and in Table 15.1.

Table 15.1 Oracy skills within the module

Physical	Linguistic	Cognitive	Social and emotional
Voice Pace of speaking Tonal variation Clarity of pronunciation Voice projection Stress of important words	**Vocabulary** Appropriate and accurate academic vocabulary relating to the topic Appropriate sign-posting language to guide the listener Appropriate reflective language for self and peer feedback Oral citation conveying source credibility	**Content** Choice of content to convey meaning and intention Evidence of using oral and written sources	**Working with others** Guiding or managing interactions Turn-taking
Body language Gesture and posture Facial expression and eye contact	**Language** Register appropriate for the context Grammar accurate enough to aid comprehension	**Structure** Structure and organisation of talk	**Listening and responding** Listening actively to lecturers and peers and responding appropriately
	Rhetorical techniques Choice of vocabulary to create impact	**Self-regulation** Maintaining focus on task Time management	**Confidence in speaking** Self-assurance Liveliness and flair
		Reasoning Structured argumentation Giving reasons to support views Critically examining ideas and views expressed	**Audience awareness** Taking account of level of understanding of the audience

The development of vocabulary through talk is discussed, again in a School 21 context, by teachers Amy Gaunt and Alice Stott, who have shown through their classroom practice that oral language can provide a more effective method for learning new vocabulary than written language, because the learning is supported by physical features of talk, like intonation, emphasis and body language, and the ability to immediately self-correct, use synonyms or clarify further (Gaunt & Stott, 2019).

The difference between exploratory talk, often used to try out ideas in an incomplete fashion, and presentational talk, when the focus moves from individuals looking for meaning to an individual addressing an audience, is important (Barnes, 2008). The plethora of available resources suggests that presentational skills are being taught to a growing extent in HE, but less so the skills for effective exploratory talk. The most common type of exploratory talk in HE is group discussion, often in the form of a seminar, in which students are required to share their own ideas and engage with the ideas of others as a method of learning, so they are accountable to each other as much as to the teacher: a new educational experience for many students, and one which I would suggest requires explicit support, in the same way as academic writing, on account of the high level of oracy demanded. This has been shown to be the case in a research project carried out looking at the oracy demands of two undergraduate business modules (Heron, 2019).

Awareness of the processes we go through when talking is a pre-requisite for analysing and improving our practice through reflection. Again, this has been shown to be the case in School 21, where differing techniques to promote understanding of oracy have been tried out in the classroom. It is suggested that students' understanding of what good oracy looks like is transferable across subjects and contexts (Gaunt & Stott, 2019). The importance of this awareness will be discussed under the section "Delivery and assessment".

In classrooms in the US ten years ago, the researchers and educators Jeff Zwiers and Marie Crawford concluded that students in the classrooms they observed were not holding productive conversations. They felt that approaches to teaching in many curricula were neglecting to train students in the academic dialogue required for effective classroom interaction (Zwiers & Crawford, 2011). In response to this and stemming from many hours of analysis of classroom practice, they identified five core communication skills "that focus and deepen academic conversations" in various situations and content areas, namely: elaborating and clarifying, supporting ideas with evidence, building on and/or challenging ideas, paraphrasing, and synthesising (Zwiers & Crawford, 2011, p. 2). These skills meld closely with the cognitive strand of the Oracy Skills Framework referred to above (Oracy – Voice 21, 2020). Zwiers and Crawford identify advantages of classroom talk for personal and academic development across five categories which they describe as language and literacy, cognitive, content learning, social and cultural, and psychological. In their book *Academic Conversations*, they suggest myriad classroom practices which, according to the subtitle, encourage "classroom talk that fosters critical thinking and content understandings" (Zwiers & Crawford, 2011) across a range of discipline areas.

The research referred to above has provided a framework for my own experiment in teaching oracy in a range of academic situations. Through actual classroom practice over some years, I aim to promote more effective learning through effective classroom interactions.

Aims of the oracy module

The module provides opportunities for students to participate and be assessed in a range of academic situations, including interviews, recorded presentations, discussion and debate (see Table 15.2), which may also be work related. Through

Table 15.2 Module assessments

Assessment	Interaction requirements	Recording
Application and interview for a student job	Student/tutor – by phone, email and face-to-face or online	N/A
Student videoed presentation of a human rights case study, leading to online discussion via the VLE	Student/classmates – classroom practice or online Student/own camera Student/classmates on VLE during specific allocated timeframe	Student films him/herself
Listening to and discussion of a live lecture	Whole class/invited lecturer – in class or online Student/small discussion groups – in class or online	Tutor films/records discussion
Group debate	Student team/whole class/small invited audience – in class or online	Tutor films debate
Reflection on learning from each of the above, after completion of each task	Student choice of reflection method: written; audio recorded; face-to-face/online with tutor	Dependent on student choice

these situations, which can take place in a physical classroom or online, it aims to introduce and practise oracy skills as described in Table 15.1; the level of interaction is scaffolded, starting between the individual student and the tutor, followed by interaction between individual students and small groups, leading to interaction between teams and an audience. Table 15.1 adapts the Oracy Skills Framework (Oracy – Voice 21, 2020) to reflect the particular circumstances and requirements of the students enrolled in this module.

Throughout the module, choice of language has the largest focus, which might suggest that it is designed for non-native English speakers only. Although the majority of students who have taken the module so far are in fact non-native English speakers, it is not the case that they are the only likely beneficiaries: all students at the start of their university career can benefit their learning from raising awareness of how they use spoken language, as has been shown through the research discussed earlier. In other words, the overarching aim of the module is to develop classroom interaction to lead to improved learning for all.

Delivery and assessment

Oracy skills are delivered through preparation for five assessed tasks during the semester (see Table 15.2). The level of interaction is scaffolded throughout, starting with student–tutor interaction, and finishing with student group interaction with an audience. The content is non-discipline specific, allowing the widest possible student choice for the focus, but could easily be adapted to a specific disciplinary context. For example, the theme of human rights is introduced and discussed to allow students to choose their own human rights case study violation on which to base their recorded presentation. Once students have listened to a live lecture, their questions and responses lead to a focussed topic for group discussion. When the group debate task is introduced, students have almost free rein to choose a debate motion, but often choose one relating to research they are undertaking in a different module.

Awareness of metacognitive skills are key and are explicitly discussed at every stage. This is achieved early on in the module through short activities relating to the different elements of the Oracy Skills Framework, adapted from School 21's work, described above (Gaunt & Stott, 2019). For example, students enjoy practising the linguistic element by describing a concept (eg freedom) to a group without using any words in the same family as the target concept. As they become more familiar with these elements, they can practise by relating the assessment rubric to recorded examples of the task (see the discussion of challenges below) and through peer feedback focussing on specific skills. This also allows them to become aware of the scaffolding of the skills required as the module progresses.

Just as the level of student oral interaction amongst the group and the skills required are scaffolded, so is the use of recording equipment (see Table 15.2). At first, the student's engagement is with the tutor on a one-to-one basis, through phone calls, emails and interview. Following this, students record themselves on their own devices, allowing as much editing as they wish. Next, the tutor records a small-group discussion, but only after the students have practised similar discussion to camera and analysed their performances. Finally, they speak in a debate, which is more akin to a performance as part of a cast since each student has a particular role to play, in front of an audience whom they may or may not know. Again, this is recorded by the tutor, following filmed practice. Student reaction to this pedagogy is recorded below under 'Challenges and benefits'.

Practice for each task takes place in class time, including the introduction of guided oral peer feedback. Through role play, students can practise formal telephone calls and interviews; through presenting informally to their classmates, students can think about the differences between an audience presentation and a recorded one; through analysing online discussion, they can become more aware of the importance of signposting language to enhance effective discussion. Through giving oral peer feedback in a constructive manner, they can become aware of what they also need to develop.

Having received audio feedback from the tutor after each assessment (see discussion of audio feedback below), students reflect on their own skills development by responding to a series of prompts (see Appendix) which follow Gibbs' reflective cycle (Gibbs, 1988), a model also followed for reflection in other modules they may be taking. Skills for each assessment need to be further developed for the next, which allows students to focus on those skills which they need most.

By using an assessment rubric which refers directly to the Oracy Skills Framework (Oracy – Voice 21, 2020), and to which students have already been introduced, tutors are helped to grade appropriately for each of the four elements: physical, linguistic, cognitive, social and emotional, as discussed above.

In order to promote active listening within the context of learning through talk, the use of audio feedback may be beneficial. Results from the Sounds Good project, supported by JISC, suggest a very positive response from students towards receiving audio feedback on their assessments. They liked its personal nature and the careful consideration of their work which was evidenced – "students noted that audio made it easier to grasp what the lecturer felt was most important" (Rotherham, 2009). This is supported by experience from this module, in which 95% of students have reported (anonymously) through their self-reflections that they prefer audio feedback for a number of reasons, including that they could hear the teacher modelling the target language; spoken language can have more impact and more detail; it can seem less harsh, and more like someone is speaking to you directly.

Challenges and benefits

The following discussion is based on experience and feedback from the teaching and learning of this module over a two-year period between 2017 and 2019. Three tutors were involved (including the author) working closely together, so were able to share their experiences informally, allowing the author to note down relevant comments. Fifty students completed the module during this period, and a selection of their comments, chosen from their guided self-reflections on the university's VLE is shared below, with students' permission.

Challenges

The challenges described here fall under a variety of themes; the first two are reported by the students themselves, while the next three are reported by the tutors. Importantly, strategies are suggested to address each one.

Cultural issues: Some students report that expectations from their schooling and upbringing require them to listen attentively but only speak when invited. "A bit difficult was the discussion part because I do not like to interrupt others" is an example of a common student reaction amongst some groups. However, an awareness of this issue can be fostered amongst the group, so that others who understand the requirement to participate can be encouraged to prompt the more reticent participants.

Recording and filming: Few students report feeling confident when recording themselves or speaking in front of a camera; more often they say that the camera makes them feel inhibited because they are worried about being seen to make mistakes. "I was more anxious, less confident, because there was a video recorder." This suggests that the filmed practice sessions are potentially very important to allow a level of familiarity with being filmed. The section below under "Benefits" suggests that, although practice in front of the camera does not make perfect, it does in time lead to increased confidence.

A further challenge relates to General Data Protection Regulation requirements which must be adhered to, meaning that students must explicitly give their permission to be filmed, within a specific context and for a specific purpose. A major benefit arising from this is the bank of authentic material available as models for future teaching.

Attendance in class: In order to practise or complete most of the assessed tasks, students need an audience or a discussion group, so they need to be present in the class, whether physically or online. An absent student will not easily be able to make up the work missed, which is a problem for him/her but may well provide extrinsic motivation for future attendance because an absent student may, by default, miss out on the grade. During the period of this study, no student who completed the module missed taking part in more than one of the assessed tasks, meaning that they would only miss out on a maximum of 25% of the overall grade.

Practice: Some students may 'over-rehearse' by trying to learn by heart what they want to say; this inevitably involves using too much written-style language, less easily comprehensible to the audience; others may 'wing it', assuming they can simply react to others without any preparation. Feedback on practice sessions can alleviate such issues, fostering an awareness of appropriate register and organisation of ideas.

Grading: The biggest challenge is surely to grade the assessments fairly and objectively. When recording what is said is not appropriate or practical, there is a strong reliance on the grader's memory, note-taking and level of concentration. When the assessment is recorded, the tutor must still balance an individual student's performance against that of the rest of the group, especially since an individual's performance will often be affected by those of other group members. However much we aim to use open and transparent grading criteria, we, as graders, are still making subjective judgements, because "conversations are moving targets, morphing all the time" (Zwiers & Crawford, 2011, p. 189); unlike in certain more conventional tests, we cannot count right or wrong answers. Yet, despite this, it is possible to see and hear strengths and weaknesses, and give them a value, according to an agreed oracy framework, as discussed under 'Delivery and assessment' above. In the period of this study, issues of grading have led each semester to improving the presentation of the grading criteria, which will help students as much as tutors. For example, the five oracy strands are now colour-coded, then subdivided between different criteria in order to emphasise the key skills for a particular assessment task. Thus, for example, research skills are separated from other cognitive skills, and described as follows: 'clear reference to sources, explaining source credibility' in order to focus on spoken citation.

It seems that these challenges can be faced successfully using the strategies proposed above. Let us now assess some of the benefits perceived.

Benefits

Students report a wide range of areas of improvement, but the most positive outcome stems from a statement posed as part of the end of semester module evaluations: "I learnt a lot from this course". This statement consistently scores from 3.6 to 3.8 out of 4.0, which is regarded as very high for a mandatory skills-based, rather than a discipline-based, module. When reflecting on each assessed task, they provide detail of what they see as their learning, though they do not refer explicitly to the Oracy Skills Framework; however, examples of the language they use, as quoted in the examples below, do suggest an understanding of some of the metalanguage, and are organised according to the main headings of the framework, followed by comments about practised recording in the classroom.

Physical: The following comments suggest students are developing an awareness of the positive and negative effects of their voice and body language, and the impact that this can have on an audience.

> "I think I improved my pronunciation"; "I am learning to control my body language"; "I saw that I was touching my hair and nose too much, which is not a good thing to do"; "I have developed eye contact with the audience"; "I learnt to make a strong impact through a clear voice, confident body language, eye contact with audience and strong adjectives"; "I now know I need to pause at the end of sentences to allow the audience to think about what I have just said."

Linguistic: An understanding of the need for preparation of appropriate language prior to speaking is being demonstrated here:

> "it enables me to improve my English"; "this assignment taught me some vocabulary that I was not aware of"; "I think I became pretty good at organising the content with appropriate signposting"; "I focus now more on signposting the main body, because that is the part where people get most information"; "it made me think what phrase I should use to interact with others"; "I learnt to try to use the correct language trying to explain everything clearly"; "I have developed my communication skills, precisely appropriate and accurate academic language"; "I spoke too much in an informal way, so to avoid this mistake I now study specific vocabulary."

Cognitive: At the start of their HE, students are required to work on structure and organisation of written work, as well as citing their sources. Understanding the need to transfer those skills to oral situations is a great benefit.

> "I learnt to organise what to say in my mind first"; "I have developed the skill of explaining things as I talk"; "I learnt about citing the source

where I got the information from, even when speaking"; "now I know I must give the source for the example I am giving"; "I try to sound as credible as possible"; "comparing notes with other students helped me cultivate a better understanding"; "I've learned how to better structure my arguments. How to support them with good source evidence using relevant academic language."

Social and emotional: Improved self-confidence and the enjoyment of working with others are themes demonstrated here:

"it helped me to develop the capacity to be able to have a speech with a person who has more experience than me"; "I love discussing all sorts of topics with the others"; "practice can help me to be less nervous and automatically improve my self-confidence and help me to seem more professional"; "on debate day, everyone was excited and energised. I really enjoyed everyone's participation in it."

Practice: The problem of over-practising or not practising at all are discussed above (see "Challenges" above). Many students can find the right balance, and benefit greatly from it.

"I was able to film myself over and over again because it was a recorded presentation. In other words, I had practised a lot before posting it"; "thanks to the practice in pairs, I could be more confident when recording my own presentation"; "all the practices we did helped me to get through the assignment."

Recording: Despite initial reservations (see 'Challenges' above), the majority of students (just like any of us) adapt to the presence of the camera, and indeed take what they say more seriously because of it. Many of their comments back this up:

"I developed the ability to be comfortable with myself in front of a camera"; "I learnt that recording myself is not that terrible"; "when I first started talking to the camera I was feeling really embarrassed since I am not a native English speaker and I was scared that people would not understand me because of my accent. While recording though I started to sort of manage my fear and tried to speak as clearly as possible"; "I felt like a reporter doing a news report"; "I had great fun in filming myself and helping my peers make their videos."

These student comments accurately reflect my and colleagues' perceptions of areas of development; although we are aware that the rubric for these self-reflections tends to promote positive rather than negative responses, it is made clear that it is totally acceptable to make constructive criticism of the oracy skills approach. The absence to date of negative feedback and the plethora of positive feedback suggests that the students appreciate the approach taken in the design of this module.

Conclusion

The Oracy Skills Framework, designed originally for use in schools (Oracy – Voice 21, 2020), has proved to be eminently adaptable to a HE environment, at least at the start of a student's university career. Its clear categorisation and explicit description of separate oracy skills has allowed us to face the most major challenges: students' understanding of oracy requirements and tutors' ability to grade fairly and openly.

Describing the process of interthinking, Littleton and Mercer (2013) aim to explain how "mainly by using spoken language, people are able to think creatively and productively together" (p. 1). If we accept that classroom interaction is an example of such interthinking, then it follows that talking skills, or oracy, are crucial for students as they begin and work through their university career. Just as support in writing is provided by universities in numerous and wide-ranging forms, so it seems that support in oracy must become similarly normal.

The module described in this chapter is one approach to how such support can be provided at an early stage, in a specific university context, outside of a particular discipline. The challenge remains to identify further ways in which teaching in a range of contexts and disciplines, both in a physical classroom and online, might adapt to enhance classroom interaction, embed oracy skills, and thus promote learning through talk.

Any answer to the question posed "are we getting it right?" will surely be subjective to a large extent, given the complexities in this university of conducting a longitudinal study of students with multiple degree pathways, but evidence from the students themselves would suggest that the development of oracy skills can indeed benefit learning, through increasingly effective classroom interaction in a particular academic context. As practitioners continue to experiment and share results and good practice, we can hope that more and more will be able to affirm that they know that they are "getting it right".

Appendix

In order to reflect effectively on your learning from each assessment, please respond to the following prompts:

1   Very short description of the requirements of the assessment
2   How you felt about undertaking it
3   What challenges you faced whilst completing each stage, and how major they were
4   Which skills you developed, and the role of any formative feedback

5   What you learnt from your experience above and from your summative feedback
6   What you will work on to improve for the future, giving practical details

References

About us. (2020). Retrieved 1 June 2020, from https://oracycambridge.org/about-us/.

Barnes, D. (2008). Exploratory talk for learning. In N. Mercer & S. Hodgkinson (Eds.), *Exploring Talk in School: Inspired by the Work of Douglas Barnes*. London: Sage Publications.

Doherty, C., Kettle, M., May, L., & Caukill, E. (2011). Talking the talk: oracy demands in first year university assessment tasks. *Assessment in Education: Principles, Policy & Practice*, 18(1), 27–39.

Gaunt, A., & Stott, A. (2019). *Transform Teaching and Learning Through Talk*. London: Rowman and Littlefield.

Gibbs, G. (1988). *Learning by Doing: A Guide to Teaching and Learning Methods*. London: Further Education Unit.

Heron, M. (2019). Making the case for oracy skills in higher education: practices and opportunities. *Journal of University Teaching and Learning Practice*, 16(2). https://ro.uow.edu.au/jutlp/vol16/iss2/9.

Littleton, K., & Mercer, N. (2013). *Interthinking: Putting Talk to Work*. Abingdon: Routledge.

Mercer, N., & Littleton, K. (2007). *Dialogue and the Development of Children's Thinking*. London: Routledge.

Mission Statement – Richmond University. (2020). Retrieved 1 June 2020, from www.richmond.ac.uk/about-richmond/mission-statement/.

Oracy – Voice 21. (2020). Retrieved 1 June 2020, from https://voice21.org/oracy/.

Rotherham, B. (2009). *Sounds Good: Quicker, better assessment using audio feedback*. Retrieved 1 June 2020 from www.reading.ac.uk/web/files/EngageinFeedback/Podcast_feedback_soundsgood.pdf.

Skyrme, G. (2010). Is this a stupid question? International undergraduate students seeking help from teachers during office hours. *Journal of English For Academic Purposes*, 9(3), 211–221.

Zwiers, J., & Crawford, M. (2011). *Academic Conversations: Classroom Talk that Fosters Critical Thinking and Content Understandings*. Portland, OR: Stenhouse Publishers.

16 Conclusion

Taking classroom interaction forward

Doris Dippold and Marion Heron

Introduction

This final chapter, which summarises the contributions to this volume, was guided by four questions we asked all our authors from Parts II and III to answer. These were:

- Which theory/framework of interaction did you draw on and why?
- What were the challenges of investigating and developing classroom discourse in your context?
- What is the impact of your study on either theory and practice?
- What is the impact on student learning?

In the foreword to this volume, Olcay Sert described the field of classroom discourse and interaction as "a field *in* transformation". The chapters in this volume show that we can also describe it as "a field *of* transformation", including (1) transformations of methodology through using micro-analytical approaches, (2) transformations of student learning by enabling them to engage in learning in a more egalitarian manner, and (3) transformations of pedagogical practice through student and staff development.

In this chapter, we will discuss each of these three themes in turn. In the final part of the chapter, we will provide an outlook to the future of research in classroom interaction research, in particular the changes and new agendas which may be sparked by the move to online teaching and learning.

Theme 1: Transforming the study of classroom interaction – theories, frameworks and approaches

Chapters in this volume have drawn on a range of theories, frameworks and approaches to investigating classroom interaction in higher education. A common denominator for many of them is the fact that they use micro-analytical approaches (Connor & Michaels, 2015) which use transcribed classroom exchanges and centre in on what students and teachers actually do in the classroom.

For example, Sohn and Spilotopolous (Chapter 7) use conversation analysis (CA) to reveal how, in group work, an Asian student was systematically excluded from the interaction. Hardman (Chapter 3) draws on recorded and transcribed extracts of classroom talk to show how specific lecturer and student talk moves created a space for rich classroom dialogue. Chen and Bonacina-Pugh (Chapter 9) describe, also with a CA approach, how teachers and students implement a 'practised (language) policy' and negotiate a 'shared preferred language'.

Other chapters do not feature micro-analytical analyses per se but are either grounded in theoretical approaches that centre around micro-analysis or tools and strategies which allow a detailed look at language and interaction to improve student learning or to develop teacher classroom talk. One example is Walsh's SETTVEO project (Walsh, 2020, reported on in Chapter 2) providing opportunities for video enhanced observation and tagging of teacher talk moves. The project builds on Walsh's concept of Classroom Interactional Competence (CIC) and his SETT framework. In addition, Poore (Chapter 13) uses Hardman's (2016) dialogic pedagogy framework to discuss how such a pedagogy may enhance student results and how learners react to a teacher-directed space.

What these studies have in common is confidence in the transformative potential of micro-analytical approaches on student learning, teacher development and on addressing wider issues. For example, Hardman (Chapter 3) ends her contribution by saying that "there is a need to do further research into classroom dialogue in the context of higher education across subjects… These activities will help build a strong evidence base for informing university policy and practice with regard to implementing a dialogic pedagogy", while Sohn and Spilotopolous (Chapter 7) suggest that an analysis of small-group discussion will allow insights into how some interactions lead to marginalisation. These examples show that micro-analytical approaches have great potential to add an additional dimension to the interpretative (interviews, focus groups) approaches common to most mainstream higher education research.

Research which either draws on, or promotes, micro-analytical approaches to classroom interaction is, in this volume, complemented by an array of other frameworks and concepts, including, for example, silence (Sequeira, Chapter 4), English as a Lingua Franca (Doubleday, Chapter 10), bullying and emotions (Bell and Richardson, Chapter 14), Academic Integration (Spencer-Oatey and Dauber, Chapter 5) and Philosophy for Children (Demissie, Chapter 12) and oracy (Long, Chapter 15). Despite these different starting points, all these contributions reveal, discuss and question issues of wider significance for higher education, such as cohesion between home and international students and issues of equality and asymmetry of power (Jenkins, 2014; Dippold, 2015) These wider issues will be discussed in more detail in the next two themes, focusing on the transformative power of classroom discourse on student learning and its capacity to address inequality (Theme 2) and staff development (Theme 3).

Theme 2: Transforming student learning and addressing inequality by developing students' classroom interaction skills

Perhaps not surprisingly, there is a general agreement amongst the authors in this volume that developing students' ability to engage in classroom interaction not only allows them to better engage in learning, but also has wider benefits for higher education and beyond. For example, Poore (Chapter 13) describes the introduction of dialogic pedagogy in a drama module which had a positive impact on student attainment in module assessment, although some caution is necessary here due to the lack of a control group.

Student wellbeing and mental health are topics that have gained increasing traction in higher education (Barden & Caleb, 2019). It is not surprising therefore that some of our authors also describe how developing classroom interaction skills can benefit student wellbeing. For example, Hardman (Chapter 3) argues that classroom dialogue does not only benefit student learning but can facilitate friendships and belongingness to the university. Demissie (Chapter 12) describes how implementing a 'Philosophy for Children' approach led not only to improvements in critical thinking ability, but also a perception of personal growth. Long (Chapter 15) explains how a long-term pedagogic project led to perceived improvements on all dimensions of the oracy framework, including confidence, and Bell and Richardson (Chapter 14) discuss how awareness sessions for students and staff can improve classroom interaction and prevent bullying and harassment of international students.

The other major theme in this volume is internationalisation and its implications, with authors describing the development of classroom interaction skills purporting better relationships between students. For example, Spencer-Oatey and Dauber (Chapter 5) show, through quantitative as well as qualitative approaches, that there was often a large gap between international students' expectations of classroom interaction and their actual experiences. Students hoped to be able to share experiences from their own background, to be given opportunities to participate and for home students to adjust their language more.

Spencer-Oatey and Dauber's research reveals a common theme across the general internationalisation literature, which is also touched upon in some contributions to this volume, namely that international students often feel marginalised and 'silenced' by those speaking English as a majority language (e.g. Henderson, 2011). Most prominently, Sequeira (Chapter 4) describes these asymmetries through the example of student silence in the classroom which, seen through the lenses of a traditional Western education, can be regarded as problematic. On the issue of communication skills, Spencer-Oatey and Dauber (Chapter 5) as well as Doubleday (Chapter 10) argue that staff and students' global competencies should be actively developed, including training in accommodating to others. Cranwell et al. (Chapter 8) further argue that the development of disciplinary language would be beneficial for equality and integration in the classroom as it would allow international students to engage more effectively in the classroom.

There is thus an argument emerging from the contributions to our volume that developing classroom interaction skills will not only lead to better learning opportunities, but also has the ability to address inequalities inherent in the higher education system, an issue wrapped up for example in discussions about the BAME attainment gap (Buns et al., 2019). As most of the studies featured in this volume were on a small scale, future research should investigate these questions further, using for example experimental methods through which the results of pedagogical interventions focusing on classroom interaction can be explicitly compared. In addition, as suggested in Chapter 6, research should also try to cast their disciplinary net more widely than it currently does.

Theme 3: Transforming pedagogical practice through staff and student development

Unsurprisingly, one very large theme extending across our chapters is the question of how the abilities of students and staff to engage in classroom interaction can be developed. A related question is the issue of how subject specialists can fruitfully collaborate with teachers in English for Academic Purposes (Arnó-Macià & Mancho-Bares, 2015).

As far as staff are concerned, the most obvious way of developing skills for leading classroom interaction are teacher training courses and degrees. However, as Walsh (Chapter 2) points out, hardly any university-run teacher training courses currently include any focus on classroom interaction and discourse. The reasons for this have never been fully evaluated, but mirror more general trends in HE research which, as discussed in Chapters 1 and 11, still tends to shy away from language and discourse-focused evaluations of classroom pedagogy.

As the contributions to this volume show, a focus on language, discourse and reflection is key to developing teachers' abilities in leading classroom interaction. Walsh (Chapter 2) for example describes the SETTVEO app which allows annotation and tagging of recorded classroom videos, followed up by subsequent reflection. Similarly, Hardman (Chapter 3) also proposes a training module centred on peer-supported reflection, in a four-step process which involves target-setting, implementation, observation and analysis/interpretation.

In addition to reflection, which is presented as a key factor in other chapters, too – for example, Doubleday's contribution (Chapter 10) centring on communication strategies inherent to English as a lingua franca and Demissie's description of classroom interaction which is centred around a 'Philosophy for Children' approach (Chapter 12) – authors also argue that the development of classroom interaction skills requires an evidence base. For example, Walsh (Chapter 2) proposes the development of an international corpus of practice in HE, and Hardman (Chapter 3) and Bell and Richardson (Chapter 14) call for further research into classroom dialogue across a fuller range of subjects, which, as we have shown in Chapter 6, so far is still lacking in a HE context (Heron & Dippold, Chapter 6). Cranwell et al. (Chapter 8) indeed showed, using an analysis of discourse from the chemistry lab, that the lack of disciplinary language and the speed of delivery of content were main barriers in international students' engagement with classroom dialogue.

The chapters in this volume also address the issue of how students can develop the capabilities for classroom interaction. Long (Chapter 15) introduces a longitudinal approach to developing the whole range of speaking (oracy skills), while Demissie (Chapter 12) describes a programme built on the 'Philosophy for Children' approach. Chen and Bonacina-Pugh (Chapter 9) argue that there is a need for a greater awareness of how meaning in the classroom can be achieved through a multilingual repertoire which may include the use of national language if this suits students' interactional needs better.

In summary, chapters in this volume emphasise how, through initiatives for student and staff development, pedagogic practice can undergo fruitful transformation. In the context of UK higher education – but potentially replicated in other national contexts – transforming pedagogic practice is particularly important in view of quality assurance initiatives such as the TEF (Teaching Excellence Framework) in the UK (Department of Education, 2017), whose criteria include 'Teaching Quality' with five sub-criteria. One of these sub-criteria is 'Rigour and stretch' (TQ3), which is defined as "Curriculum, pedagogy and assessment stretch students to develop independence, knowledge and skills that reflect their potential". As discussed in various parts of this volume (e.g. Heron & Dippold, Chapter 1 or Hardman, Chapter 3), the notion of 'stretch' is encapsulated in descriptions of learning as dialogic practice, which sees talk as a key tool for learning (e.g. Mercer, 1995, 'exploratory talk'). However, the metrics for evaluating these criteria, do, at this stage, only include quantitative measures drawn from questions on the National Student Survey, such as "staff are good at explaining things", "staff have made the subject interesting" and "the course is intellectually stimulating", none of which sufficiently capture the nature of learning through talk. This suggests that the wider policy framework is not sufficiently equipped to support and encourage the transformation of pedagogic practice.

In addition, the willingness of students and staff to engage in innovative pedagogic practices centring on reflection on and experimentation with classroom discourse is dependent on students' and teachers' willingness to take risks in an environment characterised by financial pressures. For example, Poore (Chapter 13) describes the increasing casualisation of teaching in HE as a factor for teachers not engaging in developing pedagogic practices as bad module evaluations may lead to contracts not being renewed. Similarly, students may also be reluctant in engaging in innovative classroom practices as they fear a loss of control and deteriorating degree results.

This situation is likely to be exacerbated by the Covid-19 crisis, which has put huge pressures on university tutors to change their approaches to teaching with little notice, leaving very little time to engage in pedagogical research and innovation, casually employed teachers scrambling for re-employment by cash-strapped institutions and graduates having to face an uncertain job market. On the other hand, this crisis may provide opportunities for developing theory and practice in an online space not previously explored.

Learning and teaching in transformation: Online spaces

At the time of initial conception of this volume (Spring 2019), teaching and learning delivered remotely online occupied only a very small market segment in higher education and was primarily delivered by specialised providers such as the Open University. A report by Universities UK (2018) estimated that, with the Open University included, 8% of degree courses in the UK were delivered online, and 3% when excluding provision by the Open University.

At the time when we asked authors in this volume to submit final chapters (Spring/Summer 2020), universities had been forced to rapidly change their provision to teaching online, leading the way towards a blended learning model at least in the short term. But what do these changes mean for learning and teaching classroom interaction in an online space, and for researching such interactions?

Learning and teaching taking place in an online space is fundamentally different to learning in an environment of physical co-presence: different media and technologies vary in their ability to communicate complex messages, and to reduce equivocality (Daft & Lengel, 1986). Online learning can of course be delivered through a multitude of platforms, each of which has their own affordances.

Considering for example software to deliver live classroom sessions, such as Zoom or Microsoft Teams, such software is, on the one hand, relatively 'rich' in that it has the potential to convey auditory as well as visual cues in real time. However, this richness is constrained by when participants do not use their camera, and more generally by the limited visual field displayed on the screen, which does not allow participants to convey reactions (such as facial expressions) as effectively or reliably as in a face-to-face encounter. This has repercussions for classroom interaction and dialogue as, for example, the ability to take turns in speaking may be limited by a lack of ability to 'pick up' on visual cues of indicating when someone else's turn has finished.

The limitations in terms of conveying a full range of cues represents one of the many possible examples of the specific affordances of the media used to deliver teaching in an online space. Others apply to other media, such as VLE discussion boards, chat, social media. However, these new learning and teaching spaces may also offer opportunities for classroom interaction not previously exploited.

For example, learning in an online space may be able to better facilitate the use of English as a lingua franca and strategies for negotiation of meaning (Björkman, 2013) than traditional face-to-face environments. Classroom environments such as Zoom and Teams feature multiple interaction channels, the primary video/audio channel and chat (as well as, sometimes, a Q&A facility). This has the potential to allow for much more sophisticated strategies for negotiating meaning, for example by using written modes (such as the chat function) to complement, but not replace, spoken classroom interaction.

Online and blended modes of teaching may also provide for more sophisticated opportunities for teaching disciplinary vocabulary. In the traditional face-to-face classroom, with mainly spoken modes of communication, making disciplinary vocabulary explicit – with a long-term record – may be more difficult to achieve. A combination of spoken and written modes in an online learning environment may provide previously unseen opportunities, for example through the use of software and apps which allow students and staff to co-develop inventories of subject-specific terminology.

One other issue – addressed by Sequeira (Chapter 4) – is that of student 'silence' in the traditional face-to-face classroom. We certainly do not wish to follow the established tradition of 'pathologising' student silence as disengagement, as engagement cannot be measured exclusively in terms of engagement in spoken interaction. However, online and blended modes of teaching do perhaps offer a chance for students who do not wish to 'engage' through spoken contributions to interact in different ways, for example through written chat messages. This offers the potential to democratise learning and teaching spaces and give international students a voice which they may otherwise not have had.

A move to blended or hybrid learning, in which the more didactic elements of classroom learning, such as lectures, are delivered online, may also change the nature of teaching in the face-to-face elements towards a flipped classroom approach, which leaves more space for in-depth exploration of a subject area through talk. Consequently, big on the research agenda in the coming years will be the questions about the extent to which various forms of online and blended learning, and the modes through which it will be delivered, support a dialogic pedagogy. In addition, these changes will also require additional staff training to use educational talk in new and innovative ways.

Conclusion

This chapter has served as a summary of this edited volume on classroom interaction under three main themes – transforming classroom interaction research, transforming student learning, and transforming pedagogical practice. In addition, it has provided an outlook towards what the move of learning and teaching in HE into online spaces might mean for classroom interaction and its research. The chapters, and this summary, have made clear that there is a huge amount of ongoing potential for the study of classroom interaction. Further research should attempt to break more clearly into different disciplinary spaces in HE and explore the potential of training in classroom interaction to foster equality and cohesion. Most importantly however, future research should be a cornerstone for student and staff development initiatives which are research-led.

References

Arnó-Macià, E., & Mancho-Barés, G. (2015). The role of content and language in content and language integrated learning (CLIL) at university: Challenges and implications for ESP. *English for Specific Purposes*, 37, 63–73. https://doi.org/10.1016/j.esp.2014.06.007.

Barden, H., & Caleb, R. (2019). *Student mental health and wellbeing in higher education: A practical guide*. London: Sage Publications.

Björkman, B. (2013). *English as an academic lingua franca: An investigation of form and communicative effectiveness*. Boston, MA: Walter de Gruyter.

Buns, L., King, N., Saran, S. & Talib, N. (2019). Experiences of black and minority ethnic (BME) students in higher education: applying self-determination theory to understand the BME attainment gap. *Studies in Higher Education*. doi:10.1080/03075079.2019.1643305.

Connor, C., & Michaels, S. (2015). How'd you figure that...OUT? What can micro-analysis of discourse tell us about fostering academic language? *Linguistics and Education*, 31, 304–310. https://doi.org/10.1016/j.linged.2015.05.002.

Daft, R., & Lengel, R. H. (1986). Organizational information requirements, media richness and structural design. *Management Science*, 32 (5), 554–571. doi:10.1287/mnsc.32.5.554.

Department of Education (2017). *Teaching Excellence and Student Outcomes Framework Specification*. Available at: https://assets.publishing.service.gov.uk/government/uploads/system/uploads/attachment_data/file/658490/Teaching_Excellence_and_Student_Outcomes_Framework_Specification.pdf.

Dippold, D. (2015). *Classroom interaction: The internationalised Anglophone university*. Basingstoke: Routledge.

Hardman, J. (2016). Tutor–student interaction in seminar teaching: implications for professional development. *Active Learning in Higher Education*, 17, 63–76.

Henderson, J. (2011). New and not so new horizons: brief encounters between UK undergraduate native speaker and non-native speaker Englishes. *Language and Intercultural Communication*, 11 (3), 270–284. https://doi.org/10.1080/14708477.2011.583352.

Jenkins, J. (2014). *English as a Lingua Franca in the international university: The politics of academic English language policy*. Abingdon: Routledge.

Mercer, N. (1995). *The guided construction of knowledge: Talk amongst teachers and learners*. Clevedon: Multilingual Matters.

Universities UK (2018). *Flexible learning: The current state of play in UK Higher Education*. Available at: www.universitiesuk.ac.uk/policy-and-analysis/reports/Documents/2018/flexible-learning-the-current-state-of-play-in-higher-education.pdf.

Walsh, S. (2020). *Evidence-based reflection and teacher development*. British Council: ELT Research Papers 19.05. Available at: www.teachingenglish.org.uk/article/settveo-evidence-based-reflection-teacher-development.

Index